Practical Cookery

Low Fat

Practical Cookery

Low Fat

This is a Parragon Book
This edition published in 2002

Parragon
Queen Street House
4 Queen Street
Bath BA1 1HE, UK

ISBN: 0-75257-948-7

Printed in China

NOTE

Cup measurements in this book are for American cups. Tablespoons are assumed to be 15 ml. Unless otherwise stated, milk is assumed to be full fat, eggs are medium and pepper is freshly ground black pepper.

Recipes using uncooked eggs should be avoided by infants, the elderly, pregnant women and anyone suffering from an illness

Contents

Soups

Starters & Snacks

Meat Dishes

Poultry & Game

Fish & Seafood

Vegetables & Salads

Desserts

Introduction

Whether you are on a low-fat diet or simply want to introduce healthier eating habits to your lifestyle, this is the book for you. Although the majority of recipes are low in fat, some have been included because they are highly nutritious and add important variety of ingredients.

Nutritionists agree that typical modern diets usually contain too much fat and that this can be detrimental to health. Scarcely a day passes without a television programme or a magazine article giving advice on cutting down our intake of fat. In fact, so much attention is given to the subject that people could be forgiven for believing that all their health problems would be solved if they never ate another gram of fat in their lives. Nothing could be further from the truth. A moderate intake of fat is essential for good health. For example, the body requires fat-soluble vitamins. Fish oils are one of the richest sources of vitamins A and D, and vitamin E is found in vegetable oils. Fats are also a concentrated source of energy, providing over twice as much as carbohydrates or proteins. The aim should be to reduce fat in the diet, but not to cut it out altogether.

How much is too much?

The body's nutrient requirements, including how much fat is needed, vary with age, sex, general state of health, level of physical activity and even genetic inheritance. However, the proportions in which the different

nutrients are required are much the same from one person to another. The World Health Organization recommends that fats should not exceed 30 per cent of the daily intake of energy. (Energy is measured in calories, kilocalories or kilojoules.) It has conducted studies in countries with an exceptionally high rate of heart disease and the research has revealed that this almost invariably coincides with a high-fat diet, where fats comprise as much as 40 per cent of the body's daily energy intake.

If 2,000 calories a day is taken as the average, then, for good health, only 600 of them should be supplied by fats. One gram of pure fat yields nine calories, whereas one gram of pure carbohydrate or pure protein yields only one calorie. Simple arithmetic, therefore, indicates that the maximum daily intake of fats should be 600 divided by nine, or 66.6 grams of fat.

Fats are broken down and digested in a rather different way from proteins and carbohydrates and the human body is designed to store them for times of need. In the Western world, food no longer becomes scarce every winter and we do not need to rely on stored fat to provide the energy for day-to-day life. So if a lot of fat is stored, the body becomes overweight, even obese. Worse still, a mechanism that is not yet properly understood can suddenly trigger fat deposits in the arteries, resulting in their becoming narrower and eventually leading to heart disease. Anyone who is already overweight and keen to return to a healthier size can reduce their fat intake to well below the 30 per cent maximum. However, it is probably better and the long-term effects will be more permanent if the overall intake of calories is reduced, but the proportions of nutrients remains within the normal range. Everyone, overweight or not, should observe the no-more-than-30 per-cent rule to ensure long-term health and vitality.

Types of Fat

When you are thinking about reducing your intake of fat, it is important to know that fats can broadly be divided into two categories: saturated and unsaturated fat. Although they are still fats, unsaturated fats are healthier than the saturated variety and it is important to consider this when buying food.

Fats are made up of a combination of fatty acids and glycerol. Fatty acids consist of a chain of carbon atoms linked to hydrogen atoms. The way these are linked determines the type of fat – saturated or unsaturated. The type of fat you eat is just as important as the amount.

Saturated fats

Saturated fatty acids contain as many hydrogen atoms as possible – there are no empty links on the chain. They are mainly found in animal products, such as meat and dairy foods, although some vegetable oils, including palm and coconut oil, also contain them. Foods labelled as containing hydrogenated vegetable oils, such as some types of margarine, also contain saturated fats as a by-product of their processing. They are easy to recognize as they are usually solid at room temperature.

These are the fats that the body has difficulty processing and which it tends to store. They also increase cholesterol levels in the bloodstream, which can increase the risk of heart disease. It is, therefore, sensible to reduce the level of saturated fats in the diet. They should comprise no more than 30 per cent of the total fat intake or no more than nine per cent of the total energy intake.

Unsaturated fats

These fatty acids have spare links in the carbon chain and some hydrogen atoms are missing. There are two types: monounsaturated fats which have one pair of hydrogen atoms missing and polyunsaturated fats which have more than one pair missing. They are normally liquid or soft at room temperature. They are both thought to reduce the level of cholesterol in the bloodstream.

Monounsaturated fats are mainly of vegetable origin, but are also found in oily fish, such as mackerel. Other rich sources include olive oil, many kinds of nuts, and avocados.

Cooking Techniques

One of the easiest and least disruptive ways to reduce your fat intake is to change the way you cook. Trying new recipes, even with familiar ingredients, is fun and will result in the pleasure of eating delicious meals that are also healthier.

Frying

This is undoubtedly the technique that most dramatically raises the level of fats in the diet. You do not have to abandon chips or sausages completely, but it is sensible to make sure that they are only occasional treats rather than the staple diet. Fried-food fans might find it helpful to know that ingredients absorb much more fat when shallow-fried than they do during deep-frying, but even deep-frying should be used only occasionally. If you do enjoy a shallow-fried dish once in a while, invest in a good quality, heavy-based, non-stick frying pan (skillet) and you will then require much less oil. Use a vegetable oil, high in polyunsaturates, for frying rather than a solid fat and measure the quantity you add to the pan, rather than just tipping it in. A spray oil is a useful way of controlling how much you use.

Try the Chinese cooking technique of stir-frying. The ingredients are cooked very rapidly over an extremely high heat, using a small amount of oil. Consequently, they absorb little fat and, as an additional advantage, largely retain their colour, flavour, texture and nutritional content.

Grilling (Broiling)

This is a good alternative to frying, producing a similar crisp and golden coating while remaining moist and tender inside. Ingredients with a delicate texture and which can easily dry out, such as white fish or chicken breasts, will require brushing with oil, but more robust foods, such as red meat or oily fish, can usually be grilled (broiled) without additional fat, providing the heat is not too fierce. Consider marinating meat and fish in wine, soy sauce, cider, sherry, beer and herbs or spices. Not only will this tenderize meat and provide additional flavour, the marinade can be brushed on during grilling (broiling), so that additional fat will not be required. When grilling (broiling), always place the food on a rack, so that the fat drains away.

Poaching

This is an ideal technique for ingredients with a delicate texture or subtle flavour, such as chicken and fish, and is fat-free. Poached food

does not have to be bland and uninteresting. You can use all kinds of liquids, including stock, wine and acidulated water, flavoured with vegetables and herbs. The cooking liquid can be used as the basis for a sauce to provide additional flavour, as well as preserving any dissolved nutrients.

Steaming

Another fat-free technique, this is becoming an increasingly popular way of cooking meat, fish, chicken and vegetables. Ingredients retain the colour, flavour and texture, fewer nutrients are leached out and it is very economical because steamers can be stacked on top of one another. The addition of herbs and other flavourings to the cooking liquid or the ingredients being cooked, results in a wonderfully aromatic dish. An additional advantage is that when meat is steamed, the fat melts and drips into the cooking liquid. In that case, do not use the cooking liquid for making gravy or sauces.

Braising and stewing

Slow cooking techniques produce succulent dishes that are especially welcome in winter. Trim all visible fat from meat and always remove the skin from chicken. If red meat is to be browned first, consider dry-frying it in a heavy-based pan and drain off any fat before continuing with the recipe. Straining the cooking liquid, reducing it and then skimming off the fat before serving is a classic way of preparing braised food and concentrates the flavour as well as reducing the fat content.

Roasting

Fat is an integral part of this cooking technique. Without it, meat or fish would dry out and become too brown. If you are planning a roast dish, stand meat on a rack over a tray or roasting tin (pan) so that the fat drains off. When making gravy, use stock or vegetable cooking water rather than the meat juices.

Baking

Many baked dishes are virtually fat free. Foil-wrapped parcels of meat or fish are always delicious. Add a little fruit juice or wine, rather than oil or butter, for a moist texture and delicious flavour.

Microwave

Food cooked in this way rarely requires additional fat.

Basic Recipes

Chinese Stock

This basic stock is used in Chinese cooking not only as the basis for soup-making, but also whenever liquid is required instead of plain water.

MAKES 2.5L/4½ PINTS/10 CUPS

- 750 g/1 lb 10 oz chicken pieces
- 750 g/1 lb 10 oz pork spare ribs
- 3.75 litres/6½ pints/15 cups cold water
- 3-4 pieces ginger root, crushed
- 3-4 spring onions (scallions), each tied into a knot
- 3-4 tbsp Chinese rice wine or dry sherry

1 Trim off any excess fat from the chicken and spare ribs; chop them into large pieces.

2 Place the chicken and pork in a large pan with the water; add the ginger and spring onion (scallion) knots.

3 Bring to the boil, and skim off the scum. Reduce the heat and simmer uncovered for at least 2-3 hours.

4 Strain the stock, discarding the chicken, pork, ginger and spring onions (scallions); add the wine and return to the boil, simmer for 2-3 minutes.

5 Refrigerate the stock when cool; it will keep for up to 4-5 days. Alternatively, it can be frozen in small containers and be defrosted as required.

Fresh Chicken Stock

MAKES 1.75 LITRES/3 PINTS/7½ CUPS

- 1 kg/2 lb 4 oz chicken, skinned
- 2 celery sticks
- 1 onion
- 2 carrots
- 1 garlic clove
- few sprigs of fresh parsley
- 2 litres/3½ pints/9 cups water
- salt and pepper

1 Put all the ingredients into a large saucepan.

2 Bring to the boil. Skim away surface scum using a large flat spoon. Reduce the heat to a gentle simmer, partially cover, and cook for 2 hours. Allow to cool.

3 Line a sieve (strainer) with clean muslin (cheesecloth) and place over a large jug or bowl. Pour the stock through the sieve (strainer). The cooked chicken can be used in another recipe. Discard the other solids. Cover the stock and chill.

4 Skim away any fat that forms before using. Store in the refrigerator for 3-4 days, until required, or freeze in small batches.

Fresh Vegetable Stock

This can be kept chilled for up to three days or frozen for up to three months. Salt is not added when cooking the stock: it is better to season it according to the dish in which it its to be used.

MAKES 1.5 LITRES/2¾ PINTS/6¼ CUPS

- 250 g/9 oz shallots
- 1 large carrot, diced
- 1 celery stalk, chopped
- ½ fennel bulb
- 1 garlic clove
- 1 bay leaf
- a few fresh parsley and tarragon sprigs
- 2 litres/ 3½ pints/8¾ cups water
- pepper

1 Put all the ingredients in a large saucepan and bring to the boil.

2 Skim off the surface scum with a flat spoon and reduce to a gentle simmer. Partially cover and cook for 45 minutes. Leave to cool.

3 Line a sieve (strainer) with clean muslin (cheesecloth) and put over a large jug or bowl. Pour the stock through the sieve (strainer). Discard the herbs and vegetables.

4 Cover and store in small quantities in the refrigerator for up to three days.

Fresh Lamb Stock

MAKES 1.75 LITRES/3 PINTS/7½ CUPS

- about 1 kg/2 lb 4 oz bones from a cooked joint or raw chopped lamb bones
- 2 onions, studded with 6 cloves, or sliced or chopped coarsely
- 2 carrots, sliced
- 1 leek, sliced
- 1-2 celery sticks, sliced
- 1 Bouquet Garni
- about 2.25 litres/4 pints/2 quarts water

1 Chop or break up the bones and place in a large saucepan with the other ingredients.

2 Bring to the boil and remove any scum from the surface with a perforated spoon. Cover and simmer gently for 3-4 hours. Strain the stock and leave to cool.

3 Remove any fat from the surface and chill. If stored for more than 24 hours the stock must be boiled every day, cooled quickly and chilled again. The stock may be frozen for up to 2 months; place in a large plastic bag and seal, leaving at least 2.5 cm/1 inch of headspace to allow for expansion.

Fresh Fish Stock

MAKES 1.75 LITRES/3 PINTS/7½ CUPS

- 1 head of a cod or salmon, etc, plus the trimmings, skin and bones or just the trimmings, skin and bones
- 1-2 onions, sliced
- 1 carrot, sliced
- 1-2 celery sticks, sliced
- good squeeze of lemon juice
- 1 Bouquet Garni or 2 fresh or dried bay leaves

1 Wash the fish head and trimmings and place in a saucepan. Cover with water and bring to the boil.

2 Remove any scum with a perforated spoon, then add the remaining ingredients. Cover and simmer for about 30 minutes.

3 Strain and cool. Store in ther refrigerator and use within 2 days.

Cornflour (cornstarch) Paste

Cornflour (cornstarch) paste is made by mixing 1 part cornflour (cornstarch) with about 1½ parts of cold water. Stir until smooth. The paste is used to thicken sauces.

Plain Rice

Use long-grain rice or patna rice, or better still, try fragrant Thai rice

SERVES 4

- 250 g/9 oz long-grain rice
- about 250 ml/9 fl oz/1 cup cold water
- pinch of salt
- ½ tsp oil (optional)

1 Wash and rinse the rice just once. Place the rice in a saucepan and add enough water so that there is no more than 2 cm/¾ inch of water above the surface of the rice.

2 Bring to the boil, add salt and oil (if using), and stir to prevent the rice sticking to the bottom of the pan.

3 Reduce the heat to very, very low, cover and cook for 15-20 minutes.

4 Remove from the heat and let stand, covered, for 10 minutes or so. Fluff up the rice with a fork or spoon before serving.

How to Use This Book

Each recipe contains a wealth of useful information, including a breakdown of nutritional quantities, preparation and cooking times, and level of difficulty. All of this information is explained in detail below.

This amount of time represents the actual cooking time.

The nutritional information provided for each recipe is per serving or per portion. Optional ingredients, variations or serving suggestions have not been included in the calculations.

The number of chef's hats represents the difficulty of each recipe, ranging from easy (1 chef's hat) to difficult (5 chef's hats).

This amount of time represents the preparation of ingredients, including cooling, chilling and soaking times.

The ingredients for each recipe are listed in the order that they are used.

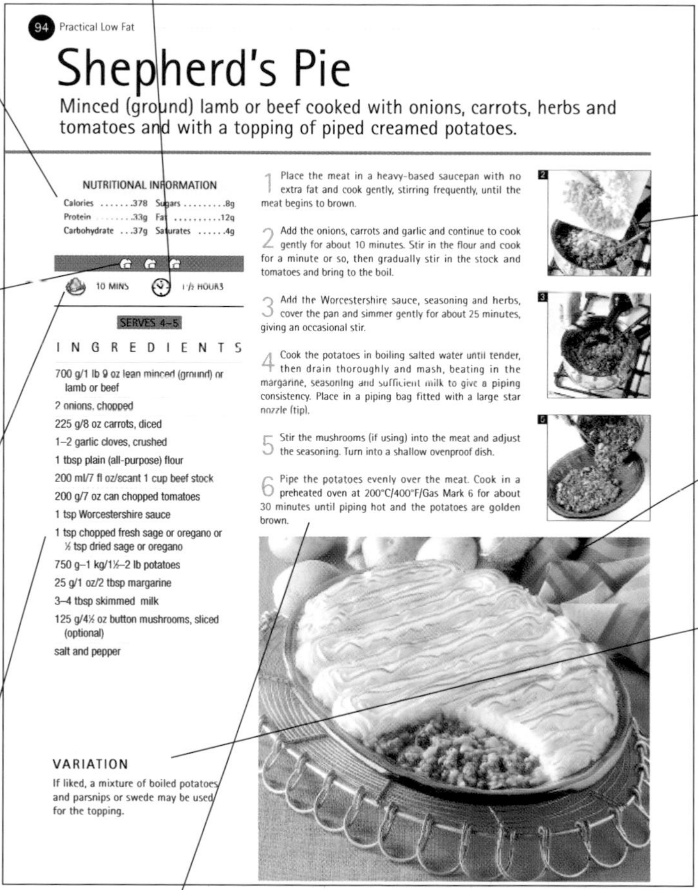

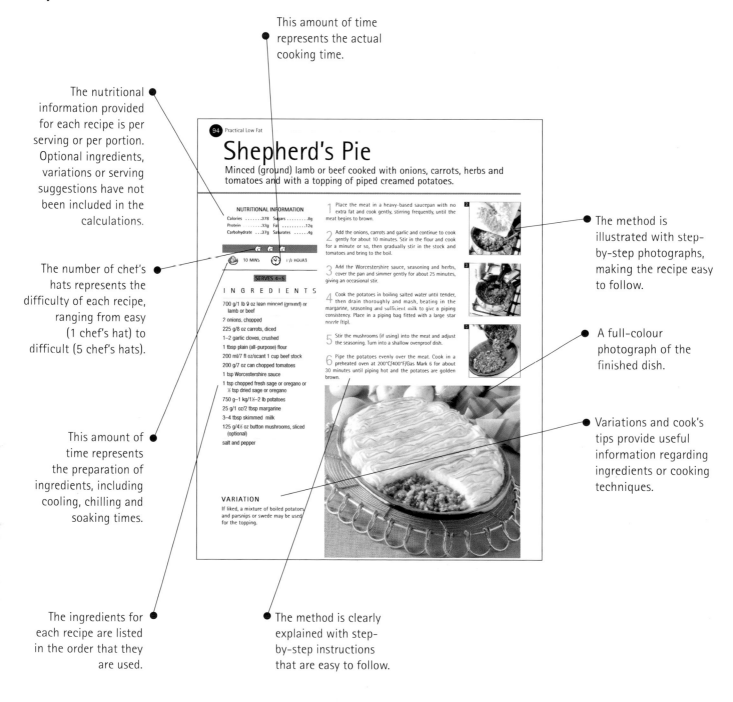

94 Practical Low Fat

Shepherd's Pie

Minced (ground) lamb or beef cooked with onions, carrots, herbs and tomatoes and with a topping of piped creamed potatoes.

NUTRITIONAL INFORMATION

Calories	378	Sugars	8g
Protein	33g	Fat	12g
Carbohydrate	37g	Saturates	4g

10 MINS 1½ HOURS

SERVES 4–5

INGREDIENTS

700 g/1 lb 9 oz lean minced (ground) or lamb or beef
2 onions, chopped
225 g/8 oz carrots, diced
1–2 garlic cloves, crushed
1 tbsp plain (all-purpose) flour
200 ml/7 fl oz/scant 1 cup beef stock
200 g/7 oz can chopped tomatoes
1 tsp Worcestershire sauce
1 tsp chopped fresh sage or oregano or ½ tsp dried sage or oregano
750 g–1 kg/1½–2 lb potatoes
25 g/1 oz/2 tbsp margarine
3–4 tbsp skimmed milk
125 g/4½ oz button mushrooms, sliced (optional)
salt and pepper

1 Place the meat in a heavy-based saucepan with no extra fat and cook gently, stirring frequently, until the meat begins to brown.

2 Add the onions, carrots and garlic and continue to cook gently for about 10 minutes. Stir in the flour and cook for a minute or so, then gradually stir in the stock and tomatoes and bring to the boil.

3 Add the Worcestershire sauce, seasoning and herbs, cover the pan and simmer gently for about 25 minutes, giving an occasional stir.

4 Cook the potatoes in boiling salted water until tender, then drain thoroughly and mash, beating in the margarine, seasoning and sufficient milk to give a piping consistency. Place in a piping bag fitted with a large star nozzle (tip).

5 Stir the mushrooms (if using) into the meat and adjust the seasoning. Turn into a shallow ovenproof dish.

6 Pipe the potatoes evenly over the meat. Cook in a preheated oven at 200°C/400°F/Gas Mark 6 for about 30 minutes until piping hot and the potatoes are golden brown.

VARIATION

If liked, a mixture of boiled potatoes and parsnips or swede may be used for the topping.

The method is illustrated with step-by-step photographs, making the recipe easy to follow.

A full-colour photograph of the finished dish.

Variations and cook's tips provide useful information regarding ingredients or cooking techniques.

The method is clearly explained with step-by-step instructions that are easy to follow.

Soups

The traditional way to start a meal is with a soup, but they can also be a satisfying meal in themselves, depending on their ingredients or if they are served with crusty bread. For best results use homemade stock – use the liquor left after cooking vegetables and the juices from fish and meat that have been used as the base of casseroles. Ready-made

stocks in the form of cubes or granules tend to contain large amounts of salt and flavourings which can overpower the delicate flavours. Although making fresh stock takes a little longer, it is well worth it for the superior taste. It is a good idea to make a large batch and freeze the remainder, in smaller quantities, for later use. Potato can be added to thicken soups rather than stirring in the traditional thickener of flour and water – or, worse, flour and fat.

Mixed Bean Soup

This is a really hearty soup, filled with colour, flavour and goodness, which may be adapted to any vegetables that you have at hand.

NUTRITIONAL INFORMATION

Calories	190	Sugars	9g
Protein	10g	Fat	4g
Carbohydrate	30g	Saturates	0.5g

5 MINS

40 MINS

SERVES 4

INGREDIENTS

- 1 tbsp vegetable oil
- 1 red onion, halved and sliced
- 100 g/3½ oz/⅔ cup potato, diced
- 1 carrot, diced
- 1 leek, sliced
- 1 green chilli, sliced
- 3 garlic cloves, crushed
- 1 tsp ground coriander
- 1 tsp chilli powder
- 1 litre/1¾ pints/4 cups vegetable stock
- 450 g/1 lb mixed canned beans, such as red kidney, borlotti, black eye or flageolet, drained
- salt and pepper
- 2 tbsp chopped coriander (cilantro), to garnish

1

3

5

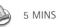

1 Heat the vegetable oil in a large saucepan and add the prepared onion, potato, carrot and leek. Sauté for about 2 minutes, stirring, until the vegetables are slightly softened.

2 Add the sliced chilli and crushed garlic and cook for 1 minute.

3 Stir in the ground coriander, chilli powder and the vegetable stock.

4 Bring the soup to the boil, reduce the heat and cook for 20 minutes or until the vegetables are tender.

5 Stir in the beans, season well with salt and pepper and cook for a further 10 minutes, stirring occasionally.

6 Transfer the soup to a warm tureen or individual bowls, garnish with chopped coriander (cilantro) and serve.

COOK'S TIP

Serve this soup with slices of warm corn bread or a cheese loaf.

Red (Bell) Pepper Soup

This soup has a real Mediterranean flavour, using sweet red (bell) peppers, tomato, chilli and basil. It is great served with a warm olive bread.

NUTRITIONAL INFORMATION

Calories	55	Sugar	10g
Protein	2g	Fats	0.5g
Carbohydrates	11g	Saturates	0.1g

5 MINS 25 MINS

SERVES 4

INGREDIENTS

- 225 g/8 oz red (bell) peppers, seeded and sliced
- 1 onion, sliced
- 2 garlic cloves, crushed
- 1 green chilli, chopped
- 300 ml/½ pint/1½ cups passata (sieved tomatoes)
- 600 ml/1 pint/2½ cups vegetable stock
- 2 tbsp chopped basil
- fresh basil sprigs, to garnish

1 Put the (bell) peppers in a large saucepan with the onion, garlic and chilli. Add the passata (sieved tomatoes) and vegetable stock and bring to the boil, stirring well.

2 Reduce the heat to a simmer and cook for 20 minutes or until the (bell) peppers have softened. Drain, reserving the liquid and vegetables separately.

3 Sieve the vegetables by pressing through a sieve (strainer) with the back of a spoon. Alternatively, blend in a food processor until smooth.

4 Return the vegetable purée to a clean saucepan with the reserved cooking liquid. Add the basil and heat through until hot. Garnish the soup with fresh basil sprigs and serve.

1

3

4

VARIATION

This soup is also delicious served cold with 150 ml/¼ pint/¼ cup of natural (unsweetened) yogurt swirled into it.

Tomato & (Bell) Pepper Soup

Sweet red (bell) peppers and tangy tomatoes are blended together in a smooth vegetable soup that makes a perfect starter or light lunch.

NUTRITIONAL INFORMATION

Calories	52	Sugar	9g
Protein	3g	Fats	0.4g
Carbohydrates	10g	Saturates	0g

1¼ HOURS 35 MINS

SERVES 4

INGREDIENTS

- 2 large red (bell) peppers
- 1 large onion, chopped
- 2 sticks celery, trimmed and chopped
- 1 garlic clove, crushed
- 600 ml/1 pint/2½ cups Fresh Vegetable Stock (see page 14)
- 2 bay leaves
- 2 x 400 g/14 oz cans plum tomatoes
- salt and pepper
- 2 spring onions (scallions), finely shredded, to garnish
- crusty bread, to serve

1 Preheat the grill (broiler) to hot. Halve and deseed the (bell) peppers, arrange them on the grill (broiler) rack and cook, turning occasionally, for 8–10 minutes until softened and charred.

2 Leave to cool, then carefully peel off the charred skin. Reserving a small piece for garnish, chop the (bell) pepper flesh and place in a large saucepan.

3 Mix in the onion, celery and garlic. Add the stock and the bay leaves. Bring to the boil, cover and simmer for 15 minutes. Remove from the heat.

4 Stir in the tomatoes and transfer to a blender. Process for a few seconds until smooth. Return to the saucepan.

5 Season to taste and heat for 3–4 minutes until piping hot. Ladle into warm bowls and garnish with the reserved (bell) pepper cut into strips and the spring onion (scallion). Serve with crusty bread.

1

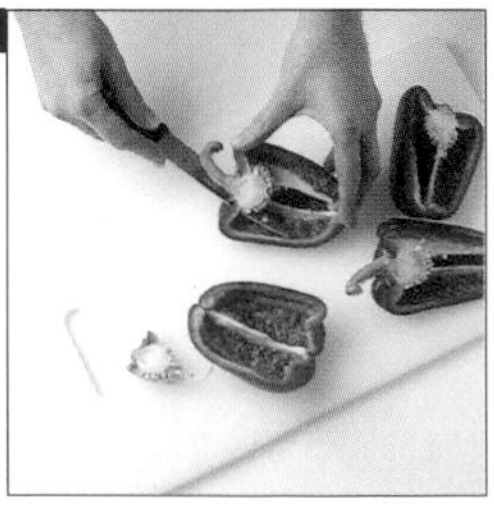

2

4

COOK'S TIP

If you prefer a coarser, more robust soup, lightly mash the tomatoes with a wooden spoon and omit the blending process in step 4.

Cucumber & Tomato Soup

Although this chilled soup is not an authentic Indian dish, it is wonderful served as a 'cooler' between hot, spicy courses.

NUTRITIONAL INFORMATION

Calories 73	Sugar 16g
Protein 2g	Fats 1g
Carbohydrates ...16g	Saturates 0.2g

12 HOURS 0 MINS

SERVES 6

INGREDIENTS

- 4 tomatoes, peeled and deseeded
- 1.5 kg/3 lb 5 oz watermelon, seedless if available
- 10 cm/4 inch piece cucumber, peeled and deseeded
- 2 spring onions (scallions), green part only, chopped
- 1 tbsp chopped fresh mint
- salt and pepper
- fresh mint sprigs, to garnish

1 Using a sharp knife, cut 1 tomato into 1 cm/½ inch dice.

2 Remove the rind from the melon, and remove the seeds if it is not seedless.

3 Put the 3 remaining tomatoes into a blender or food processor and, with the motor running, add the deseeded cucumber, chopped spring onions (scallions) and watermelon. Blend until smooth.

4 If not using a food processor, push the deseeded watermelon through a sieve (strainer). Stir the diced tomatoes and mint into the melon mixture. Adjust the seasoning to taste. Chop the cucumber, spring onions (scallions) and the 3 remaining tomatoes finely and add to the melon.

5 Chill the cucumber and tomato soup overnight in the refrigerator. Check the seasoning and transfer to a serving dish. Garnish with mint sprigs.

COOK'S TIP

Although this soup does improve if chilled overnight, it is also delicious as a quick appetizer if whipped up just before a meal, and served immediately.

1

4

4

Chilled Cucumber Soup

Serve this soup over ice on a warm summer day as a refreshing starter. It has the fresh tang of yogurt and a dash of spice from the Tabasco sauce.

NUTRITIONAL INFORMATION

Calories	83	Sugars	7g
Protein	12g	Fat	1g
Carbohydrate	7g	Saturates	0.3g

3½ HOURS 0 MINS

SERVES 4

INGREDIENTS

- 1 cucumber, peeled and diced
- 400 ml/14 fl oz/1⅔ cups Fresh Fish Stock, chilled (see page 15)
- 150 ml/5 fl oz/⅔ cup tomato juice
- 150 ml/5 fl oz/⅔ cup low-fat natural (unsweetened) yogurt
- 150 ml/5 fl oz/⅔ cup low-fat fromage frais (or double the quantity of yogurt)
- 125 g/4½ oz peeled prawns (shrimp), thawed if frozen, roughly chopped
- few drops Tabasco sauce
- 1 tbsp fresh mint, chopped
- salt and white pepper
- ice cubes, to serve

TO GARNISH

- sprigs of mint
- cucumber slices
- whole peeled prawns (shrimp)

1. Place the diced cucumber in a blender or food processor and work for a few seconds until smooth. Alternatively, chop the cucumber finely and push through a sieve.

2. Transfer the cucumber to a bowl. Stir in the stock, tomato juice, yogurt, fromage frais (if using) and prawns (shrimp), and mix well.

3. Add the Tabasco sauce and season to taste.

4. Stir in the chopped mint, cover and chill for at least 2 hours.

5. Ladle the soup into glass bowls and add a few ice cubes. Serve garnished with mint, cucumber slices and whole prawns (shrimp).

2

3

4

VARIATION

Instead of prawns (shrimp), add white crab meat or minced chicken. For a vegetarian version of this soup, omit the prawns (shrimp) and add an extra 125 g/4½ oz finely diced cucumber. Use fresh vegetable stock instead of fish stock.

Beetroot & Potato Soup

A deep red soup makes a stunning first course. Adding a swirl of soured cream and a few sprigs of dill gives a very pretty effect.

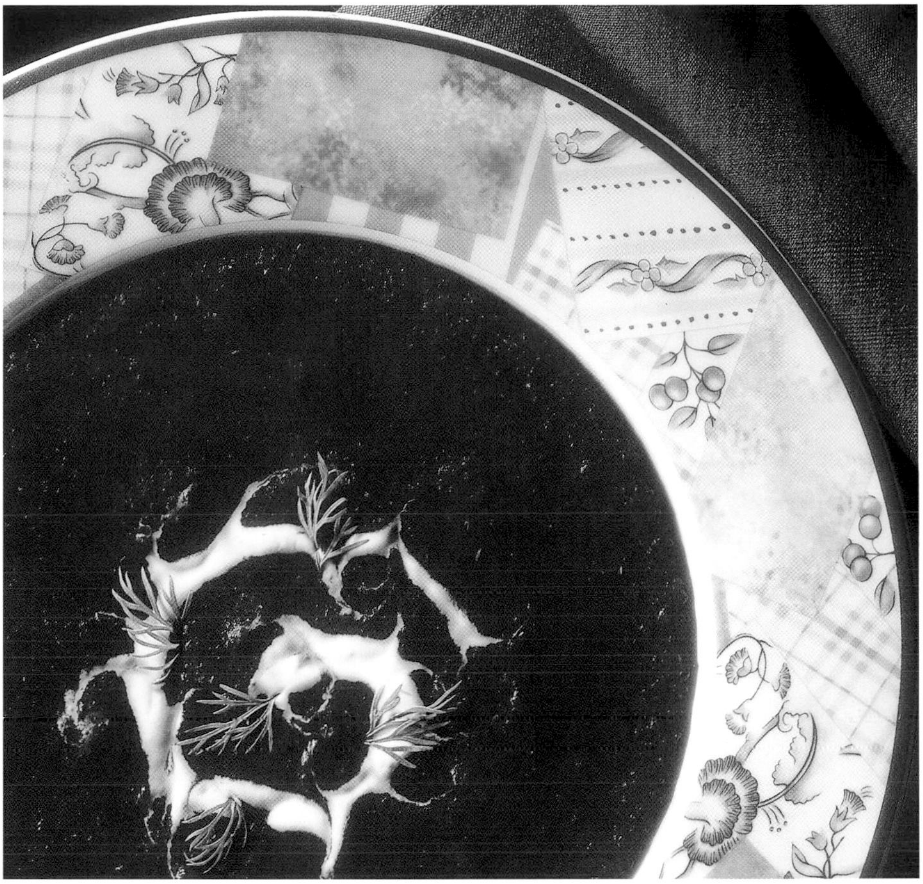

NUTRITIONAL INFORMATION

Calories 120	Sugars 11g
Protein 4g	Fat 2g
Carbohydrate ...22g	Saturates 1g

20 MINS 30 MINS

SERVES 6

INGREDIENTS

- 1 onion, chopped
- 350 g/12 oz potatoes, diced
- 1 small cooking apple, peeled, cored and grated
- 3 tbsp water
- 1 tsp cumin seeds
- 500 g/1 lb 2 oz cooked beetroot, peeled and diced
- 1 dried bay leaf
- pinch of dried thyme
- 1 tsp lemon juice
- 600 ml/1 pint/2½ cups hot vegetable stock
- 4 tbsp soured cream
- salt and pepper
- few sprigs of fresh dill, to garnish

1 Place the onion, potatoes, apple and water in a large bowl. Cover and cook on HIGH power for 10 minutes.

2 Stir in the cumin seeds and cook on HIGH power for 1 minute.

3 Stir in the beetroot, bay leaf, thyme, lemon juice and stock. Cover and cook on HIGH power for 12 minutes, stirring halfway through. Leave to stand, uncovered, for 5 minutes.

2

3

5

4 Remove and discard the bay leaf. Strain the vegetables and reserve the liquid in a jug.

5 Purée the vegetables with a little of the reserved liquid in a food processor or blender, until they are smooth and creamy. Alternatively, either mash the soup or press it through a sieve (strainer).

6 Pour the vegetable purée into a clean bowl with the reserved liquid and mix well. Season with salt and pepper to taste. Cover and cook on HIGH power for 4–5 minutes until piping hot.

7 Serve the soup in warmed bowls. Swirl 1 tablespoon of soured cream into each serving and garnish with a few sprigs of fresh dill.

Spiced Fruit Soup

This delicately flavoured apple and apricot soup is gently spiced with ginger and allspice, and finished with a swirl of soured cream.

NUTRITIONAL INFORMATION

Calories	147	Sugar	28g
Protein	3g	Fats	0.4g
Carbohydrates	29g	Saturates	0g

7¾ HOURS 25 MINS

SERVES 4–6

INGREDIENTS

- 125 g/4½oz/⅔ cup dried apricots, soaked overnight or no-need-to-soak dried apricots
- 500 g/1 lb 2 oz dessert apples, peeled, cored and chopped
- 1 small onion, chopped
- 1 tbsp lemon or lime juice
- 700 ml/1¼ pints/3 cups Fresh Chicken Stock (see page 14)
- 150 ml/¼ pint/⅔ cup dry white wine
- ¼ tsp ground ginger
- good pinch of ground allspice
- salt and pepper

TO GARNISH

- 4–6 tbsp soured cream or natural fromage frais
- little ground ginger or ground allspice

1 Drain the apricot if necessary and chop.

2 Put in a saucepan and add the apples, onion, lemon or lime juice and stock. Bring to the boil, cover and simmer gently for about 20 minutes.

3 Leave the soup to cool a little, then press through a sieve (strainer) or blend in a food processor or blender until smooth. Next pour the fruit soup into a clean pan.

4 Add the wine and spices and season to taste. Bring back to the boil, then leave to cool. If too thick, add a little more stock or water and then chill thoroughly.

5 Put a spoonful of soured cream or fromage frais on top of each portion and lightly dust with ginger or allspice.

VARIATION

Other fruits can be combined with apples to make fruit soups – try raspberries, blackberries, blackcurrants or cherries. If the fruits have a lot of pips or stones (pits), the soup should be sieved (strained) after puréeing.

1

2

3

Yogurt & Spinach Soup

Whole young spinach leaves add vibrant colour to this unusual soup. Serve with hot, crusty bread for a nutritious light meal.

NUTRITIONAL INFORMATION	
Calories 227	Sugars 13g
Protein 14g	Fat 7g
Carbohydrate ...29g	Saturates 2g

15 MINS 30 MINS

SERVES 4

INGREDIENTS

- 600 ml/1 pint/2½ cups chicken stock
- 60 g/2 oz/4 tbsp long-grain rice, rinsed and drained
- 4 tbsp water
- 1 tbsp cornflour (cornstarch)
- 600 ml/1 pint/2½ cups low-fat natural yogurt
- juice of 1 lemon
- 3 egg yolks, lightly beaten
- 350 g/12 oz young spinach leaves, washed and drained
- salt and pepper

1 Pour the stock into a large pan, season and bring to the boil. Add the rice and simmer for 10 minutes, until barely cooked. Remove from the heat.

2 Combine the water and cornflour (cornstarch) to make a smooth paste.

3 Pour the yogurt into a second pan and stir in the cornflour (cornstarch) mixture. Set the pan over a low heat and bring the yogurt slowly to the boil, stirring with a wooden spoon in one direction only. This will stabilize the yogurt and prevent it from separating or curdling on contact with the hot stock. When the yogurt has reached boiling point, stand the pan on a heat diffuser and leave to simmer slowly for 10 minutes. Remove the pan from the heat and allow the mixture to cool slightly before stirring in the beaten egg yolks.

4 Pour the yogurt mixture into the stock, stir in the lemon juice and stir to blend thoroughly. Keep the soup warm, but do not allow it to boil.

5 Blanch the washed and drained spinach leaves in a large pan of boiling, salted water for 2-3 minutes until they begin to soften but have not wilted. Tip the spinach into a colander, drain well and stir it into the soup. Let the spinach warm through. Taste the soup and adjust the seasoning if necessary. Serve in wide shallow soup plates, with hot, fresh crusty bread.

Minted Pea & Yogurt Soup

A deliciously refreshing soup that is full of goodness. It is also extremely tasty served chilled.

NUTRITIONAL INFORMATION

Calories	208	Sugars	9g
Protein	10g	Fat	7g
Carbohydrate	26g	Saturates	2g

10 MINS 25 MINS

SERVES 4

INGREDIENTS

- 2 tbsp vegetable ghee or oil
- 2 onions, peeled and coarsely chopped
- 225 g/8 oz potato, peeled and coarsely chopped
- 2 garlic cloves, peeled
- 2.5 cm/1 inch ginger root, peeled and chopped
- 1 tsp ground coriander
- 1 tsp ground cumin
- 1 tbsp plain (all-purpose) flour
- 850 ml/1½ pints/3½ cups vegetable stock
- 500 g/1 lb 2 oz frozen peas
- 2-3 tbsp chopped fresh mint, to taste
- salt and freshly ground black pepper
- 150 ml/¼ pint/⅔ cup low-fat natural yogurt
- ½ tsp cornflour (cornstarch)
- 300 ml/½ pint/1¼ cups skimmed milk
- a little extra yogurt, for serving (optional)
- mint sprigs, to garnish

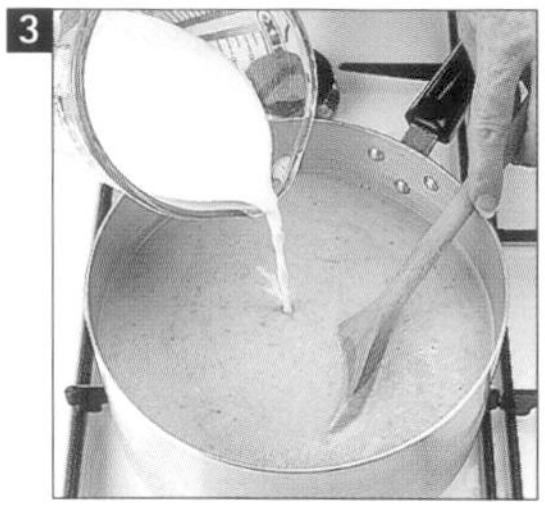

1 Heat the ghee or oil in a saucepan, add the onions and potato and cook gently for 3 minutes. Stir in the garlic, ginger, coriander, cumin and flour and cook for 1 minute, stirring. Add the stock, peas and half the mint and bring to the boil, stirring. Reduce the heat, cover and simmer gently for 15 minutes.

2 Purée the soup in a blender or food processor. Return the mixture to the pan and season with salt and pepper to taste. Blend the yogurt with the cornflour (cornstarch) and stir into the soup.

3 Add the milk and bring almost to the boil, stirring all the time. Cook very gently for 2 minutes. Serve hot, sprinkled with the remaining mint and a swirl of extra yogurt, if wished.

COOK'S TIP

The yogurt is mixed with a little cornflour (cornstarch) before being added to the hot soup – this helps to stabilize the yogurt and prevents it separating when heated.

Red Lentil Soup with Yogurt

Tasty red lentil soup flavoured with chopped coriander (cilantro). The yogurt adds a light piquancy to the soup .

NUTRITIONAL INFORMATION

Calories 280	Sugars 6g
Protein 17g	Fat 7g
Carbohydrate ...40g	Saturates 4g

5 MINS

30 MINS

SERVES 4

INGREDIENTS

25 g/1 oz/2 tbsp butter
1 onion, chopped finely
1 celery stick, chopped finely
1 large carrot, grated
1 dried bay leaf
225 g/8 oz/1 cup red lentils
1.2 litres/2 pints/5 cups hot vegetable or chicken stock
2 tbsp chopped fresh coriander (cilantro)
4 tbsp low-fat natural (unsweetened) yogurt
salt and pepper
fresh coriander (cilantro) sprigs, to garnish

1

2

4

1 Place the butter, onion and celery in a large bowl. Cover and cook on HIGH power for 3 minutes.

2 Add the carrot, bay leaf and lentils. Pour over the stock. Cover and cook on HIGH power for 15 minutes, stirring halfway through.

3 Remove from the microwave oven and stand, covered, for 5 minutes.

4 Remove the bay leaf, then blend in batches in a food processor, until smooth. Alternatively, press the soup through a sieve (strainer).

5 Pour into a clean bowl. Season with salt and pepper to taste and stir in the coriander (cilantro). Cover and cook on HIGH power for 4–5 minutes until piping hot.

6 Serve in warmed bowls. Stir 1 tablespoon of yogurt into each serving and garnish with sprigs of fresh coriander (cilantro).

COOK'S TIP

For an extra creamy soup try adding low-fat crème fraîche or soured cream instead of yogurt.

Spicy Lentil Soup

For a warming, satisfying meal on a cold day, this lentil dish is packed full of taste and goodness.

NUTRITIONAL INFORMATION

Calories	155	Sugars	4g
Protein	11g	Fat	3g
Carbohydrate	22g	Saturates	0.4g

1 HOUR

1¼ HOURS

SERVES 4

INGREDIENTS

125 g/4½ oz/½ cup red lentils
2 tsp vegetable oil
1 large onion, chopped finely
2 garlic cloves, crushed
1 tsp ground cumin
1 tsp ground coriander
1 tsp garam masala
2 tbsp tomato purée (paste)
1 litre/1¾ pints/4½ cups Fresh Vegetable Stock (see page 14)
about 350 g/12 oz can sweetcorn, drained
salt and pepper

TO SERVE

low-fat natural (unsweetened) yogurt
chopped fresh parsley
warmed pitta (pocket) bread

2

3

4

1 Rinse the red lentils in cold water. Drain the lentils well and put to one side for a while.

2 Heat the oil in a large non-stick saucepan and fry the onion and garlic gently until softened but not browned.

3 Stir in the cumin, coriander, garam masala, tomato purée (paste) and 4 tablespoons of the stock. Mix well and simmer gently for 2 minutes.

4 Add the lentils and pour in the remaining stock. Bring to the boil, reduce the heat and simmer, covered, for 1 hour until the lentils are tender and the soup thickened. Stir in the sweetcorn and heat through for 5 minutes. Season well.

5 Ladle into warmed soup bowls and top each with a spoonful of yogurt and a sprinkling of parsley. Serve with warmed pitta (pocket) bread.

COOK'S TIP

Many of the ready-prepared ethnic breads available today either contain fat or are brushed with oil before baking. Always check the ingredients list for fat content.

Sweet Potato & Onion Soup

This simple recipe uses the sweet potato with its distinctive flavour and colour, combined with a hint of orange and coriander (cilantro).

NUTRITIONAL INFORMATION	
Calories 320	Sugars 26g
Protein 7g	Fat 7g
Carbohydrate . . .62g	Saturates 1g

15 MINS   30 MINS

SERVES 4

INGREDIENTS

- 2 tbsp vegetable oil
- 900 g/2 lb sweet potatoes, diced
- 1 carrot, diced
- 2 onions, sliced
- 2 garlic cloves, crushed
- 600 ml/1 pint/2½ cups vegetable stock
- 300 ml/½ pint/1¼ cups unsweetened orange juice
- 225 ml/8 fl oz/1 cup low-fat natural yogurt
- 2 tbsp chopped fresh coriander (cilantro)
- salt and pepper

TO GARNISH

- coriander (cilantro) sprigs
- orange rind

1 Heat the vegetable oil in a large saucepan and add the diced sweet potatoes and carrot, sliced onions and garlic. Sauté the vegetables together gently for 5 minutes, stirring constantly.

2 Pour in the vegetable stock and orange juice and bring them to the boil.

3 Reduce the heat to a simmer, cover the saucepan and cook the vegetables for 20 minutes or until the sweet potato and carrot cubes are tender.

4 Transfer the mixture to a food processor or blender in batches and process for 1 minute until puréed. Return the purée to the rinsed-out saucepan.

5 Stir in the natural yogurt and chopped coriander (cilantro) and season to taste.

6 Serve the soup in warm bowls and garnish with coriander (cilantro) sprigs and orange rind.

VARIATION

This soup can be chilled before serving, if preferred. If chilling it, stir the yogurt into the dish just before serving. Serve in chilled bowls.

Fish & Crab Chowder

Packed full of flavour, this delicious fish dish is a meal in itself, but it is ideal accompanied with a crisp side salad.

NUTRITIONAL INFORMATION

Calories	440	Sugars	10g
Protein	49g	Fat	7g
Carbohydrate	43g	Saturates	1g

1¼ HOURS 25 MINS

SERVES 4

INGREDIENTS

- 1 large onion, chopped finely
- 2 celery sticks, chopped finely
- 150 ml/¼ pint/⅔ cup dry white wine
- 600 ml/1 pint/2½ cups Fresh Fish Stock (see page 15)
- 600 ml/1 pint/2½ cups skimmed milk
- 1 dried bay leaf
- 225 g/8 oz/1½ cups smoked cod fillets, skinned and cut into 2.5 cm/1 inch cubes
- 225 g/8 oz undyed smoked haddock fillets, skinned and cut into 2.5 cm/1 inch cubes
- 2 x 175 g/6 oz cans crab meat, drained
- 225 g/8 oz blanched French (green) beans, sliced into 2.5 cm/1 inch pieces
- 225 g/8 oz/1½ cups cooked brown rice
- 4 tsp cornflour (cornstarch) mixed with 4 tablespoons cold water
- salt and pepper
- chopped fresh parsley to garnish
- mixed green salad, to serve

1

3

4

1 Place the onion, celery and wine in a large non-stick saucepan. Bring to the boil, cover and cook for 5 minutes.

2 Uncover and cook for 5 minutes until the liquid has evaporated.

3 Pour in the stock and milk and add the bay leaf. Bring to a simmer and stir in the cod and haddock. Simmer gently, uncovered, for 5 minutes.

4 Add the crab meat, French (green) beans and rice and cook gently for 2–3 minutes until heated through. Remove the bay leaf with a perforated spoon.

5 Stir in the cornflour (cornstarch) mixture until thickened slightly. Season to taste and ladle into 4 warmed soup bowls. Garnish with chopped parsley and serve with a mixed salad.

Mushroom & Ginger Soup

Thai soups are very quickly and easily put together, and are cooked so that each ingredient can still be tasted in the finished dish.

NUTRITIONAL INFORMATION

Calories 74	Sugars 1g
Protein 3g	Fat 3g
Carbohydrate 9g	Saturates 0.4g

1½ HOURS   15 MINS

SERVES 4

INGREDIENTS

- 15 g/½ oz/¼ cup dried Chinese mushrooms or 125 g/4½ oz/1⅓ cups field or chestnut (crimini) mushrooms
- 1 litre/1¾ pints/4 cups hot Fresh Vegetable Stock (see page 14)
- 125 g/4½ oz thread egg noodles
- 2 tsp sunflower oil
- 3 garlic cloves, crushed
- 2.5 cm/1 inch piece ginger, shredded finely
- ½ tsp mushroom ketchup
- 1 tsp light soy sauce
- 125 g/4½ oz/2 cups bean sprouts
- coriander (cilantro) leaves, to garnish

1 Soak the dried Chinese mushrooms (if using) for at least 30 minutes in 300 ml/½ pint/1¼ cups of the hot vegetable stock. Remove the stalks and discard, then slice the mushrooms. Reserve the stock.

2 Cook the noodles for 2–3 minutes in boiling water. Drain and rinse. Set them aside.

3 Heat the oil over a high heat in a wok or large, heavy frying pan (skillet). Add the garlic and ginger, stir and add the mushrooms. Stir over a high heat for 2 minutes.

4 Add the remaining vegetable stock with the reserved stock and bring to the boil. Add the mushroom ketchup and soy sauce.

5 Stir in the bean sprouts and cook until tender. Put some noodles in each bowl and ladle the soup on top. Garnish with coriander (cilantro) leaves and serve.

2

4

5

COOK'S TIP

Rice noodles contain no fat and are ideal for for anyone on a low-fat diet.

Carrot & Cumin Soup

Carrot soups are very popular and and here cumin, tomato, potato and celery give the soup both richness and depth.

NUTRITIONAL INFORMATION

Calories	114	Sugars	8g
Protein	3g	Fat	6g
Carbohydrate	12g	Saturates	4g

2½ HOURS 45 MINS

SERVES 4–6

INGREDIENTS

- 45 g/1½ oz/3 tbsp butter or margarine
- 1 large onion, chopped
- 1–2 garlic cloves, crushed
- 350 g/12 oz carrots, sliced
- 900 ml/1½ pints/3½ cups Chicken or Vegetable Stock (see page 14)
- ¾ tsp ground cumin
- 2 celery sticks, sliced thinly
- 125 g/4 oz potato, diced
- 2 tsp tomato purée (paste)
- 2 tsp lemon juice
- 2 fresh or dried bay leaves
- about 300 ml/½ pint/1¼ cups skimmed milk
- salt and pepper
- celery leaves to garnish

1 Melt the butter or margarine in a large saucepan. Add the onion and garlic and fry very gently until the onion begins to soften.

2 Add the carrots and continue to fry gently for a further 5 minutes, stirring frequently and taking care they do not brown.

3 Add the stock, cumin, seasoning, celery, potato, tomato purée (paste), lemon juice and bay leaves and bring to the boil. Cover and simmer gently for about 30 minutes until all the vegetables are very tender.

4 Discard the bay leaves, cool the soup a little and then press it through a sieve (strainer) or blend in a food processor or blender until smooth.

5 Pour the soup into a clean pan, add the milk and bring slowly to the boil. Taste and adjust the seasoning.

6 Garnish each serving with a small celery leaf and serve.

2

4

5

COOK'S TIP

This soup can be frozen for up to 3 months. Add the milk when reheating.

Spicy Dhal & Carrot Soup

This delicious, warming and nutritious soup includes a selection of spices to give it a 'kick'. It is simple to make and extremely good to eat.

NUTRITIONAL INFORMATION

Calories	173	Sugars	11g
Protein	9g	Fat	5g
Carbohydrate	24g	Saturates	1g

10 MINS

50 MINS

SERVES 6

INGREDIENTS

- 125 g/4½ oz split red lentils
- 1.2 litres/2 pints/5 cups vegetable stock
- 350 g/12 oz carrots, peeled and sliced
- 2 onions, peeled and chopped
- 1 x 250 g/9 oz can chopped tomatoes
- 2 garlic cloves, peeled and chopped
- 2 tbsp vegetable ghee or oil
- 1 tsp ground cumin
- 1 tsp ground coriander
- 1 fresh green chilli, seeded and chopped, or use 1 tsp minced chilli (from a jar)
- ½ tsp ground turmeric
- 15 ml/1 tbsp lemon juice
- salt
- 300 ml/½ pint/1¼ cups skimmed milk
- 30 ml/2 tbsp chopped fresh coriander (cilantro)
- yogurt, to serve

1

2

5

1 Place the lentils in a sieve and wash well under cold running water. Drain and place in a large saucepan with 850 ml/1½ pints/3½ cups of the vegetable stock, the carrots, onions, tomatoes and garlic. Bring the mixture to the boil, reduce the heat, cover and simmer for 30 minutes.

2 Meanwhile, heat the ghee or oil in a small pan, add the cumin, coriander, chilli and turmeric and fry gently for 1 minute.

3 Remove from the heat and stir in the lemon juice and salt to taste.

4 Purée the soup in batches in a blender or food processor. Return the soup to the saucepan, add the spice mixture and the remaining 300 ml/½ pint/1¼ cups stock or water and simmer for 10 minutes.

5 Add the milk to the soup and adjust the seasoning according to taste.

6 Stir in the chopped coriander (cilantro) and reheat gently. Serve hot, with a swirl of yogurt.

Indian Potato & Pea Soup

A slightly hot and spicy Indian flavour is given to this soup with the use of garam masala, chilli, cumin and coriander.

NUTRITIONAL INFORMATION

Calories	153	Sugars	6g
Protein	6g	Fat	6g
Carbohydrate	18g	Saturates	1g

5 MINS 35 MINS

SERVES 4

INGREDIENTS

- 2 tbsp vegetable oil
- 225 g/8 oz floury (mealy) potatoes, diced
- 1 large onion, chopped
- 2 garlic cloves, crushed
- 1 tsp garam masala
- 1 tsp ground coriander
- 1 tsp ground cumin
- 900 ml/1½ pints/3¾ cups vegetable stock
- 1 red chilli, chopped
- 100 g/3½ oz frozen peas
- 4 tbsp low-fat natural yogurt
- salt and pepper
- chopped fresh coriander (cilantro), to garnish

1

2

3

1 Heat the vegetable oil in a large saucepan and add the diced potatoes, onion and garlic. Sauté gently for about 5 minutes, stirring constantly. Add the ground spices and cook for 1 minute, stirring all the time.

2 Stir in the vegetable stock and chopped red chilli and bring the mixture to the boil. Reduce the heat, cover the pan and simmer for 20 minutes.

3 Add the peas and cook for a further 5 minutes. Stir in the yogurt and season to taste.

4 Pour the soup into warmed bowls, garnish with the chopped fresh coriander (cilantro) and serve hot with warm bread.

COOK'S TIP

For slightly less heat, deseed the chilli before adding it to the soup. Always wash your hands after handling chillies as they contain volatile oils that can irritate the skin and make your eyes burn if you touch your face.

Consommé

A traditional clear soup made from beef bones and lean minced (ground) beef. Thin strips of vegetables provide a colourful garnish.

NUTRITIONAL INFORMATION

Calories	109	Sugars	6g
Protein	13g	Fat	3g
Carbohydrate	7g	Saturates	1g

6¼ HOURS — 1¼ HOURS

SERVES 4–6

INGREDIENTS

- 1.25 litres/2¼ pints/5 cups strong beef stock
- 225 g/8 oz/1 cup extra lean minced (ground) beef
- 2 tomatoes, skinned, seeded and chopped
- 2 large carrots, chopped
- 1 large onion, chopped
- 2 celery sticks, chopped
- 1 turnip, chopped (optional)
- 1 Bouquet Garni
- 2–3 egg whites
- shells of 2–4 eggs, crushed
- 1–2 tbsp sherry (optional)
- salt and pepper
- Melba Toast, to serve

TO GARNISH

- julienne strips of raw carrot, turnip, celery or celeriac (celery root) or a one-egg omelette, cut into julienne strips

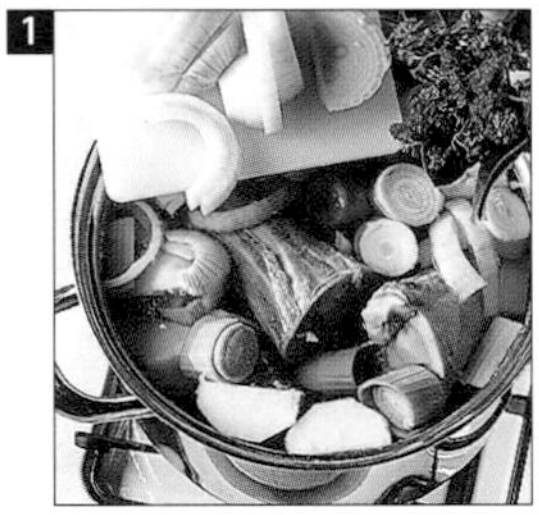

1 Put the stock and minced (ground) beef in a saucepan. Leave for 1 hour. Add the tomatoes, carrots, onion, celery, turnip (if using), bouquet garni, 2 of the egg whites, the crushed shells of 2 of the eggs and plenty of seasoning. Bring to almost boiling point, whisking hard all the time with a flat whisk.

2 Cover and simmer for 1 hour, taking care not to allow the layer of froth on top of the soup to break.

3 Pour the soup through a jelly bag or scalded fine cloth, keeping the froth back until the last, then pour the ingredients through the cloth again into a clean pan. The resulting liquid should be completely clear.

4 If the soup is not quite clear, return it to the pan with another egg white and the crushed shells of 2 more eggs. Repeat the whisking process as before and then boil for 10 minutes; strain again.

5 Add the sherry (if using) to the soup and reheat gently. Place the garnish in the warmed soup bowls and carefully pour in the soup. Serve with melba toast.

Beef & Vegetable Soup

This comforting broth is perfect for a cold day and is just as delicious made with lean lamb or pork fillet.

NUTRITIONAL INFORMATION

Calories	138	Sugars	2g
Protein	13g	Fat	3g
Carbohydrate	15g	Saturates	1g

12 HOURS   1 1/4 HOURS

SERVES 4

INGREDIENTS

- 60 g/2 oz/⅓ cup pearl barley, soaked overnight
- 1.2 litres/2 pints/5 cups fresh beef stock
- 1 tsp dried mixed herbs
- 225 g/8 oz lean rump or sirloin beef
- 1 large carrot, diced
- 1 leek, shredded
- 1 medium onion, chopped
- 2 sticks celery, sliced
- salt and pepper
- 2 tbsp fresh parsley, chopped, to garnish
- crusty bread, to serve

1 Place the pearl barley in a large saucepan. Pour over the stock and add the mixed herbs. Bring to the boil, cover and simmer gently over a low heat for 10 minutes.

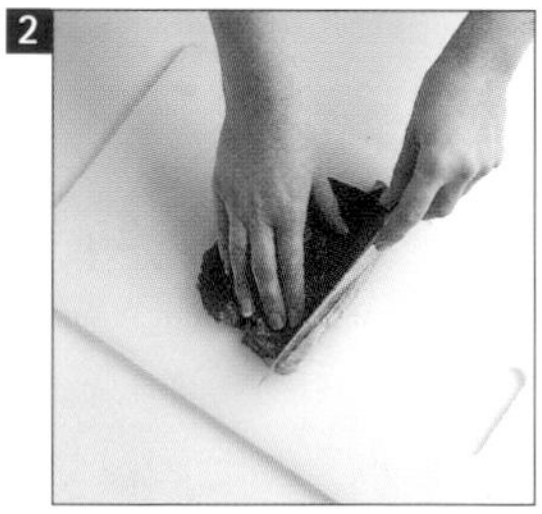

2 Meanwhile, trim any fat from the beef and cut the meat into thin strips.

3 Skim away any scum that has risen to the top of the stock with a flat ladle.

4 Add the beef, carrot, leek, onion and celery to the pan. Bring back to the boil, cover and simmer for about 1 hour or until the barley, meat and vegetables are just tender.

5 Skim away any remaining scum that has risen to the top of the soup with a flat ladle. Blot the surface with absorbent kitchen paper to remove any fat. Adjust the seasoning according to your taste.

6 Ladle the soup into warm bowls and sprinkle with freshly chopped parsley. Serve piping hot, and accompanied with crusty bread.

VARIATION

A vegetarian version can be made by omitting the beef and beef stock and using vegetable stock instead. Just before serving, stir in 175 g/6 oz fresh bean curd (tofu), drained and diced.

Chunky Potato & Beef Soup

This is a real winter warmer – pieces of tender beef and chunky mixed vegetables are cooked in a liquor flavoured with sherry.

NUTRITIONAL INFORMATION

Calories 187	Sugars 3g
Protein 14g	Fat 9g
Carbohydrate ...12g	Saturates 2g

5 MINS

35 MINS

SERVES 4

INGREDIENTS

2 tbsp vegetable oil

225 g/8 oz lean braising or frying steak, cut into strips

225 g/8 oz new potatoes, halved

1 carrot, diced

2 celery sticks, sliced

2 leeks, sliced

850 ml/1½ pints/3¾ cups beef stock

8 baby sweetcorn cobs, sliced

1 bouquet garni

2 tbsp dry sherry

salt and pepper

chopped fresh parsley, to garnish

1 Heat the vegetable oil in a large saucepan.

2 Add the strips of meat to the saucepan and cook for 3 minutes, turning constantly.

3 Add the halved potatoes, diced carrot and sliced celery and leeks. Cook for a further 5 minutes, stirring.

4 Pour the beef stock into the saucepan and bring to the boil. Reduce the heat until the liquid is simmering, then add the sliced baby sweetcorn cobs and the bouquet garni.

5 Cook the soup for a further 20 minutes or until cooked through.

6 Remove the bouquet garni from the saucepan and discard. Stir the dry sherry into the soup and then season to taste with salt and pepper.

7 Pour the soup into warmed bowls and garnish with the chopped fresh parsley. Serve at once with crusty bread.

COOK'S TIP

Make double the quantity of soup and freeze the remainder in a rigid container for later use. When ready to use, leave in the refrigerator to defrost thoroughly, then heat until piping hot.

Split Pea & Ham Soup

You can use either yellow or green split peas in this recipe, but both types must be well washed and soaked overnight before use.

NUTRITIONAL INFORMATION

Calories	323	Sugars	9g
Protein	17g	Fat	9g
Carbohydrate	45g	Saturates	4g

12¼ HOURS

2¾ HOURS

SERVES 6

INGREDIENTS

- 300 g/10½ oz/1¼ cups dried yellow split peas
- 1.75 litres/3 pints/7½ cups water
- 2 onions, chopped finely
- 1 small turnip, chopped finely
- 2 carrots, chopped finely
- 2–4 celery sticks, chopped finely
- 1 lean ham knuckle
- 1 Bouquet Garni
- ½ tsp dried thyme
- ½ tsp ground ginger
- 1 tbsp white wine vinegar
- salt and pepper

1 Wash the dried peas thoroughly, then place in a bowl with half of the water and leave to soak overnight.

2 Put the soaked peas and their liquor, the remaining water, the onions, turnip, carrots and celery into a large saucepan, then add the ham knuckle, bouquet garni, dried thyme and ginger. Bring slowly to the boil.

3 Remove any scum from the surface of the soup, cover the pan and simmer gently for 2–2½ hours until the peas are very tender.

4 Remove the ham knuckle and bouquet garni. Strip about 125–175 g/4½–6 oz/¾–1 cup meat from the knuckle and chop it finely.

5 Add the chopped ham and vinegar to the soup and season to taste.

6 Bring back to the boil and simmer for 3–4 minutes. Serve.

VARIATION

If preferred, this soup can be sieved (strained) or blended in a food processor or blender until smooth. You can vary the vegetables, depending on what is available. Leeks, celeriac (celery root), or chopped or canned tomatoes are particularly good.

Lentil & Ham Soup

This is a good hearty soup, based on a stock made from a ham knuckle, with plenty of vegetables and red lentils to thicken it and add flavour.

NUTRITIONAL INFORMATION

Calories	219	Sugars	4g
Protein	17g	Fat	3g
Carbohydrate	33g	Saturates	1g

2¼ HOURS 1¾ HOURS

SERVES 4–6

INGREDIENTS

- 225 g/8 oz/1 cup red lentils
- 1.5 litres/2¾ pints/6¼ cups stock or water
- 2 onions, chopped
- 1 garlic clove, crushed
- 2 large carrots, chopped
- 1 lean ham knuckle or 175 g/6 oz lean bacon, chopped
- 4 large tomatoes, skinned and chopped
- 2 fresh or dried bay leaves
- 250 g/9 oz potatoes, chopped
- 1 tbsp white wine vinegar
- ¼ tsp ground allspice
- salt and pepper
- chopped spring onions (scallions) or chopped fresh parsley, to garnish

1 Put the lentils and stock or water in a saucepan and leave to soak for 1–2 hours.

2 Add the onions, garlic, carrots, ham knuckle or bacon, tomatoes, bay leaves and seasoning.

3 Bring the mixture in the saucepan to the boil, cover and simmer for about 1 hour until the lentils are tender, stirring occasionally to prevent the lentils from sticking to the bottom of the pan.

4 Add the potatoes and continue to simmer for about 20 minutes until the potatoes and ham knuckle are tender.

5 Discard the bay leaves. Remove the knuckle and chop 125 g/4½ oz/¾ cup of the meat and reserve. If liked, press half the soup through a sieve (strainer) or blend in a food processor or blender until smooth. Return to the pan with the rest of the soup.

6 Adjust the seasoning, add the vinegar and allspice and the reserved chopped ham. Simmer gently for a further 5–10 minutes. Serve sprinkled liberally with spring onions (scallions) or chopped parsley.

2

3

4

Bacon, Bean & Garlic Soup

A mouth-wateringly healthy vegetable, bean and bacon soup with a garlic flavour. Serve with granary or wholemeal (whole wheat) bread.

NUTRITIONAL INFORMATION

Calories	261	Sugars	5g
Protein	23g	Fat	8g
Carbohydrate	25g	Saturates	2g

5 MINS 20 MINS

SERVES 4

INGREDIENTS

- 225 g/8 oz lean smoked back bacon slices
- 1 carrot, sliced thinly
- 1 celery stick, sliced thinly
- 1 onion, chopped
- 1 tbsp oil
- 3 garlic cloves, sliced
- 700 ml/1¼ pints/3 cups hot vegetable stock
- 200 g/7 oz can chopped tomatoes
- 1 tbsp chopped fresh thyme
- about 400 g/14 oz can cannellini beans, drained
- 1 tbsp tomato purée (paste)
- salt and pepper
- grated Cheddar cheese, to garnish

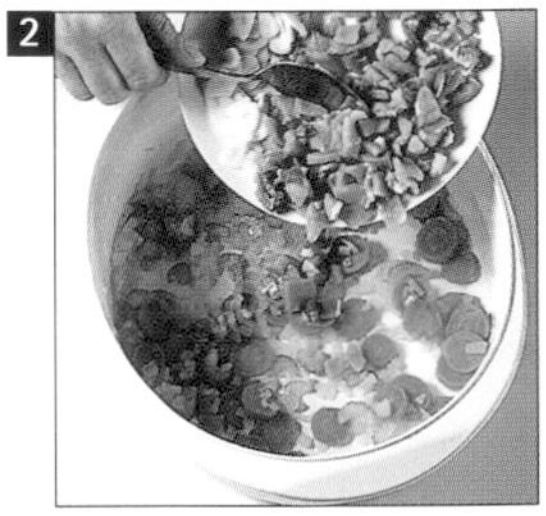

COOK'S TIP

For a more substantial soup add 60 g/2 oz cup small pasta shapes or short lengths of spaghetti when you add the stock and tomatoes. You will also need to add an extra 150 ml/¼ pint/⅔ cup vegetable stock.

1 Chop 2 slices of the bacon and place in a bowl. Cook on HIGH power for 3–4 minutes until the fat runs out and the bacon is well cooked. Stir the bacon halfway through cooking to separate the pieces. Transfer to a plate lined with kitchen towels and leave to cool. When cool, the bacon pieces should be crisp and dry. Place the carrot, celery, onion and oil in a large bowl. Cover and cook on HIGH power for 4 minutes.

2 Chop the remaining bacon and add to the bowl with the garlic. Cover and cook on HIGH power for 2 minutes.

3 Add the stock, the contents of the can of tomatoes, the thyme, beans and tomato purée (paste). Cover and cook on HIGH power for 8 minutes, stirring halfway through. Season to taste. Ladle the soup into warmed bowls and sprinkle with the crisp bacon and grated cheese.

Lamb & Barley Broth

Warming and nutritious, this broth is perfect for a cold winter's day. The slow cooking allows you to use one of the cheaper cuts of meat.

NUTRITIONAL INFORMATION

Calories	304	Sugars	4g
Protein	29g	Fat	14g
Carbohydrate	16g	Saturates	6g

15 MINS

2¼ HOURS

SERVES 4

INGREDIENTS

- 1 tbsp vegetable oil
- 500 g/1 lb 2 oz lean neck of lamb
- 1 large onion, sliced
- 2 carrots, sliced
- 2 leeks, sliced
- 1 litre/1¾ pints/4 cups vegetable stock
- 1 bay leaf
- few sprigs of fresh parsley
- 60 g/2 oz/⅓ cup pearl barley

1 Heat the vegetable oil in a large, heavy-based saucepan and add the pieces of lamb, turning them to seal and brown on both sides.

2 Lift the lamb out of the pan and set aside until required.

3 Add the onion, carrots and leeks to the saucepan and cook gently for about 3 minutes.

4 Return the lamb to the saucepan and add the vegetable stock, bay leaf, parsley and pearl barley to the saucepan.

5 Bring the mixture in the pan to the boil, then reduce the heat. Cover and simmer for 1½–2 hours.

6 Discard the parsley sprigs. Lift the pieces of lamb from the broth and allow them to cool slightly.

7 Remove the bones and any fat and chop the meat. Return the lamb to the broth and reheat gently.

8 Ladle the lamb and parsley broth into warmed bowls and serve immediately.

COOK'S TIP

This broth will taste even better if made the day before, as this allows the flavours to fully develop. It also means that any fat will solidify on the surface so you can then lift it off. Keep the broth in the refrigerator until required.

1

3

4

Chicken & Leek Soup

This satisfying soup can be served as a main course. You can add rice and (bell) peppers to make it even more hearty, as well as colourful.

NUTRITIONAL INFORMATION

Calories	183	Sugar	4g
Protein	21g	Fats	9g
Carbohydrates	4g	Saturates	5g

5 MINS

1¼ HOURS

SERVES 4–6

INGREDIENTS

- 25 g/1 oz/2 tbsp butter
- 350 g/12 oz boneless chicken
- 350 g/12 oz leeks, cut into 2.5-cm/ 1-inch pieces
- 1.2 litres/2 pints/5 cups Fresh Chicken Stock (see page 14)
- 1 bouquet garni sachet
- 8 pitted prunes, halved
- salt and white pepper
- cooked rice and diced (bell) peppers (optional)

1 Melt the butter in a large saucepan.

2 Add the chicken and leeks to the saucepan and fry for 8 minutes.

3 Add the chicken stock and bouquet garni sachet and stir well.

4 Season well with salt and pepper to taste.

5 Bring the soup to the boil and simmer for 45 minutes.

6 Add the prunes to the saucepan with some cooked rice and diced (bell) peppers (if using) and simmer for about 20 minutes.

7 Remove the bouquet garni sachet from the soup and discard. Serve the chicken and leek soup immediately.

2

3

6

VARIATION

Instead of the bouquet garni sachet, you can use a bunch of fresh mixed herbs, tied together with string. Choose herbs such as parsley, thyme and rosemary.

Chicken & Coconut Soup

This fragrant, Thai-style soup combines citrus flavours with coconut and a hint of piquancy from chillies.

NUTRITIONAL INFORMATION	
Calories 345	Sugar 2g
Protein 28g	Fats 24g
Carbohydrates 5g	Saturates 18g

2¾ HOURS — 15 MINS

SERVES 4

INGREDIENTS

- 350 g/12 oz/1¾ cups cooked, skinned chicken breast
- 125 g/4½ oz/1⅓ cups unsweetened desiccated coconut
- 500 ml/18 fl oz/2 cups boiling water
- 500 ml/18 fl oz/2 cups Fresh Chicken Stock (see page 14)
- 4 spring onions (scallions), white and green parts, sliced thinly
- 2 stalks lemon grass
- 1 lime
- 1 tsp grated ginger root
- 1 tbsp light soy sauce
- 2 tsp ground coriander
- 2 large fresh red chillies
- 1 tbsp chopped fresh coriander (cilantro)
- 1 tbsp cornflour (cornstarch) mixed with 2 tbsp cold water
- salt and white pepper
- chopped red chilli, to garnish

1

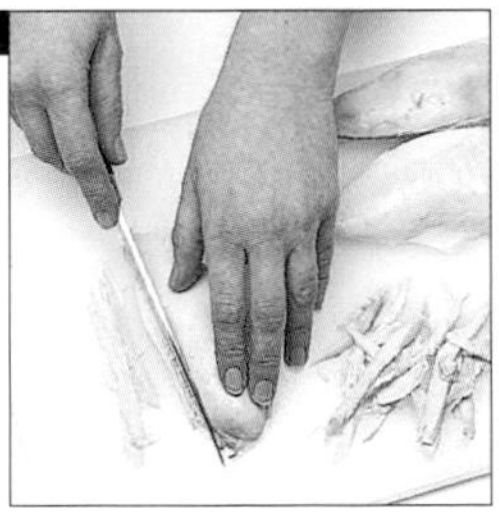

2

3

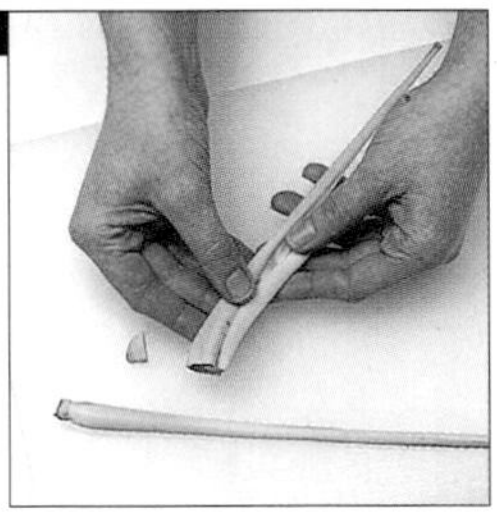

1 Slice the chicken into thin strips. Place the coconut in a heatproof bowl and pour the boiling water over.

2 Place a fine sieve (strainer) over another bowl and pour in the coconut water. Work the coconut through the sieve (strainer).

3 Add the coconut water, the stock and the spring onions (scallions) to a large saucepan. Slice the base of each lemon grass and discard the damaged leaves. Bruise the stalks and add to the saucepan.

4 Peel the rind from the lime, keeping it in large strips. Slice the lime in half and extract the juice. Add the lime strips, juice, ginger, soy sauce and ground coriander to the saucepan.

5 Bruise the chillies with a fork then add to the pan. Heat the pan to just below boiling point. Add the chicken and fresh coriander (cilantro) to the pan, bring to the boil, then simmer for 10 minutes.

6 Discard the lemon grass, lime rind and chillies. Pour the blended cornflour (cornstarch) mixture into the saucepan and stir until slightly thickened. Season, then garnish with the red chilli.

Mediterranean Fish Soup

Juicy chunks of fish and sumptuous shellfish are cooked in a flavoursome stock. Serve with toasted bread rubbed with garlic.

NUTRITIONAL INFORMATION

Calories	316	Sugar	4g
Protein	53g	Fats	7g
Carbohydrates	5g	Saturates	1g

1 HOUR   15 MINS

SERVES 4

INGREDIENTS

- 1 tbsp olive oil
- 1 large onion, chopped
- 2 garlic cloves, finely chopped
- 425 ml/15 fl oz/1¾ cups Fresh Fish Stock (see page 15)
- 150 ml/5 fl oz/⅔ cup dry white wine
- 1 bay leaf
- 1 sprig each fresh thyme, rosemary and oregano
- 450 g/1 lb firm white fish fillets (such as cod, monkfish or halibut), skinned and cut into 2.5 cm/1 inch cubes
- 450 g/1 lb fresh mussels, prepared
- 400 g/14 oz can chopped tomatoes
- 225 g/8 oz peeled prawns (shrimp), thawed if frozen
- salt and pepper
- sprigs of thyme, to garnish

TO SERVE

- lemon wedges
- 4 slices toasted French bread, rubbed with cut garlic clove

1 Heat the olive oil in a large saucepan and gently fry the onion and garlic for 2–3 minutes until just softened.

2 Pour in the stock and wine and bring to the boil.

3 Tie the bay leaf and herbs together with clean string and add to the saucepan together with the fish and mussels. Stir well, cover and simmer for 5 minutes.

4 Stir in the tomatoes and prawns (shrimp) and continue to cook for a further 3–4 minutes until piping hot and the fish is cooked through.

5 Discard the herbs and any mussels that have not opened. Season to taste, then ladle into warm bowls.

6 Garnish with sprigs of fresh thyme and serve with lemon wedges and toasted bread.

1

3

4

Coconut & Crab Soup

Thai red curry paste is quite fiery, but adds a superb flavour to this dish. It is available in jars or packets from supermarkets.

NUTRITIONAL INFORMATION

Calories	122	Sugar	9g
Protein	11g	Fats	4g
Carbohydrates	11g	Saturates	1g

5 MINS 10 MINS

SERVES 4

INGREDIENTS

- 1 tbsp groundnut oil
- 2 tbsp Thai red curry paste
- 1 red (bell) pepper, deseeded and sliced
- 600 ml/1 pint/2½ cups coconut milk
- 600 ml/1 pint/2½ cups fish stock
- 2 tbsp fish sauce
- 225 g/8 oz canned or fresh white crab meat
- 225 g/8 oz fresh or frozen crab claws
- 2 tbsp chopped fresh coriander (cilantro)
- 3 spring onions (scallions), trimmed and sliced

1 Heat the oil in a large preheated wok.

2 Add the red curry paste and red (bell) pepper to the wok and stir-fry for 1 minute.

3 Add the coconut milk, fish stock and fish sauce and bring to the boil.

4 Add the crab meat, crab claws, coriander (cilantro) and spring onions (scallions) to the wok.

5 Stir the mixture well and heat thoroughly for 2–3 minutes or until everything is warmed through.

6 Transfer the soup to warm bowls and serve hot.

COOK'S TIP

Clean the wok after use by washing it with water, using a mild detergent if necessary, and a soft cloth or brush. Do not scrub or use any abrasive cleaner as this will scratch the surface. Dry thoroughly then wipe the surface all over with a little oil to protect the surface.

Partan Bree

This traditional Scottish soup is thickened with a purée of rice and crab meat cooked in milk. Add soured cream, if liked, at the end of cooking.

NUTRITIONAL INFORMATION

Calories 112	Sugars 5g
Protein 7g	Fat 2g
Carbohydrate ...18g	Saturates 0.3g

1 HOUR   35 MINS

SERVES 6

INGREDIENTS

- 1 medium-sized boiled crab
- 90 g/3 oz/scant ½ cup long-grain rice
- 600 ml/1 pint/2½ cups skimmed milk
- 600 ml/1 pint/2½ cups Fish Stock (see page 15)
- 1 tbsp anchovy essence (paste)
- 2 tsp lime or lemon juice
- 1 tbsp chopped fresh parsley or I tsp chopped fresh thyme
- 3–4 tbsp soured cream (optional)
- salt and pepper
- snipped chives, to garnish

1

3

5

1 Remove and reserve all the brown and white meat from the crab, then crack the claws and remove and chop that meat; reserve the claw meat.

2 Put the rice and milk into a saucepan and bring slowly to the boil. Cover and simmer gently for about 20 minutes.

3 Add the reserved white and brown crab meat and seasoning and simmer for a further 5 minutes.

4 Cool a little, then press through a sieve (strainer), or blend in a food processor or blender until smooth.

5 Pour the soup into a clean saucepan and add the fish stock and the reserved claw meat. Bring slowly to the boil, then add the anchovy essence (paste) and lime or lemon juice and adjust the seasoning to taste.

6 Simmer for a further 2–3 minutes. Stir in the parsley or thyme and then swirl soured cream (if using) through each serving. Garnish with snipped chives.

COOK'S TIP

If you are unable to buy a whole crab, use about 175 g/6 oz frozen crab meat and thaw thoroughly before use; or a 175 g/6 oz can of crab meat which just needs thorough draining.

Smoked Haddock Soup

Smoked haddock gives this soup a wonderfully rich flavour, while the mashed potatoes and cream thicken and enrich the stock.

NUTRITIONAL INFORMATION

Calories	169	Sugars	8g
Protein	16g	Fat	5g
Carbohydrate	16g	Saturates	3g

25 MINS   40 MINS

SERVES 4–6

INGREDIENTS

- 225 g/8 oz smoked haddock fillet
- 1 onion, chopped finely
- 1 garlic clove, crushed
- 600 ml/1 pint/2½ cups water
- 600 ml/1 pint/2½ cups skimmed milk
- 225–350 g/8–12 oz/1–1½ cups hot mashed potatoes
- 30 g/1 oz/2 tbsp butter
- about 1 tbsp lemon juice
- 6 tbsp low-fat natural fromage frais
- 4 tbsp fresh parsley, chopped
- salt and pepper

2

3

5

1 Put the fish, onion, garlic and water into a saucepan. Bring to the boil, cover and simmer for 15–20 minutes.

2 Remove the fish from the pan, strip off the skin and remove all the bones. Flake the flesh finely.

3 Return the skin and bones to the cooking liquor and simmer for 10 minutes. Strain, discarding the skin and bone. Pour the liquor into a clean pan.

4 Add the milk, flaked fish and seasoning to the pan, bring to the boil and simmer for about 3 minutes.

5 Gradually whisk in sufficient mashed potato to give a fairly thick soup, then stir in the butter and sharpen to taste with lemon juice.

6 Add the fromage frais and 3 tablespoons of the chopped parsley. Reheat gently and adjust the seasoning. Sprinkle with the remaining parsley and serve immediately.

COOK'S TIP

Undyed smoked haddock may be used in place of the bright yellow fish; it will give a paler colour but just as much flavour. Alternatively, use smoked cod or smoked whiting.

Starters & Snacks

If you prefer not to start your meal with soup, this chapter contains a range of appetizers from all around the world to whet your appetite. This is a truly international

selection of low-fat dishes from as far afield as India, Mexico and Italy. Some of them are extremely easy to make, such as some of the pâté and pasta recipes, while others take a little longer to make; all, however, are delicious. Whether cooking a cosy family supper or hoping to impress your friends around the dinner table, you will find many innovative new starter ideas here alonside some old favourites.

Minted Onion Bhajis

Gram flour (also known as besan flour) is a fine yellow flour made from chick peas and is available from supermarkets and Asian food shops.

NUTRITIONAL INFORMATION

Calories	251	Sugars	7g
Protein	7g	Fat	8g
Carbohydrate	39g	Saturates	1g

5 MINS

15 MINS

MAKES 12

INGREDIENTS

- 125 g/4½ oz/1 cup gram flour
- ¼ tsp cayenne pepper
- ¼–½ tsp ground coriander
- ¼–½ tsp ground cumin
- 1 tbsp chopped fresh mint
- 4 tbsp strained thick low-fat yogurt
- 65 ml/2½ fl oz/¼ cup cold water
- 1 large onion, quartered and thinly sliced
- vegetable oil, for frying
- salt and pepper
- sprigs of mint, to garnish

1

2

3

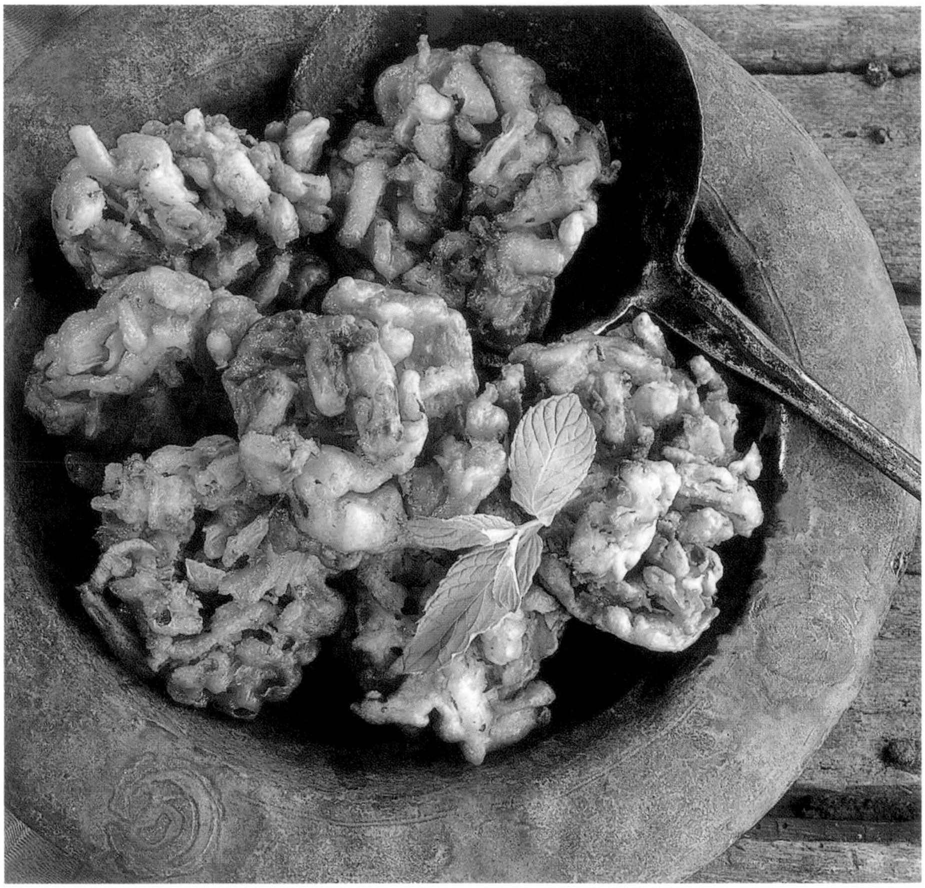

1 Put the gram flour into a bowl, add the cayenne pepper, coriander, cumin and mint and season with salt and pepper to taste. Stir in the yogurt, water and sliced onion and mix well together.

2 One-third fill a large, deep frying pan with oil and heat until very hot. Drop heaped spoonfuls of the mixture, a few at a time, into the hot oil and use two forks to neaten the mixture into rough ball-shapes.

3 Fry the bhajis until golden brown and cooked through, turning frequently.

4 Drain the bhajis on absorbent kitchen paper (paper towels) and keep warm while cooking the remainder in the same way.

5 Arrange the bhajis on a platter and garnish with sprigs of fresh mint. Serve hot or warm.

COOK'S TIP

Gram flour is excellent for making batter and is used in India in place of flour. It can be made from ground split peas as well as chickpeas (garbanzo beans).

Vegetables with Tahini Dip

This tasty dip is great for livening-up simply-cooked vegetables. You can vary the vegetables according to the season.

NUTRITIONAL INFORMATION

Calories	126	Sugars	7g
Protein	11g	Fat	6g
Carbohydrate	8g	Saturates	1g

5 MINS — 20 MINS

SERVES 4

INGREDIENTS

- 225 g/8 oz small broccoli florets
- 225 g/8 oz small cauliflower florets
- 225 g/8 oz asparagus, sliced into 5 cm/2 inch lengths
- 2 small red onions, quartered
- 1 tbsp lime juice
- 2 tsp toasted sesame seeds
- 1 tbsp chopped fresh chives, to garnish

HOT TAHINI & GARLIC DIP

- 1 tsp sunflower oil
- 2 garlic cloves, crushed
- ½–1 tsp chilli powder
- 2 tsp tahini (sesame seed paste)
- 150 ml/¼ pint/⅔ cup low-fat natural fromage frais
- 2 tbsp chopped fresh chives
- salt and pepper

1

3

4

1 Line the base of a steamer with baking parchment and arrange the vegetables on top.

2 Bring a wok or large saucepan of water to the boil, and place the steamer on top. Sprinkle with lime juice and steam for 10 minutes.

3 To make the hot tahini & garlic dip, heat the sunflower oil in a small non-stick saucepan, add the garlic, chilli powder and seasoning to taste and fry gently for 2–3 minutes until the garlic is softened.

4 Remove the saucepan from the heat and stir in the tahini (sesame seed paste) and fromage frais. Return to the heat and cook gently for 1–2 minutes without boiling. Stir in the chives.

5 Remove the vegetables from the steamer and place on a warmed serving platter. Sprinkle with the sesame seeds and garnish with chopped chives. Serve with the hot dip.

Spinach Cheese Moulds

These flavour-packed little moulds are a perfect starter or a tasty light lunch. Serve them with warm pitta bread.

NUTRITIONAL INFORMATION

Calories 119	Sugars 2g
Protein 6g	Fat 9g
Carbohydrate 2g	Saturates 6g

1¼ HOURS 50 MINS

SERVES 4

INGREDIENTS

100 g/3½ oz fresh spinach leaves

300 g/10½ oz skimmed milk soft cheese

2 garlic cloves, crushed

sprigs of fresh parsley, tarragon and chives, finely chopped

salt and pepper

TO SERVE

salad leaves and fresh herbs

pitta bread

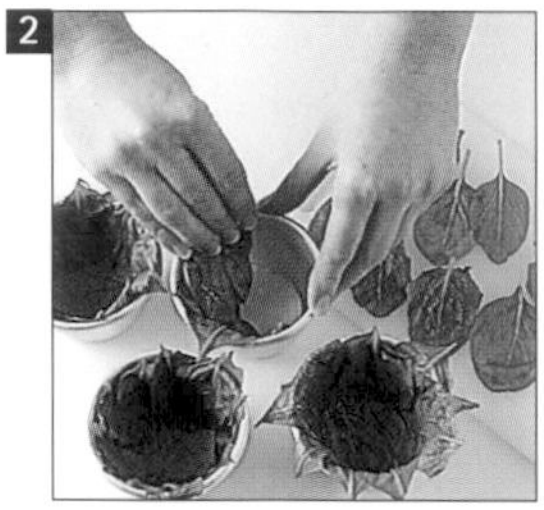

1 Trim the stalks from the spinach leaves and rinse the leaves under running water. Pack the leaves into a saucepan while still wet, cover and cook for 3–4 minutes until wilted – they will cook in the steam from the wet leaves (do not overcook). Drain well and pat dry with absorbent kitchen paper (paper towels).

2 Base-line 4 small pudding basins or individual ramekin dishes with baking parchment. Line the basins or ramekins with spinach leaves so that the leaves overhang the edges if they are large enough to do so.

3 Place the cheese in a bowl and add the garlic and herbs. Mix together thoroughly and season to taste.

4 Spoon the cheese and herb mixture into the basins or ramekins and pull over the overlapping spinach to cover the cheese, or lay extra leaves to cover the top. Place a greaseproof (waxed) paper circle on top of each dish and weigh down with a 100 g/3½ oz weight. Leave to chill in the refrigerator for 1 hour.

5 Remove the weights and peel off the paper. Loosen the moulds gently by running a small palette knife (spatula) around the edges of each dish and turn them out on to individual serving plates. Serve the moulds with a mixture of salad leaves and fresh herbs, and warm pitta bread.

Lentil Pâté

Red lentils are used in this spicy recipe for speed as they do not require pre-soaking. If you use other lentils, soak and pre-cook them first.

NUTRITIONAL INFORMATION	
Calories 267	Sugars 12g
Protein 14g	Fat 8g
Carbohydrate . . .37g	Saturates 1g

25 MINS

1¼ HOURS

SERVES 4

INGREDIENTS

- 1 tbsp vegetable oil, plus extra for greasing
- 1 onion, chopped
- 2 garlic cloves, crushed
- 1 tsp garam masala
- ½ tsp ground coriander
- 850 ml/1½ pints/1¼ cups vegetable stock
- 175 g/6 oz/¾ cup red lentils
- 1 small egg
- 2 tbsp milk
- 2 tbsp mango chutney
- 2 tbsp chopped parsley
- chopped parsley, to garnish
- salad leaves and warm toast, to serve

1 Heat the vegetable oil in a large saucepan and sauté the onion and garlic for 2–3 minutes, stirring. Add the spices and cook for a further 30 seconds. Stir in the stock and lentils and bring the mixture to the boil. Reduce the heat and simmer for 20 minutes until the lentils are cooked and softened. Remove the pan from the heat and drain off any excess moisture.

2 Put the mixture in a food processor and add the egg, milk, mango chutney and parsley. Blend until smooth.

3 Grease and line the base of a 450 g/ 1 lb loaf tin (pan) and spoon the mixture into the tin (pan). Cover and cook in a preheated oven at 200°C/400°F/Gas Mark 6 for 40–45 minutes or until firm.

4 Allow the pâté to cool in the tin (pan) for 20 minutes, then transfer to the refrigerator to cool completely. Slice the pâté and garnish with chopped parsley. Serve with salad leaves and warm toast.

VARIATION

Use other spices, such as chilli powder or Chinese five-spice powder, to flavour the pâté and add tomato relish or chilli relish instead of the mango chutney, if you prefer.

1

2

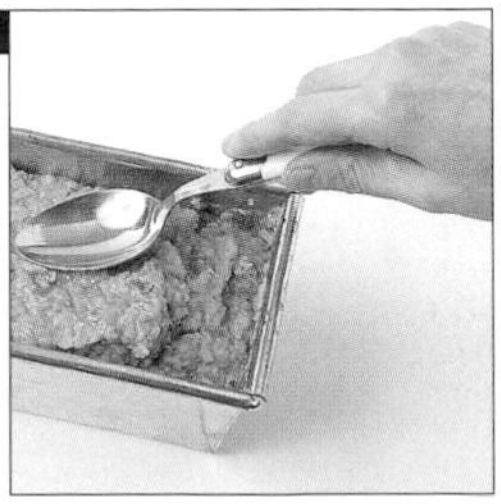
3

Potato & Bean Pâté

This pâté is easy to prepare and may be stored in the refrigerator for up to two days. Serve with small toasts, Melba toast or crudités.

NUTRITIONAL INFORMATION

Calories	94	Sugars	5g
Protein	6g	Fat	1g
Carbohydrate	17g	Saturates	0.2g

5 MINS

10 MINS

SERVES 4

INGREDIENTS

- 100 g/3½ oz floury (mealy) potatoes, diced
- 225 g/8 oz mixed canned beans, such as borlotti, flageolet and kidney beans, drained
- 1 garlic clove, crushed
- 2 tsp lime juice
- 1 tbsp chopped fresh coriander (cilantro)
- 2 tbsp low-fat natural yogurt
- salt and pepper
- chopped fresh coriander (cilantro), to garnish

1 Cook the potatoes in a saucepan of boiling water for 10 minutes until tender. Drain well and mash.

2 Transfer the potato to a food processor or blender and add the beans, garlic, lime juice and the fresh coriander (cilantro).

3 Season the mixture with salt and pepper and process for 1 minute to make a smooth purée. Alternatively, mix the beans with the potato, garlic, lime juice and coriander (cilantro) and mash.

4 Turn the purée into a bowl and add the yogurt. Mix well and season with salt and pepper to taste.

1

3

4

5 Spoon the pâté into a serving dish and garnish with the chopped coriander (cilantro). Serve at once or leave to chill.

COOK'S TIP

If you do not have a food processor or you would prefer to make a chunkier pâté, simply mash the ingredients with a fork.

Potato Skins with Guacamole

Although avocados do contain fat, if they are used in small quantities you can still enjoy their creamy texture.

NUTRITIONAL INFORMATION

Calories 399	Sugars 4g
Protein 10g	Fat 15g
Carbohydrate ...59g	Saturates 4g

45 MINS — $1^{3}/_{4}$ HOURS

SERVES 4

INGREDIENTS

- 4 x 225 g/8 oz baking potatoes
- 2 tsp olive oil
- coarse sea salt and pepper
- chopped fresh chives, to garnish

GUACAMOLE DIP

- 175 g/6 oz ripe avocado
- 1 tbsp lemon juice
- 2 ripe, firm tomatoes, chopped finely
- 1 tsp grated lemon rind
- 100 g/3½ oz/½ cup low-fat soft cheese with herbs and garlic
- 4 spring onions (scallions), chopped finely
- a few drops of Tabasco sauce
- salt and pepper

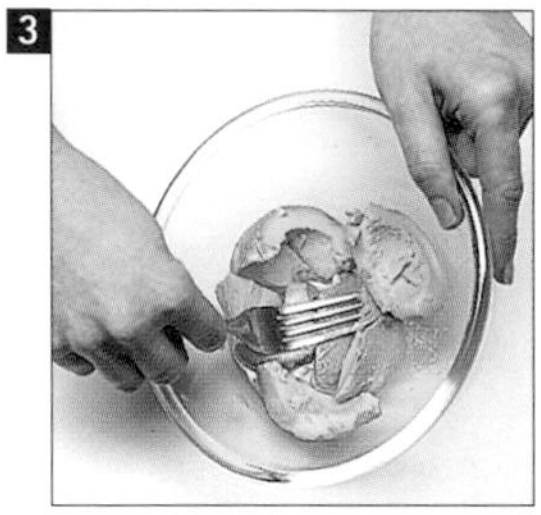

1 Bake the potatoes in a preheated oven at 200°C/400°F/Gas Mark 6 for $1^{1}/_{4}$ hours. Remove from the oven and allow to cool for 30 minutes. Reset the oven to 220°C/425°F/Gas Mark 7.

2 Halve the potatoes lengthwise and scoop out 2 tablespoons of the flesh. Slice in half again. Place on a baking tray (cookie) sheet and brush the flesh side lightly with oil. Sprinkle with salt and pepper. Bake for a further 25 minutes until golden and crisp.

3 To make the guacamole dip, mash the avocado with the lemon juice. Add the remaining ingredients and mix.

4 Drain the potato skins on paper towels and transfer to a warmed serving platter. Garnish with chives. Pile the avocado mixture into a serving bowl.

COOK'S TIP

Mash the leftover potato flesh with natural yogurt and seasoning, and serve as an accompaniment to meat, fish and vegetarian dishes.

Potato & Mushroom Hash

This is a quick one-pan dish which is ideal for a quick snack. Packed with colour and flavour, you can add any other vegetable you have at hand.

NUTRITIONAL INFORMATION

Calories	378	Sugars	14g
Protein	18g	Fat	26g
Carbohydrate	20g	Saturates	7g

10 MINS

35 MINS

SERVES 4

INGREDIENTS

- 675 g/1½ lb potatoes, cubed
- 1 tbsp olive oil
- 2 garlic cloves, crushed
- 1 green (bell) pepper, cubed
- 1 yellow (bell) pepper, cubed
- 3 tomatoes, diced
- 75 g/2¾ oz/1 cup button mushrooms, halved
- 1 tbsp Worcester sauce
- 2 tbsp chopped basil
- salt and pepper
- fresh basil sprigs, to garnish
- warm, crusty bread, to serve

1 Cook the potatoes in a saucepan of boiling salted water for 7–8 minutes. Drain well and reserve.

2 Heat the oil in a large, heavy-based frying pan (skillet) and cook the potatoes for 8–10 minutes, stirring until browned.

3 Add the garlic and (bell) peppers to the frying pan (skillet) and cook for 2–3 minutes.

4 Stir in the tomatoes and mushrooms and cook, stirring, for 5–6 minutes.

5 Stir in the Worcester sauce and basil and season well. Garnish with the fresh basil and serve with crusty bread.

COOK'S TIP

Most brands of Worcester sauce contain anchovies. If cooking for vegetarians, make sure you choose a vegetarian variety.

Spicy Jacket Potatoes

These twice-baked potatoes have an unusual filling of the Middle Eastern flavours of chickpeas (garbanzo beans), cumin and coriander (cilantro).

NUTRITIONAL INFORMATION

Calories	451	Sugars	6g
Protein	18g	Fat	4g
Carbohydrate	91g	Saturates	0.5g

20 MINS   1½ HOURS

SERVES 4

INGREDIENTS

- 4 baking potatoes, each about 300 g/10½ oz
- 1 tbsp vegetable oil (optional)
- 430 g/15½ oz can chickpeas (garbanzo beans), drained
- 1 tsp ground coriander
- 1 tsp ground cumin
- 4 tbsp fresh coriander (cilantro), chopped
- 150 ml/5 fl oz/⅔ cup low-fat natural (unsweetened) yogurt
- salt and pepper

SALAD

- 2 tomatoes
- 4 tbsp fresh coriander (cilantro)
- ½ cucumber
- ½ red onion

1 Preheat the oven to 200°C/400°F/Gas Mark 6.

2 Scrub the potatoes and pat them dry with absorbent kitchen paper (paper towels). Prick the potatoes all over with a fork, brush with oil (if using) and season with salt and pepper.

3 Place the potatoes on a baking sheet and bake for 1–1¼ hours or until cooked through. Cool for 10 minutes.

4 Meanwhile, place the chickpeas (garbanzo beans) in a large mixing bowl and mash with a fork or potato masher.

4

5 Stir in the ground coriander, cumin and half the chopped fresh coriander (cilantro). Cover the bowl with cling film (plastic wrap) and set aside.

6 Halve the cooked potatoes and scoop the flesh into a bowl, keeping the shells intact. Mash the flesh until smooth and gently mix into the chickpea (garbanzo bean) mixture with the natural (unsweetened) yogurt. Season well with salt and pepper to taste.

6

7 Place the potato shells on a baking tray (cookie sheet) and fill with the potato and chickpea (garbanzo bean) mixture. Return the potatoes to the oven and bake for 10–15 minutes until heated through.

7

8 Meanwhile, make the salad. Using a sharp knife, chop the tomatoes and fresh coriander (cilantro). Slice the cucumber and cut the red onion into thin slices. Toss all the ingredients together in a serving dish.

9 Serve the potatoes sprinkled with the remaining chopped coriander (cilantro) and the prepared salad.

Bruschetta

Traditionally, this Italian savoury is enriched with olive oil. Here, sun-dried tomatoes are a good substitute and only a little oil is used.

NUTRITIONAL INFORMATION

Calories	178	Sugars	2g
Protein	8g	Fat	6g
Carbohydrate	24g	Saturates	2g

45 MINS 5 MINS

SERVES 4

INGREDIENTS

- 60 g/2 oz/¼ cup dry-pack sun-dried tomatoes
- 300 ml/½ pint/1¼ cups boiling water
- 35 cm/14 inch long Granary or wholemeal (whole wheat) stick of French bread
- 1 large garlic clove, halved
- 25 g/1 oz/¼ cup pitted black olives in brine, drained and quartered
- 2 tsp olive oil
- 2 tbsp chopped fresh basil
- 40 g/1½ oz/⅓ cup grated low-fat Italian Mozzarella cheese
- salt and pepper
- fresh basil leaves, to garnish

1 Place the sun-dried tomatoes in a heatproof bowl and pour over the boiling water.

2 Set aside for 30 minutes to soften. Drain well and pat dry with paper towels. Slice into thin strips and set aside.

3 Trim and discard the ends from the bread and cut into 12 slices. Arrange on a grill (broiler) rack and place under a preheated hot grill (broiler) and cook for 1–2 minutes on each side until lightly golden.

4 Rub both sides of each piece of bread with the cut sides of the garlic. Top with strips of sun-dried tomato and olives.

5 Brush lightly with olive oil and season well. Sprinkle with the basil and Mozzarella cheese and return to the grill (broiler) for 1–2 minutes until the cheese is melted and bubbling.

6 Transfer to a warmed serving platter and garnish with fresh basil leaves.

1

3

4

COOK'S TIP

If you use sun-dried tomatoes packed in oil, drain them, rinse well in warm water and drain again on kitchen paper (paper towels) to remove as much oil as possible. Sun-dried tomatoes give a rich, full flavour to this dish, but thinly-sliced fresh tomatoes can be used instead.

Cheese, Herb & Onion Rolls

A great texture and flavour are achieved by mixing white and granary flours together with minced onion, grated cheese and fresh herbs.

NUTRITIONAL INFORMATION

Calories 529	Sugars 2g
Protein 24g	Fat 7g
Carbohydrate . . .98g	Saturates 4g

2 HOURS — 15 MINS

SERVES 4

INGREDIENTS

- 225 g/8 oz/2 cups strong white flour
- 1½ tsp salt
- 1 tsp dried mustard powder
- good pinch of pepper
- 225 g/8 oz/2 cups granary or malted wheat flour
- 2 tbsp chopped fresh mixed herbs
- 2 tbsp finely chopped spring onions (scallions)
- 125–175 g/4½–6 oz/1–1½ cups mature (sharp) low-fat Cheddar cheese, grated
- 15 g/½ oz/½ cake fresh (compressed) yeast; or 1½ tsp dried yeast plus 1 tsp caster (superfine) sugar; or 1 sachet easy-blend yeast plus 1 tbsp oil
- 300 ml/½ pint/1¼ cups warm water

3

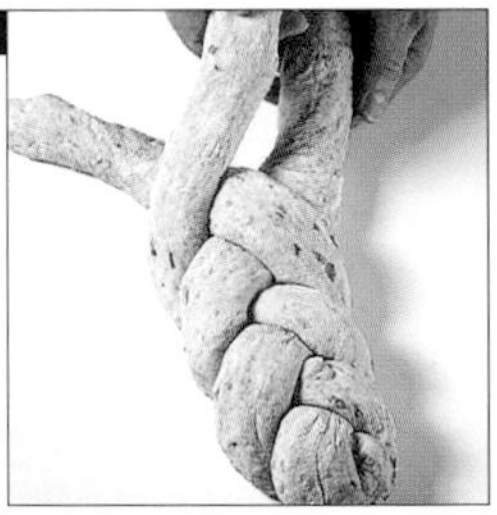

4

4

1 Sift the white flour with the salt, mustard and pepper into a bowl. Mix in the granary flour, herbs, spring onions (scallions) and most of the cheese.

2 Blend the fresh yeast with the warm water or, if using dried yeast, dissolve the sugar in the water, sprinkle the yeast on top and leave in a warm place for about 10 minutes until frothy. Add the yeast mixture of your choice to the dry ingredients and mix to form a firm dough, adding more flour if necessary.

3 Knead until smooth and elastic. Cover with an oiled polythene bag and leave in a warm place to rise for 1 hour or until doubled in size. Knock back (punch down) and knead the dough until smooth. Divide into 10–12 pieces and shape into round or long rolls, coils or knots.

4 Alternatively, make one large plaited loaf. Divide the dough into 3 even pieces and roll each into a long thin sausage and join at one end. Beginning at the joined end, plait to the end and secure. Place on greased baking sheets, cover with an oiled sheet of polythene and leave to rise until doubled in size. Remove the polythene.

5 Sprinkle with the rest of the cheese. Bake in a preheated oven at 200°C/400°F/Gas Mark 6 for 15–20 minutes for the rolls, or 30–40 minutes for the loaf.

Cheese & Chive Scones

These tea-time classics have been given a healthy twist by the use of low-fat soft cheese and reduced-fat Cheddar cheese.

NUTRITIONAL INFORMATION

Calories	297	Sugars	3g
Protein	13g	Fat	7g
Carbohydrate	49g	Saturates	4g

10 MINS 20 MINS

MAKES 10

INGREDIENTS

- 225 g/8 oz self-raising flour
- 1 tsp powdered mustard
- ½ tsp cayenne pepper
- ½ tsp salt
- 100 g/3½ oz low-fat soft cheese with added herbs
- 2 tbsp fresh snipped chives, plus extra to garnish
- 100 ml/3½ fl oz and 2 tbsp skimmed milk
- 60 g/2 oz reduced-fat mature (sharp) Cheddar cheese, grated
- low-fat soft cheese, to serve

1 Preheat the oven to 200°C/400°F/Gas Mark 6. Sift the flour, mustard, cayenne and salt into a mixing bowl.

2 Add the soft cheese to the mixture and mix together until well incorporated. Stir in the snipped chives.

3 Make a well in the centre of the ingredients and gradually pour in 100 ml/3½ fl oz milk, stirring as you pour, until the mixture forms a soft dough.

4 Turn the dough on to a floured surface and knead lightly. Roll out until 2 cm/¾ inch thick and use a 5 cm/2 inch plain pastry cutter to stamp out as many rounds as you can. Transfer the rounds to a baking sheet.

5 Re-knead the dough trimmings together and roll out again. Stamp out more rounds – you should be able to make 10 scones in total.

6 Brush the scones with the remaining milk and sprinkle with the grated cheese. Bake in the oven for 15–20 minutes until risen and golden. Transfer to a wire rack to cool. Serve warm with low-fat soft cheese, garnished with chives.

2

4

6

VARIATION

For sweet scones, omit the mustard, cayenne pepper, chives and grated cheese. Replace the flavoured soft cheese with plain low-fat soft cheese. Add 75 g/2¾ oz currants and 25 g/1 oz caster (superfine) sugar. Serve with low-fat soft cheese and fruit spread.

Savoury (Bell) Pepper Bread

This flavoursome bread contains only the minimum amount of fat. Serve with a bowl of hot soup for a filling and nutritious light meal.

NUTRITIONAL INFORMATION

Calories	468	Sugars	11g
Protein	16g	Fat	5g
Carbohydrate	97g	Saturates	1g

2 HOURS — 50 MINS

SERVES 4

INGREDIENTS

- 1 small red (bell) pepper
- 1 small green (bell) pepper
- 1 small yellow (bell) pepper
- 60 g/2 oz dry-pack sun-dried tomatoes
- 50 ml/2 fl oz/¼ cup boiling water
- 2 tsp dried yeast
- 1 tsp caster (superfine) sugar
- 150 ml/5 fl oz/⅔ cup tepid water
- 450 g/1 lb/4 cups strong white bread flour
- 2 tsp dried rosemary
- 2 tbsp tomato purée (paste)
- 150 ml/5 fl oz/⅔ cup low-fat natural fromage frais (unsweetened yogurt)
- 1 tbsp coarse salt
- 1 tbsp olive oil

1 Preheat the oven to 220°C/425°F/Gas Mark 7 and the grill (broiler) to hot. Halve and deseed the (bell) peppers, arrange on the grill (broiler) rack and cook until the skin is charred. Leave to cool for 10 minutes, peel off the skin and chop the flesh. Slice the tomatoes into strips, place in a bowl and pour over the boiling water. Leave to soak.

2 Place the yeast and sugar in a small jug, pour over the tepid water and leave for 10–15 minutes until frothy. Sift the flour into a bowl and add 1 tsp dried rosemary. Make a well in the centre and pour in the yeast mixture.

3 Add the tomato purée (paste), tomatoes and soaking liquid, (bell) peppers, fromage frais (yogurt) and half the salt. Mix to form a soft dough. Turn out on to a lightly floured surface and knead for 3–4 minutes until smooth and elastic. Place in a lightly floured bowl, cover and leave in a warm room for 40 minutes until doubled in size.

4 Knead the dough again and place in a lightly greased 23 cm/9 inch round spring-clip cake tin. Using a wooden spoon, form 'dimples' in the surface. Cover and leave for 30 minutes. Brush with oil and sprinkle with rosemary and salt. Bake for 35–40 minutes, cool for 10 minutes and release from the tin. Leave to cool on a rack and serve.

COOK'S TIP

For a quick, filling snack serve the bread with a bowl of hot soup in winter, or a crisp leaf salad in summer.

Pasta Provençale

A combination of Italian vegetables tossed in a tomato dressing, served on a bed of assorted salad leaves, makes an appetizing meal.

NUTRITIONAL INFORMATION

Calories 197	Sugars 5g
Protein 10g	Fat 5g
Carbohydrate ...30g	Saturates 1g

10 MINS — 15 MINS

SERVES 4

INGREDIENTS

- 225 g/8 oz penne (quills)
- 1 tbsp olive oil
- 25 g/1 oz pitted black olives, drained and chopped
- 25 g/1 oz dry-pack sun-dried tomatoes, soaked, drained and chopped
- 400 g/14 oz can artichoke hearts, drained and halved
- 115 g/4 oz baby courgettes (zucchini), trimmed and sliced
- 115 g/4 oz baby plum tomatoes, halved
- 100 g/3½ oz assorted baby salad leaves
- salt and pepper
- shredded basil leaves, to garnish

DRESSING

- 4 tbsp passata (sieved tomatoes)
- 2 tbsp low-fat natural fromage frais (unsweetened yogurt)
- 1 tbsp unsweetened orange juice
- 1 small bunch fresh basil, shredded

2

3

4

1 Cook the penne (quills) according to the instructions on the packet. Do not overcook the pasta – it should still have 'bite'. Drain well and return to the pan.

2 Stir in the olive oil, salt and pepper, olives and sun-dried tomatoes. Leave to cool.

3 Gently mix the artichokes, courgettes (zucchini) and plum tomatoes into the cooked pasta. Arrange the salad leaves in a serving bowl.

4 To make the dressing, mix all the ingredients together and toss into the vegetables and pasta.

5 Spoon the mixture on top of the salad leaves and garnish with shredded basil leaves.

Spicy Chickpea Snack

You can use fresh chickpeas (garbanzo beans), soaked overnight, for this popular Indian snack, but the canned variety is just as flavoursome.

NUTRITIONAL INFORMATION

Calories	190	Sugars	4g
Protein	9g	Fat	3g
Carbohydrate	34g	Saturates	0.3g

5 MINS   10 MINS

SERVES 4

INGREDIENTS

- 400 g/14 oz can chickpeas (garbanzo beans), drained
- 2 medium potatoes
- 1 medium onion
- 2 tbsp tamarind paste
- 6 tbsp water
- 1 tsp chilli powder
- 2 tsp sugar
- 1 tsp salt

TO GARNISH

- 1 tomato, sliced
- 2 fresh green chillies, chopped
- fresh coriander (cilantro) leaves

1 Place the chickpeas (garbanzo beans) in a bowl.

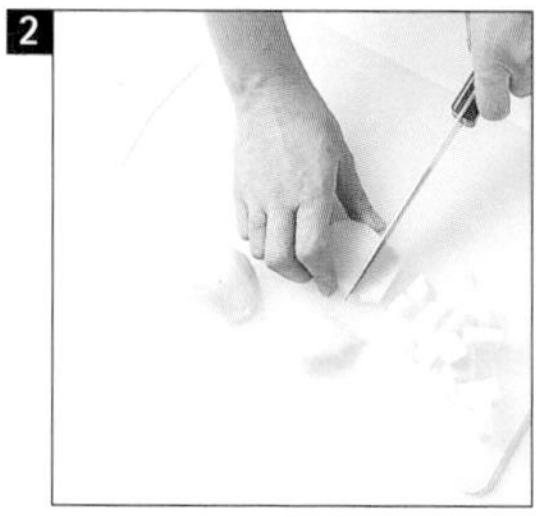

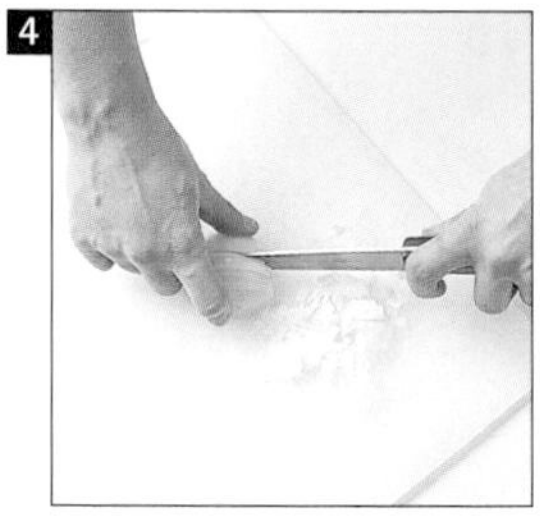

2 Using a sharp knife, cut the potatoes into dice.

3 Place the potatoes in a saucepan of water and boil until cooked through. Test by inserting the tip of a knife into the potatoes – they should feel soft and tender. Set the potatoes aside.

4 Using a sharp knife, finely chop the onion. Set aside until required.

5 Mix together the tamarind paste and water. Add the chilli powder, sugar and salt and mix again. Pour the mixture over the chickpeas (garbanzo beans).

6 Add the onion and the diced potatoes, and stir to mix. Season to taste.

7 Transfer to a serving bowl and garnish with tomatoes, chillies and coriander (cilantro) leaves.

COOK'S TIP

Chickpeas (garbanzo beans) have a nutty flavour and slightly crunchy texture. Indian cooks also grind these to make a flour called gram or besan, which is used to make breads, thicken sauces, and to make batters for deep-fried dishes.

Baked Stuffed Onions

Spanish onions are ideal for this recipe, as they have a milder, sweeter flavour that is not too overpowering.

NUTRITIONAL INFORMATION

Calories	182	Sugars	6g
Protein	10g	Fat	9g
Carbohydrate	18g	Saturates	5g

15 MINS — 2¼ HOURS

SERVES 4

INGREDIENTS

- 4 large Spanish onions
- 2 slices streaky bacon, diced
- ½ red (bell) pepper, deseeded and diced
- 125 g/4½ oz lean minced (ground) beef
- 1 tbsp chopped mixed fresh herbs such as parsley, thyme and rosemary or 1 tsp dried mixed herbs
- 25 g/1 oz/½ cup fresh white breadcrumbs
- 300 ml/½ pint/1¼ cups beef stock
- salt and pepper
- chopped fresh parsley to garnish
- long grain rice to serve

GRAVY

- 25 g/1 oz/2 tbsp butter
- 125 g/4½ oz mushrooms, chopped finely
- 300 ml/½ pint/1¼ cups beef stock
- 2 tbsp cornflour (cornstarch)
- 2 tbsp water

1 Put the onions in a saucepan of lightly salted water. Bring to the boil, then simmer for 15 minutes until tender.

2 Remove the onions from the pan, drain and cool slightly, then hollow out the centres and finely chop.

3 Heat a frying pan (skillet) and cook the bacon until the fat runs. Add the chopped onion and (bell) pepper and cook for 5–7 minutes, stirring frequently.

4 Add the beef to the frying pan (skillet) and cook, stirring, for 3 minutes, until browned. Remove from the heat and stir in the herbs, breadcrumbs and seasoning.

5 Grease an ovenproof dish and stand the whole onions in it. Pack the beef mixture into the centres and pour the stock around them.

6 Bake the stuffed onions in a preheated oven at 180°C/350°F/Gas Mark 4 for 1–1½ hours or until tender.

7 To make the gravy, heat the butter in a small saucepan and fry the mushrooms for 3–4 minutes. Strain the liquid from the onions and add to the pan with the stock. Cook for 2–3 minutes.

8 Mix the cornflour (cornstarch) with the water then stir into the gravy and heat, stirring, until thickened and smooth. Season with salt and pepper to taste. Serve the onions with the gravy and rice, garnished with chopped fresh parsley.

Stuffed Mushrooms

Large mushrooms have more flavour than the smaller button mushrooms. Serve these mushrooms as a side vegetable or appetizer.

NUTRITIONAL INFORMATION	
Calories 148	Sugars 1g
Protein 11g	Fat 7g
Carbohydrate 11g	Saturates 3g

10 MINS 15 MINS

SERVES 4

INGREDIENTS

- 12 open-cap mushrooms
- 4 spring onions (scallions), chopped
- 4 tsp olive oil
- 100 g/3½ oz fresh brown breadcrumbs
- 1 tsp fresh oregano, chopped
- 100 g/3½ oz low-fat mature (sharp) Cheddar cheese

1 Wash the mushrooms and pat dry with kitchen paper (paper towels). Remove the stalks and chop the stalks finely.

2 Sauté the mushroom stalks and spring onions (scallions) in half of the oil.

3 In a large bowl, mix together the mushroom stalks and spring onions (scallions).

4 Add the breadcrumbs and oregano to the mushrooms and spring onions (scallions), mix and set aside.

5 Crumble the cheese into small pieces in a small bowl. Add the cheese to the breadcrumb mixture and mix well. Spoon the stuffing mixture into the mushroom caps.

6 Drizzle the remaining oil over the mushrooms. Barbecue (grill) on an oiled rack over medium hot coals for 10 minutes or until cooked through.

7 Transfer the mushrooms to serving plates and serve hot.

VARIATION

For a change replace the cheese with finely-chopped chorizo sausage (remove the skin first), chopped hard-boiled eggs, chopped olives or chopped anchovy fillets. Mop up the juices with some crusty bread.

Soufflé Omelette

The sweet cherry tomatoes, mushrooms and peppery rocket (arugula) leaves make a mouthwatering filling for these light, fluffy omelettes.

NUTRITIONAL INFORMATION

Calories	146	Sugars	2g
Protein	10g	Fat	11g
Carbohydrate	2g	Saturates	2g

1¼ HOURS   45 MINS

SERVES 4

INGREDIENTS

- 175 g/6 oz cherry tomatoes
- 225 g/8 oz mixed mushrooms (such as button, chestnut, shiitake, oyster and wild mushrooms)
- 4 tbsp Fresh Vegetable Stock (see page 14)
- small bunch fresh thyme
- 4 medium eggs, separated
- 4 medium egg whites
- 4 tsp olive oil
- 25 g/1 oz rocket (arugula) leaves
- salt and pepper
- fresh thyme sprigs, to garnish

1 Halve the tomatoes and place them in a saucepan. Wipe the mushrooms with kitchen paper, trim if necessary and slice if large. Place the tomatoes and mushrooms in the saucepan.

2 Add the stock and thyme to the pan. Bring to the boil, cover and simmer for 5–6 minutes until tender. Drain, remove the thyme and discard, and keep the mixture warm.

3 Meanwhile, separate the eggs and whisk the egg yolks with 8 tbsp water until frothy. In a clean, grease-free bowl, mix the 8 egg whites until stiff and dry.

4 Spoon the egg yolk mixture into the egg whites and, using a metal spoon, fold together until well mixed. Take care not to knock out too much of the air.

5 For each omelette, brush a small omelette pan with 1 tsp oil and heat until hot. Pour in a quarter of the egg mixture and cook for 4–5 minutes until the mixture has set.

6 Preheat the grill (broiler) to medium and finish cooking the omelette for 2–3 minutes.

7 Transfer the omelette to a warm serving plate. Fill the omelette with a few rocket (arugula) leaves, and a quarter of the mushroom and tomato mixture. Flip over the top of the omelette, garnish with sprigs of thyme and serve.

Smoked Fish & Potato Pâté

This smoked fish pâté is given a tart fruity flavour by the gooseberries, which complement the fish perfectly.

NUTRITIONAL INFORMATION

Calories	418	Sugars	4g
Protein	18g	Fat	25g
Carbohydrate	32g	Saturates	6g

20 MINS 10 MINS

SERVES 4

INGREDIENTS

- 650 g/1 lb 7 oz floury (mealy) potatoes, diced
- 300 g/10½ oz smoked mackerel, skinned and flaked
- 75 g/2¾ oz cooked gooseberries
- 2 tsp lemon juice
- 2 tbsp low-fat crème fraîche
- 1 tbsp capers
- 1 gherkin, chopped
- 1 tbsp chopped dill pickle
- 1 tbsp chopped fresh dill
- salt and pepper
- lemon wedges, to garnish
- toast or warm crusty bread, to serve

3

4

5

1 Cook the diced potatoes in a saucepan of boiling water for 10 minutes until tender, then drain well.

2 Place the cooked potatoes in a food processor or blender.

3 Add the skinned and flaked smoked mackerel and process for 30 seconds until fairly smooth. Alternatively, place the ingredients in a bowl and mash with a fork.

4 Add the cooked gooseberries, lemon juice and crème fraîche to the fish and potato mixture. Blend for a further 10 seconds or mash well.

5 Stir in the capers, chopped gherkin and dill pickle, and chopped fresh dill. Season well with salt and pepper.

6 Turn the fish pâté into a serving dish, garnish with lemon wedges and serve with slices of toast or warm crusty bread cut into chunks or slices.

COOK'S TIP

Use stewed, canned or bottled cooked gooseberries for convenience and to save time, or when fresh gooseberries are out of season.

Crêpes with Curried Crab

Home-made crêpes are delicious – here, white crab meat is lightly flavoured with curry spices and tossed in a low-fat dressing.

NUTRITIONAL INFORMATION

Calories	279	Sugars	9g
Protein	25g	Fat	7g
Carbohydrate	31g	Saturates	1g

40 MINS 25 MINS

SERVES 4

INGREDIENTS

- 115 g/4 oz buckwheat flour
- 1 large egg, beaten
- 300 ml/½ pint/1¼ cups skimmed milk
- 125 g/4½ oz frozen spinach, thawed, well-drained and chopped
- 2 tsp vegetable oil

FILLING

- 350 g/12 oz white crab meat
- 1 tsp mild curry powder
- 1 tbsp mango chutney
- 1 tbsp reduced-calorie mayonnaise
- 2 tbsp low-fat natural (unsweetened) yogurt
- 2 tbsp fresh coriander (cilantro), chopped

TO SERVE

- green salad
- lemon wedges

1

2

3

1 Sift the flour into a bowl and remove any husks that remain in the sieve (strainer). Make a well in the centre of the flour and add the egg. Whisk in the milk, then blend in the spinach. Transfer to a jug and leave for 30 minutes.

2 To make the filling, mix together all the ingredients, except the coriander (cilantro), in a bowl, cover and chill until required. Whisk the batter. Brush a small crêpe pan with a little oil, heat until hot and pour in enough batter to cover the base thinly. Cook for 1–2 minutes, turn over and cook for 1 minute until golden. Repeat to make 8 pancakes, layering them on a plate with baking parchment.

3 Stir the coriander (cilantro) into the crab mixture. Fold each pancake into quarters. Open one fold and fill with the crab mixture. Serve warm, with a green salad and lemon wedges.

VARIATION

Try lean diced chicken in a light white sauce or peeled prawns (shrimp) instead of the crab.

Thai Potato Crab Cakes

These small crab cakes are based on a traditional Thai recipe. They make a delicious snack when served with this sweet and sour cucumber sauce.

NUTRITIONAL INFORMATION

Calories	254	Sugars	9g
Protein	12g	Fat	6g
Carbohydrate	40g	Saturates	1g

10 MINS — 30 MINS

SERVES 4

INGREDIENTS

450 g/1 lb floury (mealy) potatoes, diced

175 g/6 oz white crab meat, drained if canned

4 spring onions (scallions), chopped

1 tsp light soy sauce

½ tsp sesame oil

1 tsp chopped lemon grass

1 tsp lime juice

3 tbsp plain (all-purpose) flour

2 tbsp vegetable oil

salt and pepper

SAUCE

4 tbsp finely chopped cucumber

2 tbsp clear honey

1 tbsp garlic wine vinegar

½ tsp light soy sauce

1 chopped red chilli

TO GARNISH

1 red chilli, sliced

cucumber slices

2

3

5

1 Cook the diced potatoes in a saucepan of boiling water for 10 minutes until cooked through. Drain well and mash.

2 Mix the crab meat into the potato with the spring onions (scallions), soy sauce, sesame oil, lemon grass, lime juice and flour. Season with salt and pepper.

3 Divide the potato mixture into 8 portions of equal size and shape them into small rounds, using floured hands.

4 Heat the oil in a wok or frying pan (skillet) and cook the cakes, 4 at a time, for 5-7 minutes, turning once. Keep warm and repeat with the remaining crab cakes.

5 Meanwhile, make the sauce. In a small serving bowl, mix the cucumber, honey, vinegar, soy sauce and chopped red chilli.

6 Garnish the cakes with the sliced red chilli and cucumber slices and serve with the sauce.

Rice & Tuna (Bell) Peppers

Grilled mixed sweet (bell) peppers are filled with tender tuna, sweetcorn, nutty brown and wild rice and grated, reduced-fat cheese.

NUTRITIONAL INFORMATION

Calories	332	Sugars	13g
Protein	27g	Fat	8g
Carbohydrate	42g	Saturates	4g

10 MINS 35 MINS

SERVES 4

INGREDIENTS

- 60 g/2 oz/⅓ cup wild rice
- 60 g/2 oz/⅓ cup brown rice
- 4 assorted medium (bell) peppers
- 200 g/7 oz can tuna fish in brine, drained and flaked
- 325 g/11½ oz can sweetcorn kernels (with no added sugar or salt), drained
- 100 g/3½ oz reduced-fat mature (sharp) Cheddar cheese, grated
- 1 bunch fresh basil leaves, shredded
- 2 tbsp dry white breadcrumbs
- 1 tbsp Parmesan cheese, freshly grated
- salt and pepper
- fresh basil leaves, to garnish
- crisp salad leaves, to serve

1 Place the wild rice and brown rice in different saucepans, cover with water and cook for about 15 minutes or according to the instructions on the packet. Drain the rice well.

2 Meanwhile, preheat the grill (broiler) to medium. Halve the (bell) peppers, remove the seeds and stalks and arrange the peppers on the grill (broiler) rack, cut side down. Cook for 5 minutes, turn over and cook for a further 4–5 minutes.

3 Transfer the cooked rice to a mixing bowl and add the flaked tuna and drained sweetcorn. Gently fold in the grated cheese. Stir the basil leaves into the rice mixture and season with salt and pepper to taste.

4 Divide the tuna and rice mixture into 8 equal portions. Pile each portion into each cooked (bell) pepper half. Mix together the breadcrumbs and Parmesan cheese and sprinkle over each (bell) pepper.

5 Place the (bell) peppers back under the grill (broiler) for 4–5 minutes until hot and golden-brown.

6 Serve the (bell) peppers immediately, garnished with basil and accompanied with fresh, crisp salad leaves.

2

3

4

Red Mullet & Coconut Loaf

This fish and coconut loaf is ideal to take along on picnics, as it can be served cold as well as hot.

NUTRITIONAL INFORMATION

Calories	138	Sugars	12g
Protein	11g	Fat	1g
Carbohydrate	23g	Saturates	0g

15 MINS — $1^1/_4$ HOURS

SERVES 4–6

INGREDIENTS

- 225 g/8 oz red mullet fillets, skinned
- 2 small tomatoes, deseeded and chopped finely
- 2 green (bell) peppers, chopped finely
- 1 onion, chopped finely
- 1 fresh red chilli, chopped finely
- 150 g/5½ oz/2½ cups breadcrumbs
- 600 ml/1 pint/2½ cups coconut liquid
- salt and pepper

HOT PEPPER SAUCE

- 125 ml/4 fl oz/½ cup tomato ketchup
- 1 tsp West Indian hot pepper sauce
- ¼ tsp hot mustard

TO GARNISH

- lemon twists
- sprigs of fresh chervil

1 Finely chop the fish and mix with the tomatoes, (bell) peppers, onion and chilli.

2 Stir in the breadcrumbs, coconut liquid and seasoning. If using fresh coconut, use a hammer and screwdriver or the tip of a sturdy knife to poke out the three 'eyes' in the top of the coconut and pour out the liquid.

3 Grease and base-line a 500 g/1 lb 2 oz loaf tin (pan) and add the fish.

4 Bake in a preheated oven at 200°C/400°F/Gas Mark 6 for 1–$1^1/_4$ hours until set.

5 To make the hot pepper sauce, mix together the tomato ketchup, hot pepper sauce and mustard until smooth and creamy.

6 To serve, cut the loaf into slices, garnish with lemon twists and chervil and serve hot or cold with the hot pepper sauce.

1

2

3

COOK'S TIP

Be careful when preparing chillies because the juices can irritate the skin, especially the face. Wash your hands after handling them or wear clean rubber gloves to prepare them if preferred.

Turkey & Vegetable Loaf

This impressive-looking turkey loaf is flavoured with herbs and a layer of juicy tomatoes, and covered with courgette (zucchini) ribbons.

NUTRITIONAL INFORMATION

Calories	165	Sugars	1g
Protein	36g	Fat	2g
Carbohydrate	1g	Saturates	0.5g

10 MINS

1¼ HOURS

SERVES 6

INGREDIENTS

1 medium onion, finely chopped

1 garlic clove, crushed

900 g/2 lb lean turkey, minced (ground)

1 tbsp fresh parsley, chopped

1 tbsp fresh chives, chopped

1 tbsp fresh tarragon, chopped

1 medium egg white, lightly beaten

2 courgettes (zucchini), 1 medium, 1 large

2 medium tomatoes

salt and pepper

tomato and herb sauce, to serve

2

3

4

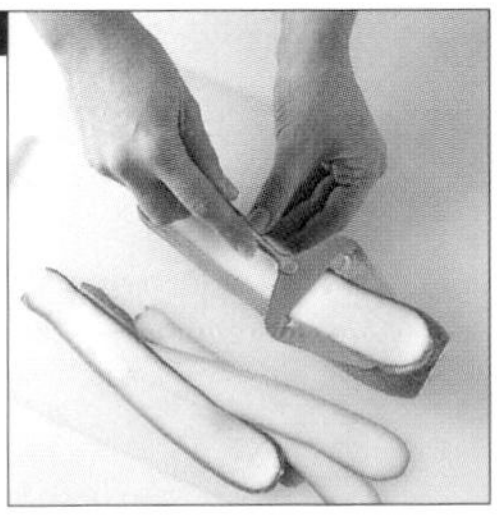

1 Preheat the oven to 190°C/375°F/Gas Mark 5 and line a non-stick loaf tin (pan) with baking parchment. Place the onion, garlic and turkey in a bowl, add the herbs and season well. Mix together with your hands, then add the egg white to bind.

2 Press half of the turkey mixture into the base of the tin (pan). Thinly slice the medium courgette (zucchini) and the tomatoes and arrange the slices over the meat. Top with the rest of the turkey and press down firmly.

3 Cover with a layer of kitchen foil and place in a roasting tin. Pour in enough boiling water to come half-way up the sides of the loaf tin. Bake in the oven for 1–1¼ hours, removing the foil for the last 20 minutes of cooking. Test the loaf is cooked by inserting a skewer into the centre – the juices should run clear. The loaf will also shrink away from the sides of the tin.

4 Meanwhile, trim the large courgette (zucchini). Using a vegetable peeler or hand-held metal cheese slicer, cut the courgette (zucchini) into thin slices. Bring a saucepan of water to the boil and blanch the courgette ribbons for 1–2 minutes until just tender. Drain and keep warm.

5 Remove the turkey loaf from the tin and transfer to a warm platter. Drape the courgette (zucchini) ribbons over the turkey loaf and serve with a tomato and herb sauce.

Cranberry Turkey Burgers

This recipe is bound to be popular with children and is easy to prepare for their supper or tea.

NUTRITIONAL INFORMATION

Calories	209	Sugars	15g
Protein	22g	Fat	5g
Carbohydrate	21g	Saturates	1g

45 MINS — 25 MINS

SERVES 4

INGREDIENTS

- 350 g/12 oz/1½ cups lean minced (ground) turkey
- 1 onion, chopped finely
- 1 tbsp chopped fresh sage
- 6 tbsp dry white breadcrumbs
- 4 tbsp cranberry sauce
- 1 egg white, size 2, lightly beaten
- 2 tsp sunflower oil
- salt and pepper

TO SERVE

- 4 toasted granary or wholemeal (whole wheat) burger buns
- ½ lettuce, shredded
- 4 tomatoes, sliced
- 4 tsp cranberry sauce

1 Mix together the turkey, onion, sage, seasoning, breadcrumbs and cranberry sauce, then bind with egg white.

2 Press into 4 x 10 cm/4 inch rounds, about 2 cm/¾ inch thick. Chill the burgers for 30 minutes.

3 Line a grill (broiler) rack with baking parchment, making sure the ends are secured underneath the rack to ensure they don't catch fire. Place the burgers on top and brush lightly with oil. Put under a preheated moderate grill (broiler) and cook for 10 minutes. Turn the burgers over, brush again with oil. Cook for a further 12–15 minutes until cooked through.

4 Fill the burger rolls with lettuce, tomato and a burger, and top with cranberry sauce.

COOK'S TIP

Look out for a variety of ready minced (ground) meats at your butchers or supermarket. If unavailable, you can mince (grind) your own by choosing lean cuts and processing them in a blender or food processor.

1

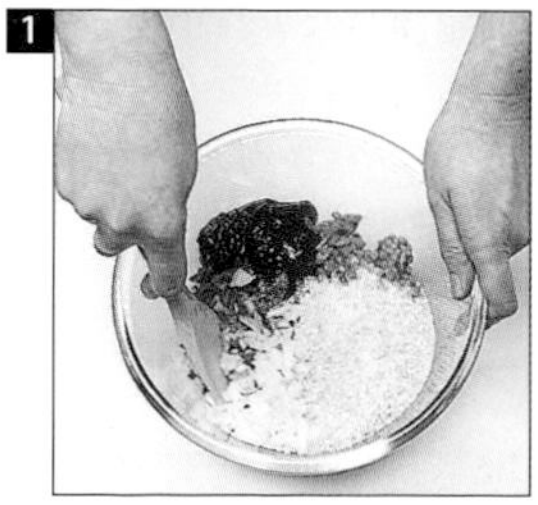

2

3

Parsley, Chicken & Ham Pâté

Pâté is easy to make at home, and this combination of lean chicken and ham mixed with herbs is especially straightforward.

NUTRITIONAL INFORMATION

Calories	119	Sugars	2g
Protein	20g	Fat	3g
Carbohydrate	2g	Saturates	1g

55 MINS

0 MINS

SERVES 4

INGREDIENTS

- 225 g/8 oz lean, skinless chicken, cooked
- 100 g/3½ oz lean ham, trimmed
- small bunch fresh parsley
- 1 tsp lime rind, grated
- 2 tbsp lime juice
- 1 garlic clove, peeled
- 125 ml/4 fl oz/½ cup low-fat natural fromage frais (unsweetened yogurt)
- salt and pepper
- 1 tsp lime zest, to garnish

TO SERVE

- wedges of lime
- crisp bread
- green salad

1 Dice the chicken and ham and place in a blender or food processor.

2 Add the parsley, lime rind and juice, and garlic to the chicken and ham, and process well until finely minced. Alternatively, finely chop the chicken, ham, parsley and garlic and place in a bowl. Mix gently with the lime rind and juice.

3 Transfer the mixture to a bowl and mix in the fromage frais (yogurt). Season with salt and pepper to taste, cover and leave to chill in the refrigerator for about 30 minutes.

4 Pile the pâté into individual serving dishes and garnish with lime zest. Serve the pâtés with lime wedges, crisp bread and a fresh green salad.

VARIATION

This pâté can be made successfully with other kinds of minced, lean, cooked meat such as turkey, beef and pork. Alternatively, replace the meat with peeled prawns (shrimp) and/or white crab meat, or with canned tuna in brine, drained.

Sweet & Sour Drumsticks

Chicken drumsticks are marinated to impart a tangy, sweet and sour flavour and a shiny glaze before being cooked on a barbecue (grill).

NUTRITIONAL INFORMATION

Calories	171	Sugars	9g
Protein	23g	Fat	5g
Carbohydrate	10g	Saturates	1g

1¼ HOURS 20 MINS

SERVES 4

INGREDIENTS

- 8 chicken drumsticks
- 4 tbsp red wine vinegar
- 2 tbsp tomato purée (paste)
- 2 tbsp soy sauce
- 2tbsp clear honey
- 1tbsp Worcestershire sauce
- 1 garlic clove
- good pinch cayenne
- salt and pepper
- crisp salad leaves, to serve

1 Skin the chicken if desired and slash 2–3 times with a sharp knife.

2 Put the chicken drumsticks into a non-metallic container.

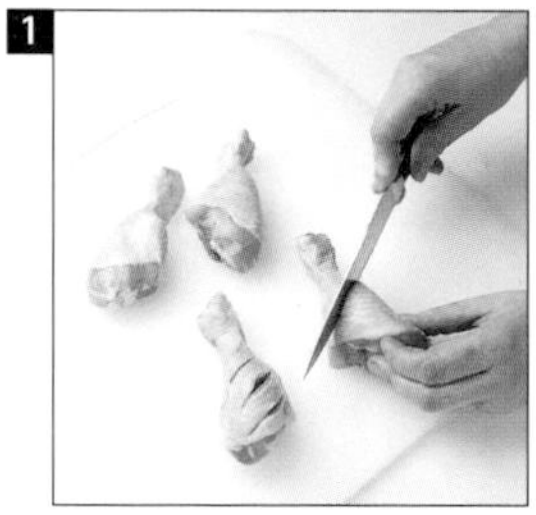

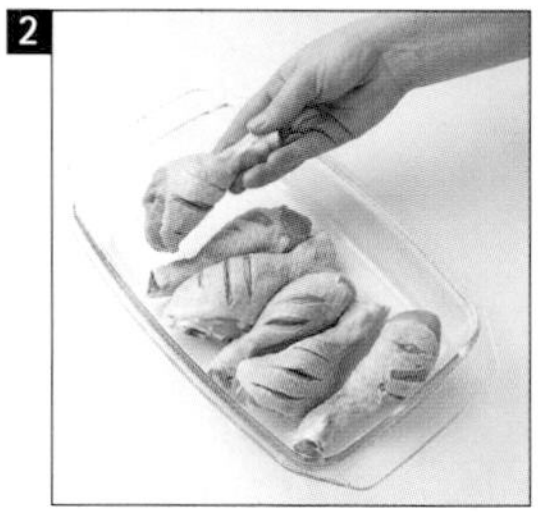

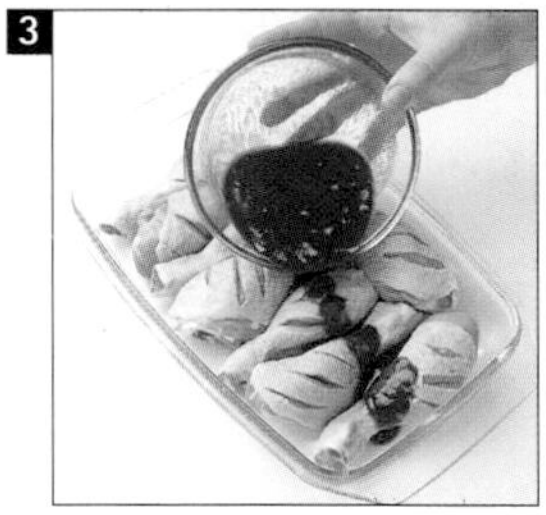

3 Mix all the remaining ingredients and pour over the chicken.

4 Leave to marinate in the refrigerator for 1 hour. Cook the drumsticks on a preheated barbecue (grill) for about 20 minutes, brushing with the glaze several times during cooking until the chicken is well browned and the juices run clear when pierced with a skewer. Serve with a crisp salad leaves.

COOK'S TIP

For a tangy flavour, add the juice of 1 lime to the marinade. While the drumsticks are grilling, check regularly to ensure that they are not burning.

Oat-Crusted Chicken Pieces

A very low-fat chicken recipe with a refreshingly light, mustard-spiced sauce, which is ideal for a healthy lunchbox or a light meal with salad.

NUTRITIONAL INFORMATION	
Calories 120	Sugars 3g
Protein 15g	Fat 3g
Carbohydrate 8g	Saturates 1g

5 MINS — 40 MINS

SERVES 4

INGREDIENTS

- 25 g/1 oz/⅓ cup rolled oats
- 1 tbsp chopped fresh rosemary
- 4 skinless chicken quarters
- 1 egg white
- 150 g/5½ oz/½ cup natural low-fat fromage frais
- 2 tsp wholegrain mustard
- salt and pepper
- grated carrot salad, to serve

1 Mix together the rolled oats, chopped fresh rosemary and salt and pepper.

2 Brush each piece of chicken evenly with egg white, then coat in the oat mixture.

3 Place the chicken pieces on a baking tray (cookie sheet) and bake in a preheated oven, 200°C/400°F/Gas Mark 6, for about 40 minutes. Test to see if the chicken is cooked by inserted a skewer into the thickest part of the chicken – the juices should run clear without a trace of pink.

4 Mix together the fromage frais and mustard, season with salt and pepper to taste.

5 Serve the chicken, hot or cold, with the sauce and a grated carrot salad.

1

2

4

Chicken & Cheese Jackets

Use the breasts from a roasted chicken to make these delicious potatoes and serve as a light lunch or supper dish.

NUTRITIONAL INFORMATION			
Calories	417	Sugars	4g
Protein	28g	Fat	10g
Carbohydrate	57g	Saturates	5g

10 MINS — 50 MINS

SERVES 4

INGREDIENTS

- 4 large baking potatoes
- 225 g/8 oz cooked, boneless chicken breasts
- 4 spring onions (scallions)
- 250 g/9 oz/1 cup low-fat soft cheese or Quark
- pepper

1 Scrub the potatoes and pat dry with absorbent kitchen paper (paper towels).

2 Prick the potatoes all over with a fork. Bake in a preheated oven, 200°C/400°F/Gas Mark 6, for about 50 minutes until tender, or cook in a microwave on HIGH/ 100% power for 12–15 minutes.

3 Using a sharp knife, dice the chicken and trim and thickly slice the spring onions (scallions). Place the chicken and spring onions (scallions) in a bowl.

4 Add the low-fat soft cheese or Quark to the chicken and spring onions (scallions) and stir well to combine.

5 Cut a cross through the top of each potato and pull slightly apart. Spoon the chicken filling into the potatoes and sprinkle with pepper.

6 Serve the chicken and cheese jackets immediately with coleslaw, green salad or a mixed salad.

COOK'S TIP

Look for Quark in the chilled section. It is a low-fat, white, fresh curd cheese made from cow's milk with a delicate, slightly sour flavour.

2

3

5

Spicy Chicken Tortillas

The chicken filling for these easy-to-prepare tortillas has a mild, mellow spicy heat and a fresh salad makes a perfect accompaniment.

NUTRITIONAL INFORMATION

Calories	650	Sugars	15g
Protein	48g	Fat	31g
Carbohydrate	47g	Saturates	10g

10 MINS

35 MINS

SERVES 4

INGREDIENTS

2 tbsp oil

8 skinless, boneless chicken thighs, sliced

1 onion, chopped

2 garlic cloves, chopped

1 tsp cumin seeds, roughly crushed

2 large dried chillies, sliced

400 g/14 oz can tomatoes

400 g/14 oz can red kidney beans, drained

150 ml/¼ pint/⅔ cup chicken stock

2 tsp sugar

salt and pepper

lime wedges, to garnish

TO SERVE

1 large ripe avocado

1 lime

8 soft tortillas

225 ml/8 fl oz/1 cup thick yogurt

1 Heat the oil in a large frying pan or wok, add the chicken and fry for 3 minutes.

2 Add the chopped onion and fry for 5 minutes, stirring until browned.

3 Add the chopped garlic, cumin and chillies, with their seeds, and cook for about 1 minute.

4 Add the tomatoes, kidney beans, stock, sugar and salt and pepper. Bring to the boil, breaking up the tomatoes. Cover and simmer for 15 minutes. Remove the lid and cook for 5 minutes, stirring occasionally until the sauce has thickened.

5 Halve the avocado, discard the stone and scoop out the flesh onto a plate. Mash the avocado with a fork.

6 Cut half of the lime into 8 thin wedges. Now squeeze the juice from the remaining lime over the mashed avocado.

7 Warm the tortillas according to the directions on the pack. Put two tortillas on each serving plate, fill with the chicken mixture and top with spoonfuls of avocado and yogurt. Garnish the tortillas with lime wedges.

Chicken & Almond Rissoles

Cooked potatoes and cooked chicken are combined to make tasty rissoles rolled in chopped almonds then served with stir-fried vegetables.

NUTRITIONAL INFORMATION

Calories	161	Sugars	3g
Protein	12g	Fat	9g
Carbohydrate	8g	Saturates	1g

35 MINS

20 MINS

SERVES 4

INGREDIENTS

- 125 g/4½ oz par-boiled potatoes
- 90 g/3 oz/½ cup carrots
- 125 g/4½ oz/1 cup cooked chicken meat
- 1 garlic clove, crushed
- ½ tsp dried tarragon or thyme
- generous pinch of ground allspice or ground coriander seeds
- 1 egg yolk, or ½ egg, beaten
- about 25 g/1 oz/¼ cup flaked (slivered) almonds
- salt and pepper

STIR-FRIED VEGETABLES

- 1 celery stick (stalk)
- 2 spring onions (scallions), trimmed
- 1 tbsp oil
- 8 baby sweetcorn cobs (corn-on-the-cob)
- about 10–12 mangetout (snow peas) or sugar snap peas, trimmed
- 2 tsp balsamic vinegar
- salt and pepper

1 Grate the boiled potatoes and raw carrots coarsely into a bowl. Chop finely or mince (grind) the chicken. Add to the vegetables with the garlic, herbs and spices and plenty of salt and pepper.

2 Add the egg and bind the ingredients together. Divide in half and shape into sausages. Chop the almonds and then evenly coat each rissole in the nuts. Place the rissoles in a greased ovenproof dish and cook in a preheated oven, 200°C/400°F/Gas Mark 6, for about 20 minutes until browned.

3 To prepare the stir-fried vegetables, cut the celery and spring onions (scallions) on the diagonal into narrow slices. Heat the oil in a frying pan (skillet) and toss in the vegetables. Cook over a high heat for 1–2 minutes, then add the sweetcorn cobs and peas, and cook for 2–3 minutes. Finally, add the balsamic vinegar and season well with salt and pepper.

4 Place the rissoles on to a platter and add the stir-fried vegetables.

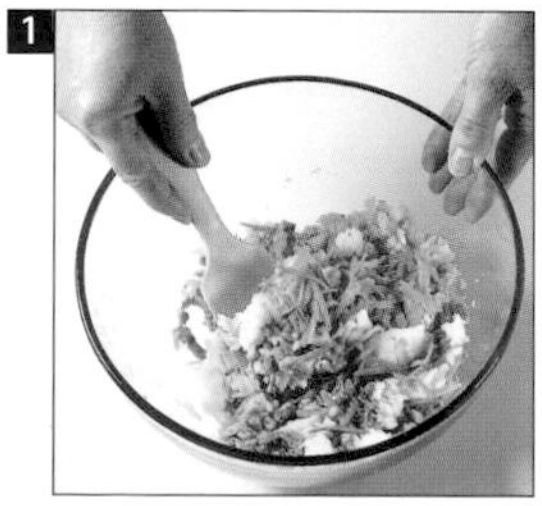

Minty Lamb Burgers

A tasty alternative to traditional hamburgers, these lamb burgers are flavoured with mint and are accompanied with a smooth minty dressing.

NUTRITIONAL INFORMATION

Calories 320	Sugars 11g
Protein 28g	Fat 10g
Carbohydrate ...33g	Saturates 4g

40 MINS — 20 MINS

SERVES 4

INGREDIENTS

- 350 g/12 oz lean lamb, minced (ground)
- 1 medium onion, finely chopped
- 4 tbsp dry wholemeal breadcrumbs
- 2 tbsp mint jelly
- salt and pepper

TO SERVE

- 4 wholemeal baps, split
- 2 large tomatoes, sliced
- small piece of cucumber, sliced
- lettuce leaves

RELISH

- 4 tbsp low-fat natural fromage frais (unsweetened yogurt)
- 1 tbsp mint jelly, softened
- 5 cm/2 inch piece cucumber, finely diced
- 1 tbsp chopped fresh mint

1

3

4

1 Place the lamb in a large bowl and mix in the onion, breadcrumbs and mint jelly. Season well, then mould the ingredients together with your hands to form a firm mixture.

2 Divide the mixture into 4 and shape each portion into a round measuring 10 cm/4 inches across. Place the rounds on a plate lined with baking parchment and leave to chill for 30 minutes.

3 Preheat the grill (broiler) to medium. Line a grill rack with baking parchment, securing the ends under the rack, and place the burgers on top. Cook for 8 minutes, then turn over the burgers and cook for a further 7 minutes or until cooked through.

4 Meanwhile, make the relish. In a small bowl, mix together the fromage frais (unsweetened yogurt), mint jelly, cucumber and freshly chopped mint. Cover the relish with cling film (plastic wrap) and leave to chill in the refrigerator for an hour or until required.

5 Drain the burgers on absorbent kitchen paper (paper towels). Serve the burgers inside the baps with sliced tomatoes, cucumber, lettuce and relish.

Lamb & Tomato Koftas

These little meatballs, served with a minty yogurt dressing, can be prepared well in advance, ready to cook when required.

NUTRITIONAL INFORMATION

Calories	183	Sugars	5g
Protein	15g	Fat	11g
Carbohydrate	5g	Saturates	4g

15 MINS

10 MINS

SERVES 4

INGREDIENTS

- 225 g/8 oz finely minced lean lamb
- 1½ onions, peeled
- 1-2 garlic cloves, peeled and crushed
- 1 dried red chilli, finely chopped (optional)
- 2-3 tsp garam masala
- 2 tbsp chopped fresh mint
- 2 tsp lemon juice
- salt
- 2 tbsp vegetable oil
- 4 small tomatoes, quartered
- mint sprigs, to garnish

YOGURT DRESSING

- 150 ml/¼ pint/⅔ cup low-fat yogurt
- 5 cm/2 inch piece cucumber, grated
- 2 tbsp chopped fresh mint
- ½ tsp toasted cumin seeds (optional)

1

2

3

1 Place the minced lamb in a bowl. Finely chop 1 onion and add to the bowl with the garlic and chilli (if using). Stir in the garam masala, mint and lemon juice and season well with salt. Mix well.

2 Divide the mixture in half, then divide each half into 10 equal portions and form each into a small ball. Roll balls in the oil to coat. Quarter the remaining onion half and separate into layers.

3 Thread 5 of the spicy meatballs, 4 tomato quarters and some of the onion layers on to each of 4 pre-soaked bamboo or metal skewers.

4 Brush the vegetables with the remaining oil and cook the koftas under a hot grill for about 10 minutes, turning frequently until they are browned all over and cooked through.

5 Meanwhile, prepare the yogurt dressing for the koftas. In a small bowl mix together the yogurt, grated cucumber, mint and toasted cumin seeds (if using).

6 Garnish the lamb and tomato koftas with mint sprigs and place on a large serving platter. Serve the koftas hot with the yogurt dressing.

Italian Platter

This popular hors d'oeuvre usually consists of vegetables soaked in olive oil and rich, creamy cheeses. Try this great low-fat version.

NUTRITIONAL INFORMATION

Calories	198	Sugars	12g
Protein	12g	Fat	6g
Carbohydrate	25g	Saturates	3g

10 MINS — 0 MINS

SERVES 4

INGREDIENTS

- 125 g/4½ oz reduced-fat Mozzarella cheese, drained
- 60 g/2 oz lean Parma ham (prosciutto)
- 400 g/14 oz can artichoke hearts, drained
- 4 ripe figs
- 1 small mango
- few plain Grissini (bread sticks), to serve

DRESSING

- 1 small orange
- 1 tbsp passata (sieved tomatoes)
- 1 tsp wholegrain mustard
- 4 tbsp low-fat natural (unsweetened) yogurt
- fresh basil leaves
- salt and pepper

1 Cut the cheese into 12 sticks, 6.5 cm/2½ inches long. Remove the fat from the ham and slice the meat into 12 strips. Carefully wrap a strip of ham around each stick of cheese and arrange neatly on a serving platter.

2 Halve the artichoke hearts and cut the figs into quarters. Arrange them on the serving platter in groups.

3 Peel the mango, then slice it down each side of the large, flat central stone. Slice the flesh into strips and arrange them so that they form a fan shape on the serving platter.

4 To make the dressing, pare the rind from half of the orange using a vegetable peeler. Cut the rind into small strips and place them in a bowl. Extract the juice from the orange and add it to the bowl containing the rind.

5 Add the passata (sieved tomatoes), mustard, yogurt and seasoning to the bowl and mix together. Shred the basil leaves and mix them into the dressing.

6 Spoon the dressing into a small dish and serve with the Italian Platter, accompanied with bread sticks.

2

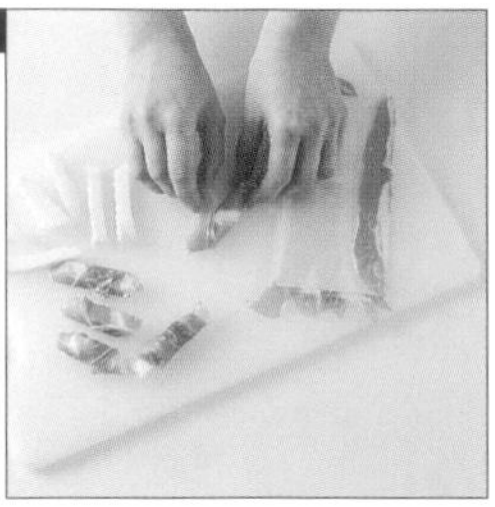

3

5

VARIATION

For a change, serve with a French stick or an Italian bread, widely available from supermarkets, and use to mop up the delicious dressing.

Cheesy Ham Savoury

Lean ham wrapped around crisp celery, topped with a light crust of cheese and spring onions (scallions), makes a delicious light lunch.

NUTRITIONAL INFORMATION

Calories	188	Sugars	5g
Protein	15g	Fat	12g
Carbohydrate	5g	Saturates	7g

10 MINS — 10 MINS

SERVES 4

INGREDIENTS

- 4 sticks celery, with leaves
- 12 thin slices of lean ham
- 1 bunch spring onions (scallions)
- 175 g/6 oz low-fat soft cheese with garlic and herbs
- 6 tbsp low-fat natural (unsweetened) yogurt
- 4 tbsp Parmesan cheese, freshly grated
- celery salt and pepper

TO SERVE

- tomato salad
- crusty bread

1 Wash the celery, remove the leaves and reserve (if wished). Slice each celery stick into 3 equal portions.

2 Cut any visible fat off the ham and lay the slices on a chopping board. Place a piece of celery on each piece of ham and roll up. Place 3 ham and celery rolls in each of 4 small, heatproof dishes.

3 Trim the spring onions (scallions), then finely shred both the white and green parts. Sprinkle the spring onions (scallions) over the ham and celery rolls and season with celery salt and pepper.

4 Mix the soft cheese and yogurt and spoon over the ham and celery rolls.

2

4

5

5 Preheat the grill (broiler) to medium. Sprinkle each portion with 1 tbsp grated Parmesan cheese and grill for 6–7 minutes until hot and the cheese has formed a crust. If the cheese starts to brown too quickly, lower the grill (broiler) setting slightly.

6 Garnish with celery leaves (if using) and serve with a tomato salad and crusty bread.

COOK'S TIP

Parmesan is useful in low-fat recipes because its intense flavour means you need to use only a small amount.

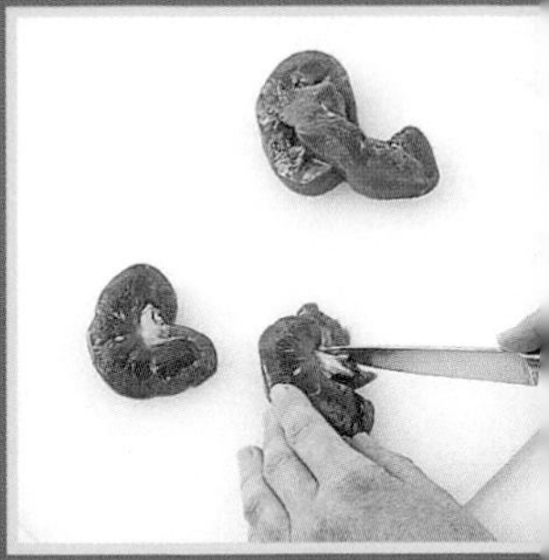

Meat Dishes

The growing awareness of the importance of healthy eating means that supermarkets and butchers now offer leaner, lower-fat cuts of meat. Although these are slightly

more expensive than standard cuts, you do not need to buy as much if you combine them with lots of tasty vegetables and low-fat sauces. It is also worth spending a little extra time cooking the meat carefully to enhance its flavour. Always remember to cut any visible fat from beef and pork before you cook it. Liver, kidney and venison are relatively low in fat. Look out for extra lean minced (ground) meats which can be dry-fried without the addition of oil or fat.

Chilli con Carne

Probably the best-known Mexican dish and one that is a great favourite with all. The chilli content can be increased to suit your taste.

NUTRITIONAL INFORMATION

Calories	443	Sugars	11g
Protein	48g	Fat	15g
Carbohydrate	30g	Saturates	4g

5 MINS

2½ HOURS

SERVES 4

INGREDIENTS

- 750 g/1 lb 10 oz lean braising or stewing steak
- 2 tbsp oil
- 1 large onion, sliced
- 2–4 garlic cloves, crushed
- 1 tbsp plain (all-purpose) flour
- 425 ml/¾ pint tomato juice
- 400 g/14 oz can tomatoes
- 1–2 tbsp sweet chilli sauce
- 1 tsp ground cumin
- salt and pepper
- 425 g/15 oz can red kidney beans, drained
- ½ teaspoon dried oregano
- 1–2 tbsp chopped fresh parsley
- chopped fresh herbs, to garnish
- boiled rice and tortillas, to serve

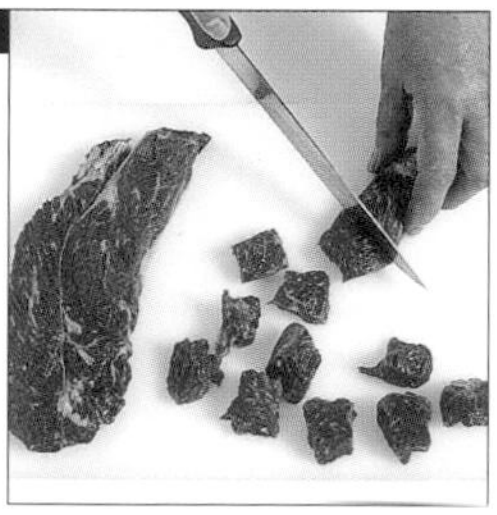

1 Cut the beef into cubes of about 2 cm/¾ inch. Heat the oil in a flameproof casserole and fry the beef until well sealed. Remove from the casserole.

2 Add the onion and garlic to the casserole and fry until lightly browned; then stir in the flour and cook for 1–2 minutes.

3 Stir in the tomato juice and tomatoes and bring to the boil. Replace the beef and add the chilli sauce, cumin and seasoning. Cover and place in a preheated oven at 160°C/325°F/Gas Mark 3 for 1½ hours, or until almost tender.

4 Stir in the kidney beans, oregano and parsley, and adjust the seasoning to taste. Cover the casserole and return to the oven for 45 minutes. Serve sprinkled with chopped fresh herbs and with boiled rice and tortillas.

COOK'S TIP

Because chilli con carne requires quite a lengthy cooking time, it saves time and fuel to prepare double the quantity you need and freeze half of it to serve on another occasion. Defrost and use within 3–4 weeks.

Beef & Orange Curry

A citrusy, spicy blend of tender chunks of tender beef with the tang of orange and the warmth of Indian spices.

NUTRITIONAL INFORMATION

Calories	345	Sugars	24g
Protein	28g	Fat	13g
Carbohydrate	31g	Saturates	3g

$5^1/_4$ HOURS $1^1/_4$ HOURS

SERVES 4

INGREDIENTS

1 tbsp vegetable oil

225 g/8 oz shallots, halved

2 garlic cloves, crushed

450 g/1 lb lean rump or sirloin beef, trimmed and cut into 2 cm/¾ inch cubes

3 tbsp curry paste

450 ml/16 fl oz/2 cups fresh beef stock

4 medium oranges

2 tsp cornflour (cornstarch)

salt and pepper

2 tbsp fresh coriander (cilantro), chopped, to garnish

basmati rice, freshly boiled, to serve

RAITA

½ cucumber, finely diced

3 tbsp chopped fresh mint

150 ml/5 fl oz/⅔ cup low-fat natural yogurt

1

3

4

1 Heat the oil in a large saucepan. Gently fry the shallots, garlic and the cubes of beef for 5 minutes, stirring occasionally, until the beef is evenly browned all over.

2 Blend together the curry paste and stock. Add the mixture to the beef and stir to mix thoroughly. Bring to the boil, cover and simmer for about 1 hour.

3 Grate the rind of one orange. Extract the juice from the orange and from one other. Peel the other two oranges, removing the pith. Slice between each segment and remove the flesh.

4 Blend the cornflour (cornstarch) with the orange juice. At the end of the cooking time, stir the orange rind into the beef along with the orange and cornflour (cornstarch) mixture. Bring to the boil and simmer, stirring, for 3–4 minutes until the sauce thickens. Season to taste and stir in the orange segments.

5 To make the raita, mix the cucumber with the mint and stir in the yogurt. Season with salt and pepper to taste.

6 Serve the curry with rice and the cucumber raita, garnished with the chopped coriander (cilantro).

Rogan Josh

This is one of the best-known curries. Rogan Josh means 'red curry', and is so-called because of the red chillies in the recipe.

NUTRITIONAL INFORMATION

Calories	248	Sugars	2g
Protein	35g	Fat	11g
Carbohydrate	2g	Saturates	5g

10 MINS

1¾ HOURS

SERVES 6

INGREDIENTS

- 2 tbsp ghee
- 1 kg/2 lb 4 oz lean braising steak, cut into 2.5 cm/1 inch cubes
- 1 onion, chopped finely
- 3 garlic cloves
- 2.5 cm/1 inch piece ginger root, grated
- 4 fresh red chillies, chopped
- 4 green cardamom pods
- 4 cloves
- 2 tsp coriander seeds
- 2 tsp cumin seeds
- 1 tsp paprika
- 1 tsp salt
- 1 bay leaf
- 125 ml/4 fl oz/½ cup low-fat yogurt
- 2.5 cm/1 inch piece cinnamon stick
- 150 ml/¼ pint/⅔ cup hot water
- ¼ tsp garam masala
- pepper

2

3

5

1 Heat the ghee in a large flameproof casserole and brown the meat in batches. Remove the meat from the casserole and set aside in a bowl.

2 Add the chopped onion to the ghee and stir over a high heat for 3–4 minutes.

3 Grind together the garlic, ginger, chillies, cardamom, cloves, coriander, cumin, paprika and salt. Add the spice paste and bay leaf to the casserole and stir until fragrant.

4 Return the meat and any juices in the bowl to the casserole and simmer for 2–3 minutes. Gradually stir the yogurt into the casserole keeping the sauce simmering.

5 Stir in the cinnamon stick and hot water, and pepper to taste.

6 Cover the casserole and cook in a preheated oven, 180°C/350°F/Gas Mark 4, for 1¼ hours until the meat is very tender and the sauce is slightly reduced. Discard the cinnamon stick and stir in the garam masala. Remove surplus oil from the surface of the casserole before serving.

Tamarind Beef Balti

Tamarind has been used in Asian cooking for centuries and gives a sour fruity flavour to the sauce.

NUTRITIONAL INFORMATION	
Calories 280	Sugars 7g
Protein 35g	Fat 12g
Carbohydrate 7g	Saturates 4g

12 HOURS 35 MINS

SERVES 4

INGREDIENTS

- 125 g/4½ oz tamarind block, broken into pieces
- 150 ml/¼ pint/⅔ cup water
- 2 tbsp tomato purée (paste)
- 1 tbsp granulated sugar
- 2.5 cm/1 inch piece ginger root, chopped
- 1 garlic clove, chopped
- ½ tsp salt
- 1 onion, chopped
- 2 tbsp oil
- 1 tsp cumin seeds
- 1 tsp coriander seeds
- 1 tsp brown mustard seeds
- 4 curry leaves
- 750 g/1 lb 10 oz lean braising steak, cut into 2.5 cm/1 inch cubes and par-cooked
- 1 red (bell) pepper, cut in half, sliced
- 2 fresh green chillies, deseeded and sliced
- 1 tsp garam masala
- 1 tbsp chopped fresh coriander (cilantro), to garnish

1 Soak the tamarind overnight in the water. Strain the soaked tamarind, keeping the liquid.

2 Put the tamarind, tomato purée (paste), sugar, ginger, garlic, salt and onion into a food processor or blender and mix to a smooth purée. Alternatively, mash the ingredients together in a bowl.

3 Heat the oil in a Balti pan or wok, add the cumin, coriander seeds, mustard seeds and curry leaves, and cook until the spices start popping.

4 Stir the beef into the spices and stir-fry for 2–4 minutes until the meat is browned.

5 Add the red (bell) pepper, chillies, garam masala, tamarind mixture and reserved tamarind liquid and cook for 20–25 minutes.

6 Serve the beef balti garnished with fresh coriander (cilantro).

2

4

5

Beef Goulash

Slow, gentle cooking is the secret to this superb goulash – it really brings out the flavour of the ingredients.

NUTRITIONAL INFORMATION

Calories 386	Sugars 10g
Protein 44g	Fat 16g
Carbohydrate ...17g	Saturates 5g

10 MINS · 2¼ HOURS

SERVES 4

INGREDIENTS

- 2 tbsp vegetable oil
- 1 large onion, chopped
- 1 garlic clove, crushed
- 750 g/1 lb 10 oz lean stewing steak
- 2 tbsp paprika
- 425 g/15 oz can chopped tomatoes
- 2 tbsp tomato purée (paste)
- 1 large red (bell) pepper, deseeded and chopped
- 175 g/6 oz mushrooms, sliced
- 600 ml/1 pint/2½ cups beef stock
- 1 tbsp cornflour (cornstarch)
- 1 tbsp water
- 4 tbsp low-fat natural yogurt
- salt and pepper
- paprika for sprinkling
- chopped fresh parsley, to garnish
- long grain rice and wild rice, to serve

1 Heat the vegetable oil in a large frying pan (skillet) and cook the onion and garlic for 3–4 minutes.

2 Cut the stewing steak into chunks and cook over a high heat for 3 minutes until browned all over. Add the paprika and stir well, then add the chopped tomatoes, tomato purée (paste), (bell) pepper and mushrooms. Cook for 2 minutes, stirring frequently.

3 Pour in the beef stock. Bring to the boil, then reduce the heat. Cover and simmer for 1½–2 hours until the meat is tender.

4 Blend the cornflour (cornstarch) with the water, then add to the saucepan, stirring until thickened and smooth. Cook for 1 minute, then season with salt and pepper to taste.

5 Put the natural yogurt in a serving bowl and sprinkle with a little paprika.

6 Transfer the beef goulash to a warm serving dish, garnish with chopped fresh parsley and serve with rice and yogurt.

Boiled Beef & Carrots

Serve this old favourite with vegetables and herby dumplings for a substantial one-pot meal.

NUTRITIONAL INFORMATION

Calories 459	Sugars 2g
Protein 31g	Fat 22g
Carbohydrate . . .35g	Saturates 10g

15 MINS

$2\frac{3}{4}$ HOURS

SERVES 6

INGREDIENTS

- about 1.75 kg/$3\frac{1}{2}$ lb joint of salted silverside or topside
- 2 onions, quartered, or 5–8 small onions
- 8–10 cloves
- 2 bay leaves
- 1 cinnamon stick
- 2 tbsp brown sugar
- 4 large carrots, sliced thickly
- 1 turnip, quartered
- $\frac{1}{2}$ swede, sliced thickly
- 1 large leek, sliced thickly
- 25 g/1 oz/2 tbsp butter or margarine
- 25 g/1 oz/4 tbsp plain (all-purpose) flour
- $\frac{1}{2}$ tsp dried mustard powder
- salt and pepper

DUMPLINGS

- 225 g/8 oz/2 cups self-raising flour
- $\frac{1}{2}$ tsp dried sage
- 90 g/3 oz/ $\frac{1}{2}$ cup shredded vegetable suet
- about 150 ml/$\frac{1}{4}$ pint/$\frac{2}{3}$ cup water

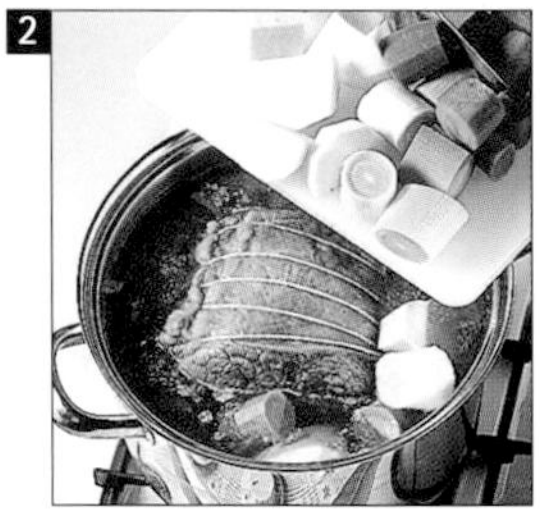

1 Put the beef in a large saucepan, add the onions, cloves, bay leaves, cinnamon and sugar and sufficient water to cover the meat. Bring slowly to the boil, remove any scum from the surface, cover and simmer gently for 1 hour.

2 Add the carrots, turnip, swede and leeks, cover and simmer for a further $1\frac{1}{4}$ hours until the beef is tender.

3 Meanwhile, make the dumplings. Sift the flour into a bowl, season well and mix in the herbs and suet. Add sufficient water to mix to a softish dough.

4 Divide the dough into 8 pieces, roughly shape into balls and place on top of the beef and vegetables. Replace the lid and simmer for 15–20 minutes.

5 Place the beef, vegetables and dumplings in a serving dish. Measure 300 ml/$\frac{1}{2}$ pint/$1\frac{1}{4}$ cups of the cooking liquid into a pan. Blend the margarine with the flour then gradually whisk into the pan. Bring to the boil and simmer until thickened. Stir in the mustard, adjust the seasoning and serve with the beef.

Shepherd's Pie

Minced (ground) lamb or beef cooked with onions, carrots, herbs and tomatoes and with a topping of piped creamed potatoes.

NUTRITIONAL INFORMATION

Calories	378	Sugars	8g
Protein	33g	Fat	12g
Carbohydrate	37g	Saturates	4g

10 MINS — $1^1/_2$ HOURS

SERVES 4–5

INGREDIENTS

- 700 g/1 lb 9 oz lean minced (ground) or lamb or beef
- 2 onions, chopped
- 225 g/8 oz carrots, diced
- 1–2 garlic cloves, crushed
- 1 tbsp plain (all-purpose) flour
- 200 ml/7 fl oz/scant 1 cup beef stock
- 200 g/7 oz can chopped tomatoes
- 1 tsp Worcestershire sauce
- 1 tsp chopped fresh sage or oregano or ½ tsp dried sage or oregano
- 750 g–1 kg/1½–2 lb potatoes
- 25 g/1 oz/2 tbsp margarine
- 3–4 tbsp skimmed milk
- 125 g/4½ oz button mushrooms, sliced (optional)
- salt and pepper

1 Place the meat in a heavy-based saucepan with no extra fat and cook gently, stirring frequently, until the meat begins to brown.

2 Add the onions, carrots and garlic and continue to cook gently for about 10 minutes. Stir in the flour and cook for a minute or so, then gradually stir in the stock and tomatoes and bring to the boil.

3 Add the Worcestershire sauce, seasoning and herbs, cover the pan and simmer gently for about 25 minutes, giving an occasional stir.

4 Cook the potatoes in boiling salted water until tender, then drain thoroughly and mash, beating in the margarine, seasoning and sufficient milk to give a piping consistency. Place in a piping bag fitted with a large star nozzle (tip).

5 Stir the mushrooms (if using) into the meat and adjust the seasoning. Turn into a shallow ovenproof dish.

6 Pipe the potatoes evenly over the meat. Cook in a preheated oven at 200°C/400°F/Gas Mark 6 for about 30 minutes until piping hot and the potatoes are golden brown.

2

3

5

VARIATION

If liked, a mixture of boiled potatoes and parsnips or swede may be used for the topping.

Steak in a Wine Marinade

Fillet, sirloin, rump and entrecôte are all suitable cuts for this dish, although rump retains the most flavour.

NUTRITIONAL INFORMATION

Calories	356	Sugars	2g
Protein	41g	Fat	9g
Carbohydrate	2g	Saturates	4g

3 HOURS 15 MINS

SERVES 4

INGREDIENTS

- 4 rump steaks, about 250 g/9 oz each
- 600 ml/1 pint/2½ cups red wine
- 1 onion, quartered
- 2 tbsp Dijon mustard
- 2 garlic cloves, crushed
- salt and pepper
- 4 large field mushrooms
- olive oil for brushing
- branch of fresh rosemary (optional)

1

2

4

1 Snip through the fat strip on the steaks in 3 places, so that the steak retains its shape when barbecued.

2 Combine the red wine, onion, mustard, garlic, salt and pepper. Lay the steaks in a shallow non-porous dish and pour over the marinade. Cover and chill for 2–3 hours.

3 Remove the steaks from the refrigerator 30 minutes before you intend to cook them to let them come to room temperature. This is especially important if the steak is thick, so that it cooks more evenly and is not well done on the outside and raw in the middle.

4 Sear both sides of the steak – about 1 minute on each side – over a hot barbecue (grill). If it is about 2.5 cm/1 inch thick, keep it over a hot barbecue (grill), and cook for about 4 minutes on each side. This will give a medium-rare steak – cook it more or less, to suit your taste. If the steak is a thicker cut, move it to a less hot part of the barbecue ((grill) or further away from the coals. To test the readiness of the meat while cooking, simply press it with your finger – the more the meat yields, the less it is cooked.

5 Brush the mushrooms with the olive oil and cook them alongside the steak, for 5 minutes, turning once. When you put the mushrooms on the barbecue (grill), put the rosemary branch (if using) in the fire to flavour the meat slightly.

6 Remove the steak and leave to rest for a minute or two before serving. Slice the mushrooms and serve alongside the meat.

Beef Daube

This dish is very French but also very, very New Orleans, especially when the beef is perked up with Tabasco and Cajun spices.

NUTRITIONAL INFORMATION

Calories	251	Sugars	2g
Protein	31g	Fat	10g
Carbohydrate	8g	Saturates	3g

10 MINS — 3¼ HOURS

SERVES 6–8

INGREDIENTS

- 2 tbsp olive oil
- 1 large onion, cut into wedges
- 2 celery sticks, chopped
- 1 green (bell) pepper, cored, seeded and chopped
- 1 kg/2¼ lb lean braising steak, cubed
- 60 g/2 oz/½ cup plain flour, seasoned with salt and pepper
- 600 ml/1 pint/2½ cups beef stock
- 2 garlic cloves, crushed
- 150 ml/¼ pint/⅔ cup red wine
- 2 tbsp red wine vinegar
- 2 tbsp tomato purée (paste)
- ½ tsp Tabasco
- 1 tsp chopped fresh thyme
- 2 bay leaves
- ½ tsp Cajun Spice Mixture
- French bread, to serve

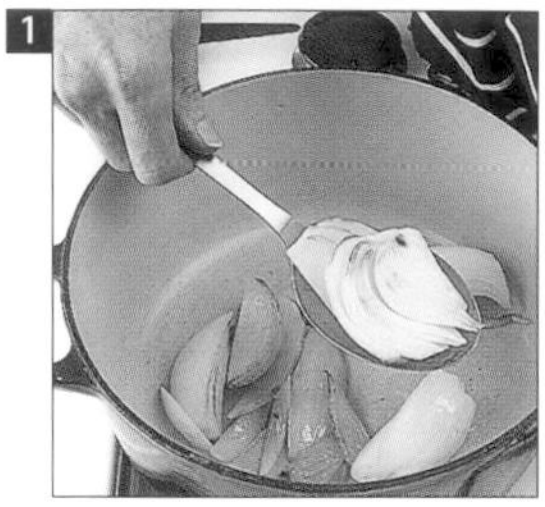
1

3

4

1 Heat the oil in a large heavy-based, flameproof casserole. Add the onion wedges and cook until browned on all sides. Remove with a slotted spoon and set aside.

2 Add the celery and (bell) pepper to the pan and cook until softened. Remove the vegetables with a slotted spoon and set aside.

3 Coat the meat in the seasoned flour, add to the pan and sauté until browned on all sides.

4 Add the stock, garlic, wine, vinegar, tomato purée (paste), Tabasco and thyme and heat gently.

5 Return the onions, celery and peppers to the pan. Tuck in the bay leaves and sprinkle with the Cajun seasoning.

6 Bring to the boil, transfer to the oven and cook for 2½–3 hours, or until the meat and vegetables are tender.

7 Serve the beef daube with French bread.

Beef Teriyaki

This Japanese-style teriyaki sauce complements barbecued (grilled) beef, but it can also be used to accompany chicken or salmon.

NUTRITIONAL INFORMATION	
Calories 184	Sugars 6g
Protein 24g	Fat 5g
Carbohydrate 8g	Saturates 2g

2¹/₄ HOURS   15 MINS

SERVES 4

INGREDIENTS

- 450 g/1 lb extra thin lean beef steaks
- 8 spring onions (scallions), trimmed and cut into short lengths
- 1 yellow (bell) pepper, deseeded and cut into chunks
- green salad, to serve

SAUCE

- 1 tsp cornflour (cornstarch)
- 2 tbsp dry sherry
- 2 tbsp white wine vinegar
- 3 tbsp soy sauce
- 1 tbsp dark muscovado sugar
- 1 clove garlic, crushed
- ½ tsp ground cinnamon
- ½ tsp ground ginger

2

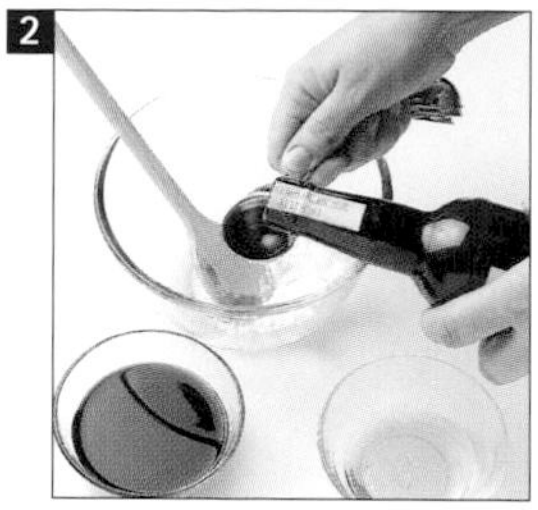

3

4

1 Place the meat in a shallow, non-metallic dish.

2 To make the sauce, combine the cornflour (cornstarch) with the sherry, then stir in the remaining sauce ingredients. Pour the sauce over the meat and leave to marinate for at least 2 hours.

3 Remove the meat from the sauce. Pour the sauce into a small saucepan.

4 Cut the meat into thin strips and thread these, concertina-style, on to pre-soaked wooden skewers, alternating each strip of meat with the prepared pieces of spring onion (scallion) and (bell) pepper.

5 Gently heat the sauce until it is just simmering, stirring occasionally.

6 Barbecue (grill) the kebabs over hot coals for 5–8 minutes, turning and basting the beef and vegetables occasionally with the reserved teriyaki sauce.

7 Arrange the skewers on serving plates and pour the remaining sauce over the kebabs. Serve with a green salad.

Ginger Beef with Chilli

Serve these fruity, hot and spicy steaks with noodles. Use a non-stick ridged frying pan (skillet) to cook with a minimum of fat.

NUTRITIONAL INFORMATION

Calories	179	Sugars	8g
Protein	21g	Fat	6g
Carbohydrate	8g	Saturates	2g

40 MINS 10 MINS

SERVES 4

INGREDIENTS

- 4 lean beef steaks (such as rump, sirloin or fillet), 100 g/3½ oz each
- 2 tbsp ginger wine
- 2.5 cm/1 inch piece root (fresh) ginger, finely chopped
- 1 garlic clove, crushed
- 1 tsp ground chilli
- 1 tsp vegetable oil
- salt and pepper
- red chilli strips, to garnish

TO SERVE

- freshly cooked noodles
- 2 spring onions (scallions), shredded

RELISH

- 225 g/8 oz fresh pineapple
- 1 small red (bell) pepper
- 1 red chilli
- 2 tbsp light soy sauce
- 1 piece stem ginger in syrup, drained and chopped

1 Trim any excess fat from the beef if necessary. Using a meat mallet or covered rolling pin, pound the steaks until 1 cm/½ inch thick. Season on both sides and place in a shallow dish.

2 Mix the ginger wine, root (fresh) ginger, garlic and chilli and pour over the meat. Cover and chill for 30 minutes.

3 Meanwhile, make the relish. Peel and finely chop the pineapple and place it in a bowl. Halve, deseed and finely chop the (bell) pepper and chilli. Stir into the pineapple together with the soy sauce and stem ginger. Cover and chill until required.

4 Brush a grill (broiler) pan with the oil and heat until very hot. Drain the beef and add to the pan, pressing down to seal. Lower the heat and cook for 5 minutes. Turn the steaks over and cook for a further 5 minutes.

5 Drain the steaks on kitchen paper and transfer to serving plates. Garnish with chilli strips, and serve with noodles, spring onions (scallions) and the relish.

1

3

4

Pork with Fennel & Aniseed

Lean pork chops, stuffed with an aniseed and orange filling, are pan-cooked with fennel in an aniseed-flavoured sweet sauce.

NUTRITIONAL INFORMATION			
Calories	298	Sugars	10g
Protein	30g	Fat	10g
Carbohydrate	18g	Saturates	3g

20 MINS 35 MINS

SERVES 4

INGREDIENTS

- 4 lean pork chops, 125 g/4½ oz each
- 60 g/2 oz/⅓ cup brown rice, cooked
- 1 tsp orange rind, grated
- 4 spring onions (scallions), trimmed and finely chopped
- ½ tsp aniseed
- 1 tbsp olive oil
- 1 fennel bulb, trimmed and thinly sliced
- 450 ml/16 fl oz/2 cups unsweetened orange juice
- 1 tbsp cornflour (cornstarch)
- 2 tbsp Pernod
- salt and pepper
- fennel fronds, to garnish
- cooked vegetables, to serve

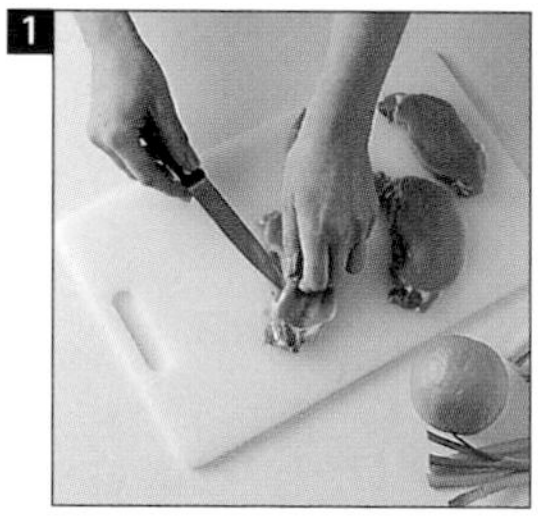

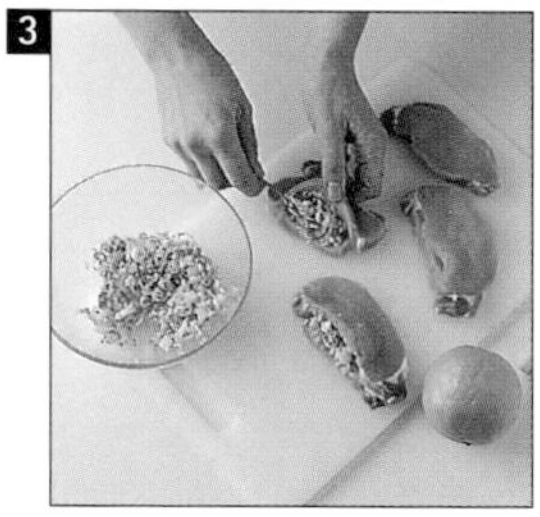

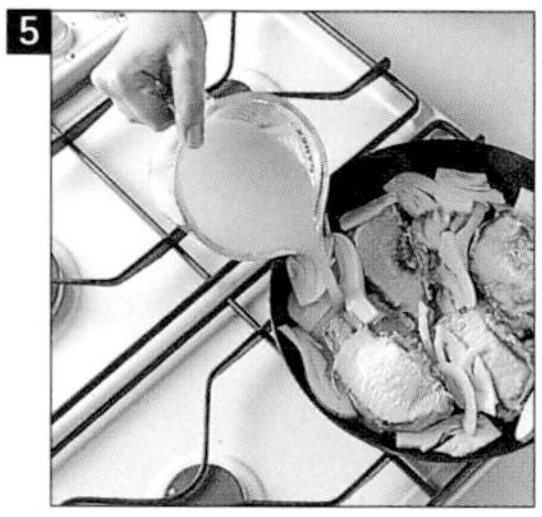

1 Trim away any excess fat from the pork chops. Using a small, sharp knife, make a slit in the centre of each chop to create a pocket.

2 Mix the rice, orange rind, spring onions (scallions), seasoning and aniseed together in a bowl.

3 Push the rice mixture into the pocket of each chop, then press gently to seal.

4 Heat the oil in a frying pan (skillet) and fry the pork chops on each side for 2–3 minutes until lightly browned.

5 Add the sliced fennel and orange juice to the pan, bring to the boil and simmer for 15–20 minutes until the meat is tender and cooked through. Remove the pork and fennel with a slotted spoon and transfer to a serving plate.

6 Blend the cornflour (cornstarch) and Pernod together in a small bowl. Add the cornflour (cornstarch) mixture to the pan and stir into the pan juices. Cook for 2–3 minutes, stirring, until the sauce thickens.

7 Pour the Pernod sauce over the pork chops, garnish with fennel fronds and serve with some cooked vegetables.

Fish-Flavoured Pork

'Fish-flavoured' is a Szechuan cookery term meaning that the dish is prepared with seasonings normally used in fish dishes.

NUTRITIONAL INFORMATION

Calories 183	Sugars 0.2g
Protein 14g	Fat 13g
Carbohydrate 3g	Saturates 3g

25 MINS 10 MINS

SERVES 4

INGREDIENTS

- about 2 tbsp dried wood ears
- 250-300 g/9-10½ oz pork fillet
- 1 tsp salt
- 2 tsp cornflour (cornstarch) paste (see page 15)
- 3 tbsp vegetable oil
- 1 garlic clove, finely chopped
- ½ tsp finely chopped ginger root
- 2 spring onions (scallions), finely chopped, with the white and green parts separated
- 2 celery stalks, thinly sliced
- ½ tsp sugar
- 1 tbsp light soy sauce
- 1 tbsp chilli bean sauce
- 2 tsp rice vinegar
- 1 tsp rice wine or dry sherry
- a few drops of sesame oil

1 Soak the wood ears in warm water for about 20 minutes, then rinse in cold water until the water is clear. Drain well, then cut into thin shreds.

2 Cut the pork into thin shreds, then mix in a bowl with a pinch of salt and about half of the cornflour (cornstarch) paste until well coated.

3 Heat 1 tablespoon of vegetable oil in a preheated wok. Add the pork strips and stir-fry for about 1 minute, or until the colour changes, then remove with a slotted spoon and set aside until required.

4 Heat the remaining oil in the wok. Add the garlic, ginger, the white parts of the spring onions (scallions), the wood ears and celery and stir-fry for about 1 minute.

5 Return the pork strips together with the salt, sugar, soy sauce, chili bean sauce, vinegar and wine or sherry. Blend well and continue stirring for 1 minute.

6 Finally, add the green parts of the spring onions (scallions) and blend in the remaining cornflour (cornstarch) paste and sesame oil. Stir until the sauce has thickened. Transfer the fish-flavoured pork to a warm serving dish and serve immediately.

1

1

3

COOK'S TIP

Also known as cloud ears, wood ears are a dried grey-black fungus widely used in Szechuan cooking. They are always soaked in warm water before using. Wood ears have a crunchy texture and a mild flavour.

Red Roast Pork in Soy Sauce

In this traditional Chinese dish the pork turns 'red' during cooking because it is basted in dark soy sauce.

NUTRITIONAL INFORMATION			
Calories	268	Sugars	20g
Protein	26g	Fat	8g
Carbohydrate	22g	Saturates	3g

$1^1/_4$ HOURS — $1^1/_4$ HOURS

SERVES 4

INGREDIENTS

- 450 g/1 lb lean pork fillets
- 6 tbsp dark soy sauce
- 2 tbsp dry sherry
- 1 tsp five-spice powder
- 2 garlic cloves, crushed
- 2.5 cm/1 inch piece root (fresh) ginger, finely chopped
- 1 large red (bell) pepper
- 1 large yellow (bell) pepper
- 1 large orange (bell) pepper
- 4 tbsp caster (superfine) sugar
- 2 tbsp red wine vinegar

TO GARNISH

- spring onions (scallions), shredded
- fresh chives, snipped

2

5

7

1 Trim away excess fat and silver skin from the pork and place in a shallow dish.

2 Mix together the soy sauce, sherry, five-spice powder, garlic and ginger. Spoon over the pork, cover and marinate in the refrigerator for at least 1 hour or until required.

3 Preheat the oven to 190°C/375°F/Gas Mark 5. Drain the pork, reserving the marinade.

4 Place the pork on a roasting rack over a roasting pan. Cook in the oven, occasionally basting with the marinade, for 1 hour or until cooked through.

5 Meanwhile, halve and deseed the (bell) peppers. Cut each (bell) pepper half into 3 equal portions. Arrange them on a baking sheet (cookie sheet) and bake alongside the pork for the last 30 minutes of cooking time.

6 Place the caster (superfine) sugar and vinegar in a saucepan and heat gently until the sugar dissolves. Bring to the boil and simmer for 3–4 minutes, until syrupy.

7 When the pork is cooked, remove it from the oven and brush with the sugar syrup. Leave for about 5 minutes, then slice and arrange on a serving platter with the (bell) peppers, garnished with the spring onions (scallions) and chives.

8 Serve garnished with the spring onions (scallions) and freshly snipped chives.

Pork Stroganoff

Tender, lean pork, cooked in a tasty, rich tomato sauce is flavoured with the extra tang of natural (unsweetened) yogurt.

NUTRITIONAL INFORMATION

Calories	223	Sugars	7g
Protein	22g	Fat	10g
Carbohydrate	12g	Saturates	3g

2¼ HOURS   30 MINS

SERVES 4

INGREDIENTS

- 350 g/12 oz lean pork fillet
- 1 tbsp vegetable oil
- 1 medium onion, chopped
- 2 garlic cloves, crushed
- 25 g/1 oz plain (all-purpose) flour
- 2 tbsp tomato purée (paste)
- 425 ml/15 fl oz/1¾ cups Fresh Chicken or Vegetable stock (see page 14)
- 125 g/4½ oz button mushrooms, sliced
- 1 large green (bell) pepper, deseeded and diced
- ½ tsp ground nutmeg
- 4 tbsp low-fat natural (unsweetened) yogurt, plus extra to serve
- salt and pepper
- white rice, freshly boiled, to serve
- ground nutmeg, to garnish

1 Trim away any excess fat and silver skin from the pork, then cut the meat into slices 1 cm/½ inch thick.

2 Heat the oil in a large saucepan and gently fry the pork, onion and garlic for 4–5 minutes until lightly browned.

3 Stir in the flour and tomato purée (paste), pour in the stock and stir to mix thoroughly.

4 Add the mushrooms, (bell) pepper, seasoning and nutmeg. Bring to the boil, cover and simmer for 20 minutes until the pork is tender and cooked through.

5 Remove the saucepan from the heat and stir in the yogurt.

6 Serve the pork and sauce on a bed of rice with an extra spoonful of yogurt, and garnish with a dusting of ground nutmeg.

2

4

5

COOK'S TIP

You can buy ready-made stock from leading supermarkets. Although more expensive, they are more nutritious than stock cubes, which are high in salt and artificial flavourings.

Pork with Ratatouille Sauce

Serve this delicious combination of meat and vegetables with baked potatoes for an appetizing supper dish.

NUTRITIONAL INFORMATION			
Calories	230	Sugars	8g
Protein	29g	Fat	9g
Carbohydrate	8g	Saturates	3g

10 MINS 35 MINS

SERVES 4

INGREDIENTS

- 4 lean, boneless pork chops, about 125 g/4½ oz each
- 1 tsp dried mixed herbs
- salt and pepper
- baked potatoes, to serve

SAUCE

- 1 medium onion
- 1 garlic clove
- 1 small green (bell) pepper, deseeded
- 1 small yellow (bell) pepper, deseeded
- 1 medium courgette (zucchini), trimmed
- 100 g/3½ oz button mushrooms
- 400 g/14 oz can chopped tomatoes
- 2 tbsp tomato purée (paste)
- 1 tsp dried mixed herbs
- 1 tsp caster (superfine) sugar

1

2

3

1 To make the sauce, peel and chop the onion and garlic. Dice the (bell) peppers. Dice the courgette (zucchini). Wipe and halve the mushrooms.

2 Place all of the vegetables in a saucepan and stir in the chopped tomatoes and tomato purée (paste). Add the dried herbs, sugar and plenty of seasoning. Bring to the boil, cover and simmer for 20 minutes.

3 Meanwhile, preheat the grill (broiler) to medium. Trim away any excess fat from the chops, then season on both sides and rub in the dried mixed herbs. Cook the chops for 5 minutes, then turn over and cook for a further 6–7 minutes or until cooked through.

4 Drain the chops on absorbent kitchen paper and serve accompanied with the sauce and baked potatoes.

COOK'S TIP

This vegetable sauce could be served with any other grilled (broiled) or baked meat or fish. It would also make an excellent alternative filling for savoury crêpes.

Fruity Pork Skewers

Prunes and apricots bring colour and flavour to these tasty pork kebabs. They are delicious eaten straight off the barbecue (grill).

NUTRITIONAL INFORMATION

Calories	205	Sugars	8g
Protein	21g	Fat	10g
Carbohydrate	8g	Saturates	3g

1¼ HOURS 15 MINS

MAKES 4

INGREDIENTS

- 4 boneless lean pork loin steaks
- 8 ready-to-eat prunes
- 8 ready-to-eat dried apricots
- 4 bay leaves
- slices of orange and lemon, to garnish

MARINADE

- 4 tbsp orange juice
- 2 tbsp olive oil
- 1 tsp ground bay leaves
- salt and pepper

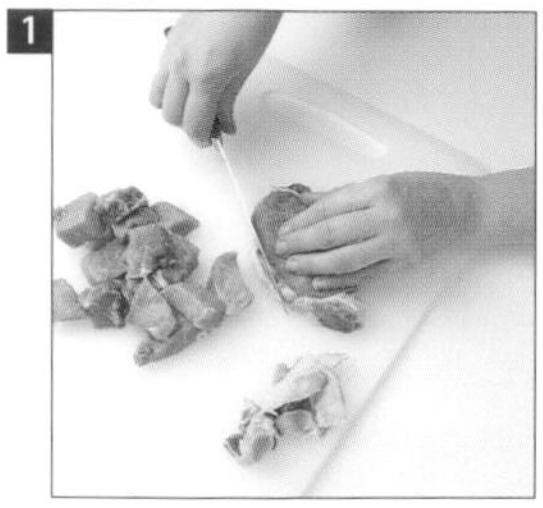

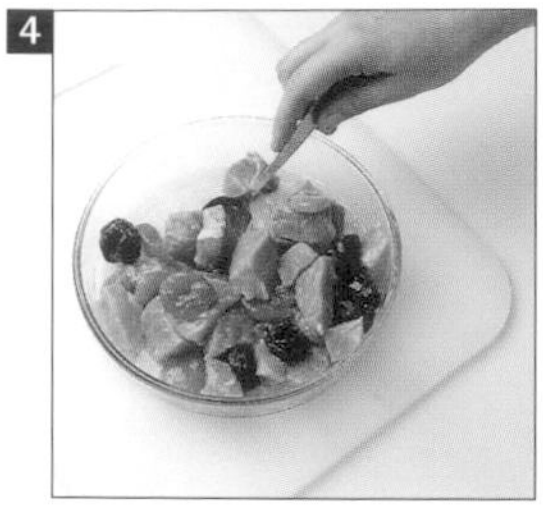

1 Trim the visible fat from the pork and cut the meat into evenly-sized chunks.

2 Place the pork in a shallow, non-metallic dish and add the prunes and apricots.

3 To make the marinade, mix together the orange juice, oil and bay leaves in a bowl. Season with salt and pepper to taste.

4 Pour the marinade over the pork and fruit and toss until well coated. Leave to marinate in the refrigerator for at least 1 hour or preferably overnight.

5 Soak 4 wooden skewers in cold water to prevent them from catching alight on the barbecue (grill).

6 Remove the pork and fruit from the marinade, using a perforated spoon, reserving the marinade for basting. Thread the pork and fruit on to the skewers, alternating with the bay leaves.

7 Barbecue (grill) the skewers on an oiled rack over medium hot coals for 10–15 minutes, turning and frequently basting with the reserved marinade, or until the pork is cooked through.

8 Transfer the pork and fruit skewers to warm serving plates. Garnish with slices of orange and lemon and serve hot.

Pork & Apple Skewers

Flavoured with mustard and served with a mustard sauce, these kebabs make an ideal lunch.

NUTRITIONAL INFORMATION

Calories 290	Sugars 11g
Protein 24g	Fat 17g
Carbohydrate 11g	Saturates 5g

10 MINS　　15 MINS

SERVES 4

INGREDIENTS

- 450 g/1 lb pork fillet
- 2 (dessert) eating apples
- a little lemon juice
- 1 lemon
- 2 tsp wholegrain mustard
- 2 tsp Dijon mustard
- 2 tbsp apple or orange juice
- 2 tbsp sunflower oil
- crusty brown bread, to serve

MUSTARD SAUCE

- 1 tbsp wholegrain mustard
- 1 tsp Dijon mustard
- 6 tbsp single (light) cream

1

4
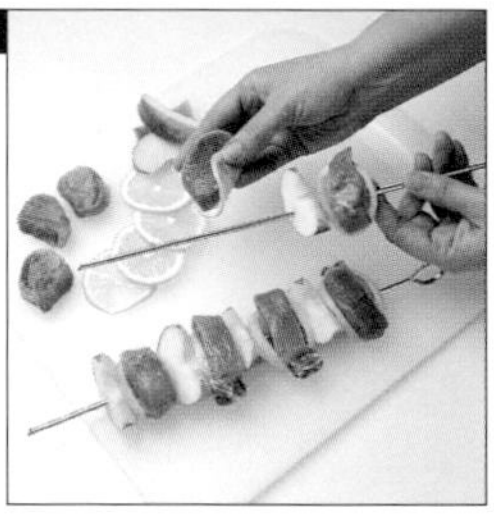

5

1 To make the mustard sauce, combine the wholegrain and Dijon mustards in a small bowl and slowly blend in the cream. Leave to stand until required.

2 Cut the pork fillet into bite-size pieces and set aside until required.

3 Core the apples, then cut them into thick wedges. Toss the apple wedges in a little lemon juice – this will prevent any discoloration. Slice the lemon.

4 Thread the pork, apple and lemon slices alternately on to 4 metal or pre-soaked wooden skewers.

5 Mix together the mustards, apple or orange juice and sunflower oil. Brush the mixture over the kebabs and barbecue (grill) over hot coals for 10–15 minutes, until cooked through, frequently turning and basting the kebabs with the mustard marinade.

6 Transfer the kebabs to warm serving plates and spoon over a little of the mustard sauce. Serve with the kebabs with fresh, crusty brown bread.

Pork with Plums

Plum sauce is often used in Chinese cooking with duck or rich meat to counteract the flavour.

NUTRITIONAL INFORMATION

Calories 281	Sugars 6g
Protein 25g	Fat 14g
Carbohydrate ...10g	Saturates 4g

35 MINS 25 MINS

SERVES 4

INGREDIENTS

- 450 g/1 lb pork fillet (tenderloin)
- 1 tbsp cornflour (cornstarch)
- 2 tbsp light soy sauce
- 2 tbsp Chinese rice wine
- 4 tsp light brown sugar
- pinch of ground cinnamon
- 5 tsp vegetable oil
- 2 garlic cloves, crushed
- 2 spring onions (scallions), chopped
- 4 tbsp plum sauce
- 1 tbsp hoisin sauce
- 150 ml/¼ pint/⅔ cup water
- dash of chilli sauce
- fried plum quarters and spring onions (scallions), to garnish

3

6

7

1 Cut the pork fillet (tenderloin) into thin slices.

2 Combine the cornflour (cornstarch), soy sauce, rice wine, sugar and cinnamon in a small bowl.

3 Place the pork in a shallow dish and pour the cornflour (cornstarch) mixture over it. Toss the meat in the marinade until it is completely coated. Cover and leave to marinate for at least 30 minutes.

4 Remove the pork from the dish, reserving the marinade.

5 Heat the oil in a preheated wok or large frying pan (skillet). Add the pork and stir-fry for 3–4 minutes, until a light golden colour.

6 Stir in the garlic, spring onions (scallions), plum sauce, hoisin sauce, water and chilli sauce. Bring the sauce to the boil. Reduce the heat, cover and leave to simmer for 8–10 minutes, or until the pork is cooked through and tender.

7 Stir in the reserved marinade and cook, stirring, for about 5 minutes.

8 Transfer the pork stir-fry to a warm serving dish and garnish with fried plum quarters and spring onions (scallions). Serve immediately.

Pan-Cooked Pork Medallions

In this dish these lean and tender cuts of meat are perfectly complemented by the eating (dessert) apples and dry (hard) cider.

NUTRITIONAL INFORMATION

Calories	256	Sugars	12g
Protein	21g	Fat	13g
Carbohydrate	12g	Saturates	3g

2½ HOURS 40 MINS

SERVES 4

INGREDIENTS

- 8 lean pork medallions, about 50 g/1¾ oz each
- 2 tsp vegetable oil
- 1 medium onion, finely sliced
- 1 tsp caster (superfine) sugar
- 1 tsp dried sage
- 150 ml/5 fl oz/⅔ cup dry (hard) cider
- 150 ml/5 fl oz/⅔ cup Fresh Chicken or Vegetable Stock (see page 14)
- 1 green-skinned apple
- 1 red-skinned apple
- 1 tbsp lemon juice
- salt and pepper
- fresh sage leaves, to garnish
- freshly cooked vegetables, to serve

1 Discard the string from the pork and trim away any excess fat. Re-tie with clean string and set aside until required.

2 Heat the oil in a frying pan (skillet) and gently fry the onion for about 5 minutes until softened. Add the sugar and cook for 3–4 minutes until golden. Add the pork to the pan and cook for 2 minutes on each side until browned.

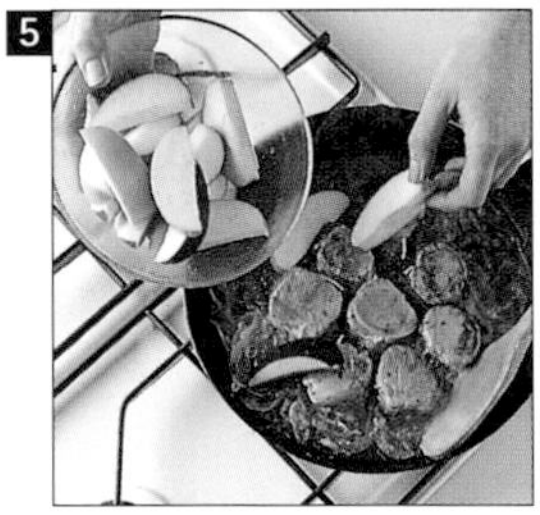

3 Add the sage, cider and stock. Bring to the boil and then simmer for 20 minutes.

4 Meanwhile, core and cut each apple into 8 wedges. Toss the apple wedges in lemon juice so that they do not turn brown when exposed to the air.

5 Add the apples to the pork and mix gently. Season and cook for a further 3–4 minutes until tender.

6 Remove the string from the pork and serve immediately, garnished with fresh sage and accompanied with freshly cooked vegetables.

Tangy Pork Fillet

Barbecued (grilled) in a parcel of kitchen foil, these tasty pork fillets are served with a tangy orange sauce.

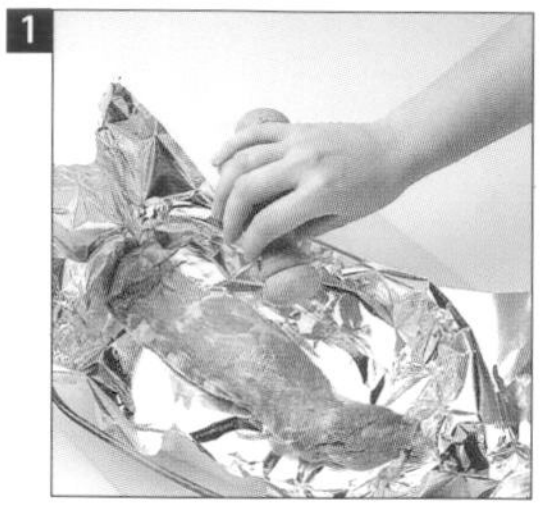

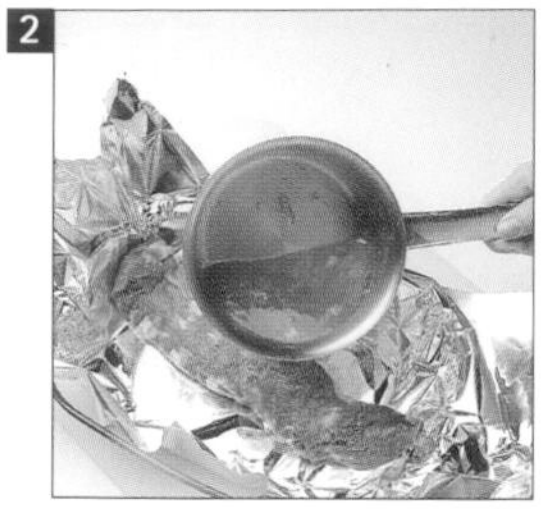

NUTRITIONAL INFORMATION

Calories	230	Sugars	16g
Protein	19g	Fat	9g
Carbohydrate	20g	Saturates	3g

10 MINS — 55 MINS

SERVES 4

INGREDIENTS

- 400 g/14 oz lean pork fillet
- 3 tbsp orange marmalade
- grated rind and juice of 1 orange
- 1 tbsp white wine vinegar
- dash of Tabasco sauce
- salt and pepper

SAUCE

- 1 tbsp olive oil
- 1 small onion, chopped
- 1 small green (bell) pepper, deseeded and thinly sliced
- 1 tbsp cornflour (cornstarch)
- 150 ml/5 fl oz/⅔ cup orange juice

TO SERVE

- cooked rice
- mixed salad leaves

1 Place a large piece of double thickness foil in a shallow dish. Put the pork fillet in the centre of the foil and season.

2 Heat the marmalade, orange rind and juice, vinegar and Tabasco sauce in a small pan, stirring until the marmalade melts and the ingredients combine. Pour the mixture over the pork and wrap the meat in foil, making sure that the parcel is well sealed so that the juices cannot run out. Place over hot coals and barbecue (grill) for about 25 minutes, turning the parcel occasionally.

3 For the sauce, heat the oil and cook the onion for 2–3 minutes. Add the (bell) pepper and cook for 3–4 minutes.

4 Remove the pork from the kitchen foil and place on to the rack. Pour the juices into the pan with the sauce.

5 Barbecue (grill) the pork for a further 10–20 minutes, turning, until cooked through and golden on the outside.

6 In a small bowl, mix the cornflour (cornstarch) with a little orange juice to form a paste. Add to the sauce with the remaining cooking juices. Cook, stirring, until the sauce thickens. Slice the pork, spoon over the sauce and serve with rice and mixed salad leaves.

Pork Chops & Spicy Beans

A tasty and substantial dish, and the spicy bean mixture, served on its own, also makes a good accompaniment to other meat or chicken dishes.

NUTRITIONAL INFORMATION

Calories 388	Sugars 5g
Protein 20g	Fat 27g
Carbohydrate ...17g	Saturates 8g

5 MINS

50 MINS

SERVES 4

INGREDIENTS

- 3 tbsp vegetable oil
- 4 lean pork chops, rind removed
- 2 onions, peeled and thinly sliced
- 2 garlic cloves, peeled and crushed
- 2 fresh green chillies, seeded and chopped or use 1-2 tsp minced chilli (from a jar)
- 2.5 cm/1 in piece ginger root, peeled and chopped
- 1½ tsp cumin seeds
- 1½ tsp ground coriander
- 600 ml/1 pint/2½ cups stock or water
- 2 tbsp tomato purée (paste)
- ½ aubergine (eggplant), trimmed and cut into 1 cm/½ inch dice
- salt
- 1 x 400 g/14 oz can red kidney beans, drained
- 4 tbsp double (heavy) cream
- sprigs of coriander (cilantro), to garnish

1 Heat the ghee or vegetable oil in a large frying pan (skillet), add the pork chops and fry until sealed and browned on both sides. Remove from the pan and set aside until required.

2 Add the sliced onions, garlic, chillies, ginger and spices and fry gently for 2 minutes. Stir in the stock or water, tomato purée (paste), diced aubergine (eggplant) and season with salt and pepper.

3 Bring the mixture to the boil, place the pork chops on top, then cover and simmer gently over medium heat for 30 minutes .

4 Remove the chops for a moment and stir the red kidney beans and double (heavy) cream into the mixture. Return the chops to the pan, cover and heat through gently for 5 minutes.

5 Taste and adjust the seasoning, if necessary. Serve hot, garnished with coriander (cilantro) sprigs.

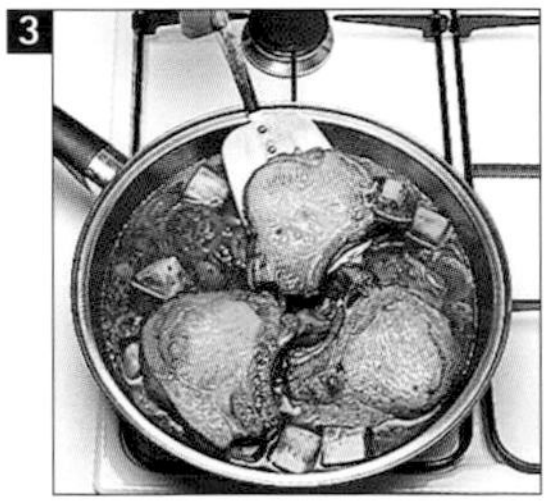

Lamb with Rosemary

This is a pretty dish of pink tender lamb fillet (tenderloin) served on a light green bed of mashed leeks and potatoes.

NUTRITIONAL INFORMATION

Calories 388	Sugars 11g
Protein 35g	Fat 12g
Carbohydrate ...38g	Saturates 5g

1¼ HOURS 55 MINS

SERVES 4

INGREDIENTS

500 g/1 lb 2 oz lean lamb fillet (tenderloin)
4 tbsp redcurrant jelly
1 tbsp chopped fresh rosemary
1 garlic clove, crushed
450 g/1 lb potatoes, diced
450 g/1 lb leeks, sliced
150 ml/¼ pint/⅔ cup Fresh Vegetable Stock, (see page 14)
4 tsp low-fat natural fromage frais
salt and pepper
freshly steamed vegetables, to serve

TO GARNISH

chopped fresh rosemary
redcurrants

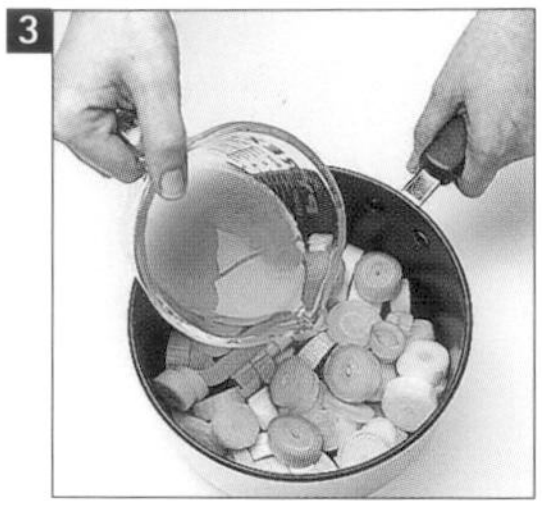

1 Put the lamb in a shallow baking tin (pan). Blend 2 tablespoons of the redcurrant jelly with the rosemary, garlic and seasoning. Brush over the lamb and cook in a preheated oven at 230°C/450°F/Gas Mark 8, brushing occasionally with any cooking juices, for 30 minutes.

2 Meanwhile, place the potatoes in a saucepan and cover with water. Bring to the boil, and cook for 8 minutes until softened. Drain well.

3 Put the leeks in a saucepan with the stock. Cover and simmer for 7–8 minutes or until soft. Drain, reserving the cooking liquid.

4 Place the potato and leeks in a bowl and mash with a potato masher. Season and stir in the fromage frais. Transfer to a warmed platter and keep warm.

5 In a saucepan, melt the remaining redcurrant jelly and stir in the leek cooking liquid. Boil for 5 minutes.

6 Slice the lamb and arrange over the mash. Spoon the sauce over the top. Garnish the lamb with rosemary and redcurrants and serve with freshly steamed vegetables.

Turkish Lamb Stew

A delicious blend of flavours with lamb, onions and tomatoes, complete with potatoes to make the perfect one-pot dish for two.

NUTRITIONAL INFORMATION

Calories 442	Sugars 5g
Protein 41g	Fat 17g
Carbohydrate ...35g	Saturates 7g

10 MINS — 1¼ HOURS

SERVES 2

INGREDIENTS

- 350 g/12 oz lean boneless lamb
- 1 large or 2 small onions
- 1 garlic clove, crushed
- ½ red, yellow or green (bell) pepper, diced roughly
- 300 ml/½ pint/1¼ cups stock
- 1 tbsp balsamic vinegar
- 2 tomatoes, peeled and chopped roughly
- 1½ tsp tomato purée (paste)
- 1 bay leaf
- ½ tsp dried sage
- ½ tsp dried dillweed
- 350 g/12 oz potatoes
- 6–8 black olives, halved and pitted
- salt and pepper

1 Cut the piece of lamb into cubes of about 2 cm/¾ inch, discarding any excess fat or gristle.

2 Place in a non-stick saucepan with no extra fat and heat gently until the fat runs and the meat begins to seal.

3 Cut the onion into 8 wedges. Add to the lamb with the garlic and fry for a further 3–4 minutes.

4 Add the (bell) pepper, stock, vinegar, tomatoes, tomato purée (paste), bay leaf, sage, dillweed and seasoning. Cover and simmer gently for 30 minutes.

5 Peel the potatoes and cut into 2 cm/¾ inch cubes. Add to the stew and stir well. If necessary, add a little more boiling stock or water if it seems a little dry. Cover the pan again and simmer for a further 25–30 minutes, or until quite tender.

6 Add the olives and adjust the seasoning. Simmer for a further 5 minutes and serve with vegetables or a salad and crusty bread.

COOK'S TIP

A good accompaniment would be a salad made of shredded white cabbage, Little Gem lettuce, coarsely grated carrot, diced avocado or cucumber and spring onions (scallions).

Lamb Hotpot

This classic recipe using lamb cutlets layered between sliced potatoes, kidneys, onions and herbs makes a perfect meal on a cold winter's day.

NUTRITIONAL INFORMATION

Calories	420	Sugars	2g
Protein	41g	Fat	15g
Carbohydrate	31g	Saturates	8g

15 MINS — 2 HOURS

SERVES 4

INGREDIENTS

- 675 g/1½ lb lean lamb neck cutlets
- 2 lamb's kidneys
- 675 g/1½ lb waxy potatoes, scrubbed and sliced thinly
- 1 large onion, sliced thinly
- 2 tbsp chopped fresh thyme
- 150 ml/¼ pint/⅔ cup lamb stock
- 25 g/1 oz/2 tbsp butter, melted
- salt and pepper
- fresh thyme sprigs, to garnish

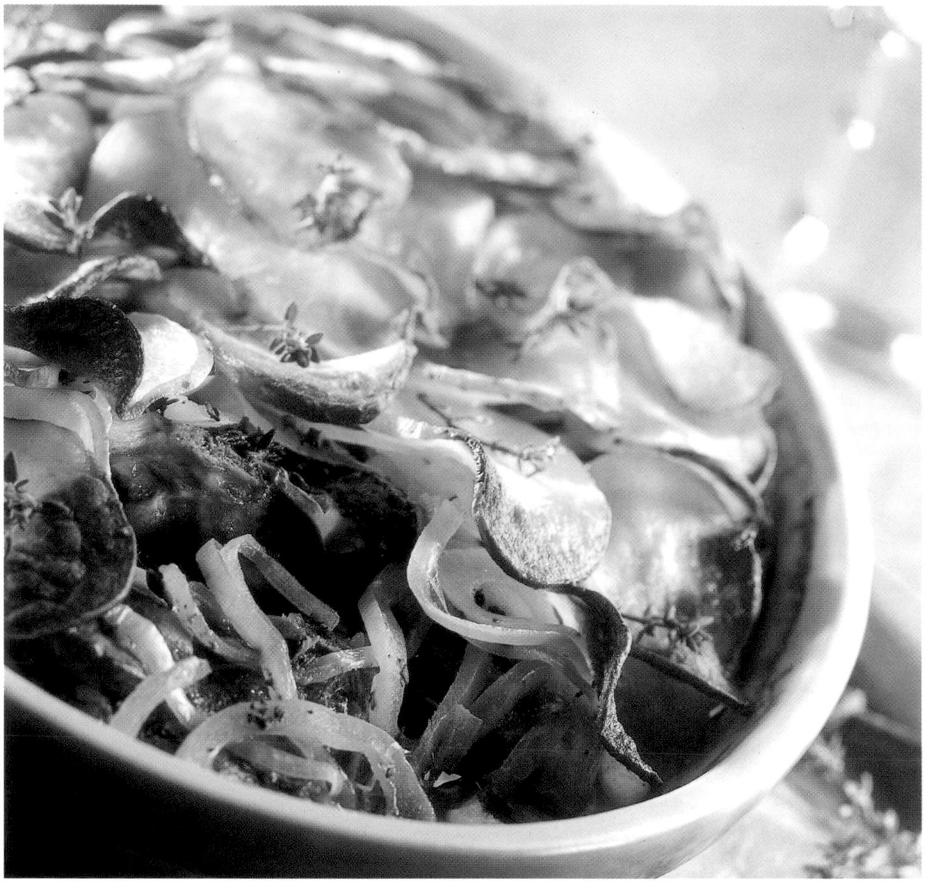

1 Remove any excess fat from the lamb. Skin and core the kidneys and cut them into slices.

2 Arrange a layer of potatoes in the base of a 1.8 litre/3 pint/3½ cup ovenproof dish.

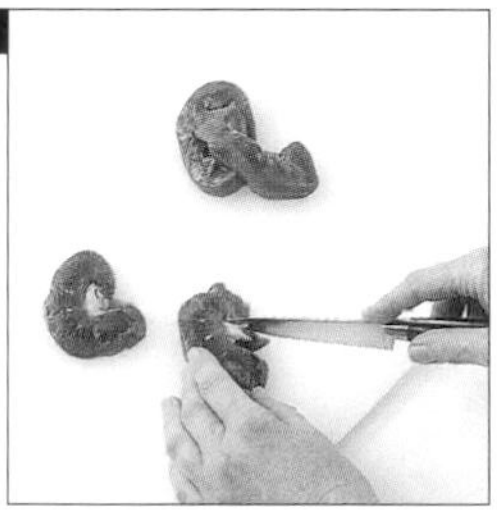

1

2

5

3 Arrange the lamb neck cutlets on top of the potatoes and cover with the sliced kidneys, onion and chopped thyme.

4 Pour the lamb stock over the meat and season to taste with salt and pepper.

5 Layer the remaining potato slices on top, overlapping to completely cover the meat and sliced onion.

6 Brush the potato slices with the butter, cover the dish and cook in a preheated oven, 180°C/350°F/Gas Mark 4, for 1½ hours.

7 Remove the lid and cook for a further 30 minutes until golden brown on top.

8 Garnish with fresh thyme sprigs and serve hot.

VARIATION

Traditionally, oysters are also included in this tasty hotpot. Add them to the layers along with the kidneys, if wished.

Sweet Lamb Fillet

Lamb fillet, enhanced by a sweet and spicy glaze, is cooked on the barbecue (grill) in a kitchen foil parcel for deliciously moist results.

NUTRITIONAL INFORMATION			
Calories	258	Sugars	13g
Protein	24g	Fat	13g
Carbohydrate	13g	Saturates	5g

5 MINS

1 HOUR

SERVES 4

INGREDIENTS

- 2 fillets of neck of lean lamb, each 225 g/8 oz
- 1 tbsp olive oil
- ½ onion, chopped finely
- 1 clove garlic, crushed
- 2.5 cm/1 inch piece root (fresh) ginger, grated
- 5 tbsp apple juice
- 3 tbsp smooth apple sauce
- 1 tbsp light muscovado sugar
- 1 tbsp tomato ketchup (catsup)
- ½ tsp mild mustard
- salt and pepper
- green salad leaves, croûtons and fresh crusty bread, to serve

1 Place the lamb fillet on a large piece of double thickness kitchen foil. Season with salt and pepper to taste.

2 Heat the oil in a small pan and fry the onion and garlic for 2–3 minutes until softened but not browned. Stir in the grated ginger and cook for 1 minute, stirring occasionally.

3 Stir in the apple juice, apple sauce, sugar, ketchup (catsup) and mustard and bring to the boil. Boil rapidly for about 10 minutes until reduced by half. Stir the mixture occasionally so that it does not burn and stick to the base of the pan.

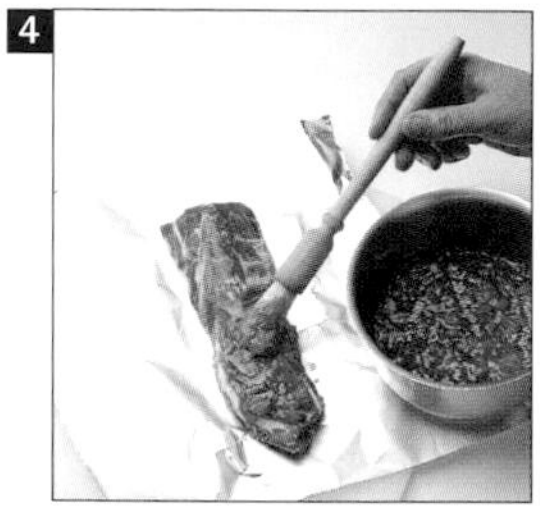

4 Brush half of the sauce over the lamb, then wrap up the lamb in the kitchen foil to completely enclose it. Barbecue (grill) the lamb parcels over hot coals for about 25 minutes, turning the parcel over occasionally.

5 Open out the kitchen foil and brush the lamb with some of the sauce. Continue to barbecue (grill) for a further 15–20 minutes or until cooked through.

6 Place the lamb on a chopping board, remove the foil and cut into thick slices. Transfer to serving plates and spoon over the remaining sauce. Serve with green salad leaves, croûtons and fresh crusty bread.

Stir-Fried Lamb with Orange

Oranges and lamb are a great combination because the tangy citrus flavour offsets the fuller flavour of the lamb.

NUTRITIONAL INFORMATION	
Calories 209	Sugars 4g
Protein 25g	Fat 10g
Carbohydrate 5g	Saturates 5g

5 MINS — 30 MINS

SERVES 4

INGREDIENTS

- 450 g/1 lb minced (ground) lamb
- 2 cloves garlic, crushed
- 1 tsp cumin seeds
- 1 tsp ground coriander
- 1 red onion, sliced
- finely grated zest and juice of 1 orange
- 2 tbsp soy sauce
- 1 orange, peeled and segmented
- salt and pepper
- snipped fresh chives, to garnish

1 Heat a wok or large, heavy-based frying pan (skillet), without adding any oil.

2 Add the minced (ground) lamb to the wok. Dry fry the minced (ground) lamb for 5 minutes, or until the lamb is evenly browned. Drain away any excess fat from the wok.

3 Add the garlic, cumin seeds, coriander and red onion to the wok and stir-fry for a further 5 minutes.

4 Stir in the finely grated orange zest and juice and the soy sauce, mixing until thoroughly combined. Cover, reduce the heat and leave to simmer, stirring occasionally, for 15 minutes.

5 Remove the lid, increase the heat and add the orange segments. Stir to mix.

6 Season with salt and pepper to taste and heat through for a further 2–3 minutes.

7 Transfer the stir-fry to warm serving plates and garnish with snipped fresh chives. Serve immediately.

COOK'S TIP

If you wish to serve wine with your meal, try light, dry white wines and lighter Burgundy-style red wines as they blend well with Oriental food.

Savoury Hotpot

This hearty lamb stew is full of vegetables and herbs, and is topped with a layer of crisp, golden potato slices.

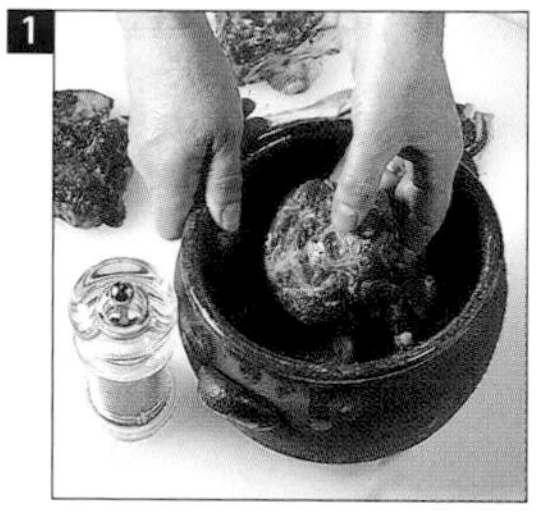

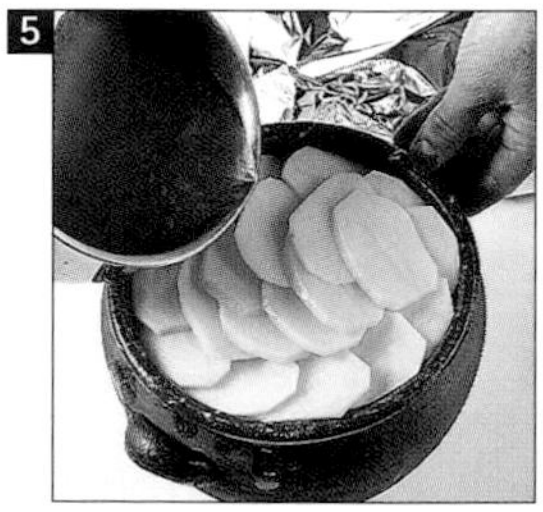

NUTRITIONAL INFORMATION			
Calories	365	Sugars	5g
Protein	23g	Fat	11g
Carbohydrate	48g	Saturates	4g

15 MINS 2 HOURS

SERVES 4

INGREDIENTS

- 8 middle neck lean lamb chops, neck of lamb or any lean stewing lamb on the bone
- 1–2 garlic cloves, crushed
- 2 lamb's kidneys (optional)
- 1 large onion, sliced thinly
- 1 leek, sliced
- 2–3 carrots, sliced
- 1 tsp chopped fresh tarragon or sage, or ½ tsp dried tarragon or sage
- 1 kg/2 lb 4 oz potatoes, sliced thinly
- 300 ml/½ pint/1¼ cups stock
- 25 g/1 oz/2 tbsp margarine, melted, or 1 tbsp vegetable oil
- salt and pepper
- chopped fresh parsley, to garnish

1 Trim any excess fat from the lamb, season well with salt and pepper and arrange in a large ovenproof casserole. Sprinkle with the garlic.

2 If using kidneys, remove the skin, halve and cut out the cores. Chop into small pieces and sprinkle over the lamb.

3 Place the vegetables over the lamb, allowing the pieces to slip in between the meat, then sprinkle with the herbs.

4 Arrange the potato slices over the meat and vegetables, in an overlapping pattern.

5 Bring the stock to the boil, season with salt and pepper to taste, then pour over the casserole.

6 Brush the potatoes with the melted margarine or vegetable oil, cover with greased foil or a lid and cook in a preheated oven at 180°C/350°F/Gas Mark 4 for 1½ hours.

7 Remove the foil or lid from the potatoes, increase the temperature to 220°C/425°F/Gas Mark 7 and return the casserole to the oven for about 30 minutes until the potatoes are browned.

8 Garnish the hotpot with the chopped fresh parsley and serve immediately.

Kibbeh

This Lebanese barbeque dish is similar to the Turkish kofte and the Indian kofta, but the spices used to flavour the meat are quite different.

NUTRITIONAL INFORMATION

Calories	232	Sugars	3g
Protein	19g	Fat	13g
Carbohydrate	9g	Saturates	4g

1 HOUR
15 MINS

SERVES 4

INGREDIENTS

- 75 g/2¾ oz couscous
- 1 small onion
- 350 g/12 oz lean minced lamb
- ½ tsp ground cinnamon
- ¼ tsp cayenne
- 4 tsp ground allspice
- green salad and onion rings, to serve

BASTE

- 2 tbsp tomato ketchup (catsup)
- 2 tbsp sunflower oil

1 Place the couscous in a large bowl, cover with cold water and leave to stand for 30 minutes or until the couscous has swelled and softened. Alternatively, soak the couscous according to the instructions on the packet.

2 Drain the couscous through a sieve and squeeze out as much moisture as you can.

3 If you have a food processor, add the onion and chop finely. Add the lamb and process briefly to chop the mince further. If you do not have a processor, grate the onion then add to the lamb.

1

2

3

4 Combine the couscous, lamb and spices and mix well together. Divide the mixture into 8 equal sized portions. Press and shape the mixture around 8 skewers, pressing the mixture together firmly so that it holds it shape. Leave to chill for at least 30 minutes or until required.

5 To make the baste, combine the oil and ketchup (catsup).

6 Barbecue (grill) the kibbeh over hot coals for 10–15 minutes, turning and basting frequently. Serve with barbecued (grilled) onion rings and green salad leaves.

Minty Lamb Kebabs

These spicy lamb kebabs go well with the cool cucumber and yogurt dip. In the summer you can barbecue (grill) the kebabs outside.

NUTRITIONAL INFORMATION

Calories	295	Sugars	4g
Protein	29g	Fat	18g
Carbohydrate	4g	Saturates	9g

5 MINS | 20 MINS

SERVES 4

INGREDIENTS

- 2 tsp coriander seeds
- 2 tsp cumin seeds
- 3 cloves
- 3 green cardamom pods
- 6 black peppercorns
- 1 cm/½ inch piece ginger root
- 2 garlic cloves
- 2 tbsp chopped fresh mint
- 1 small onion, chopped
- 400 g/14 oz/1¾ cups minced (ground) lamb
- ½ tsp salt
- lime slices to serve

DIP

- 150 ml/5 fl oz/⅔ cup low-fat natural yogurt
- 2 tbsp chopped fresh mint
- 7 cm/3 inch piece of cucumber, grated
- 1 tsp mango chutney

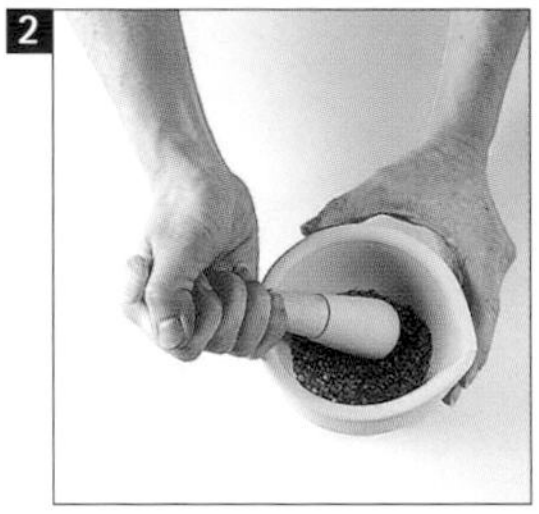

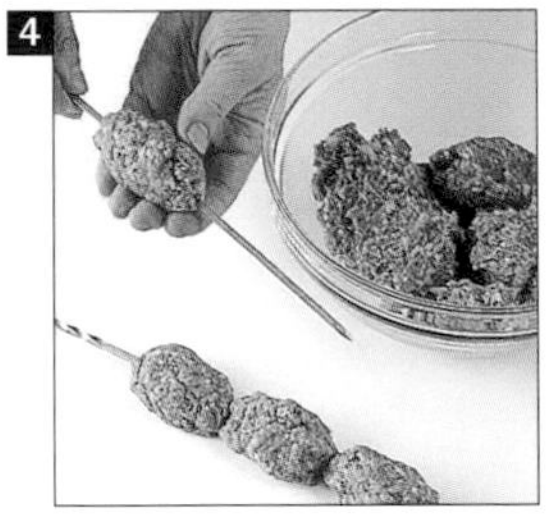

1 Heat a frying pan (skillet) and dry-fry the coriander, cumin, cloves, cardamom pods and peppercorns until they turn a shade darker and release a roasted aroma.

2 Grind the spices in a coffee grinder, spice mill or a pestle and mortar.

3 Put the ginger and garlic into a food processor or blender and process to a purée. Add the ground spices, mint, onion, lamb and salt and process until chopped finely. Alternatively, finely chop the garlic and ginger and mix with the ground spices and remaining kebab ingredients.

4 Mould the kebab mixture into small sausage shapes on 4 kebab skewers. Cook under a preheated hot grill (broiler) for 10–15 minutes, turning the skewers occasionally.

5 To make the dip, mix together the yogurt, mint, cucumber and mango chutney.

6 Serve the kebabs with lime slices and the dip.

Lamb Kebabs with Herbs

Serve the kebabs sizzling hot, and the cucumber and yogurt sauce as cool as can be – it is a delicious partnership.

NUTRITIONAL INFORMATION	
Calories 238	Sugars 7g
Protein 21g	Fat 14g
Carbohydrate 7g	Saturates 5g

2¼ HOURS | 15 MINS

SERVES 4

INGREDIENTS

- 1 kg/2 lb 4 oz lean leg of lamb, trimmed of fat
- 3 tbsp olive oil
- 1 tbsp red wine vinegar
- juice of ½ lemon
- 3 tbsp low-fat natural yogurt
- 1 tbsp dried oregano
- 2 large garlic cloves, crushed
- 2 dried bay leaves, crumbled
- 4 fresh bay leaves
- 2 tbsp chopped parsley
- salt and pepper

SAUCE

- 300 ml/½ pint/1¼ cups low-fat natural yogurt
- 1 garlic clove, crushed
- ¼ tsp salt
- ½ small cucumber, peeled and finely chopped
- 3 tbsp finely chopped mint
- pinch of paprika

1 Cut the lamb into cubes about 4-5 cm/1½-2 inches square. Pat dry with kitchen paper (paper towels) to ensure that the meat stays crisp and firm on the outside when grilled (broiled).

2 Whisk together the olive oil, wine vinegar, lemon juice and yogurt. Stir in the oregano, garlic and crumbled bay leaves and season with salt and pepper. Place the meat cubes in the marinade and stir until well coated in the mixture. Cover and place in the refrigerator for at least 2 hours.

3 Meanwhile, make the sauce. Place the natural yogurt in a large bowl. Stir in the garlic, salt, cucumber and mint. Cover with cling film (plastic wrap) and set aside in the refrigerator until required.

4 Heat the grill (broiler) to high. With a slotted spoon, lift the meat from the marinade and shake off any excess liquid. Divide the meat into 4 equal portions. Thread the meat and the fresh bay leaves on to 4 skewers.

5 Grill (broil) the kebabs for about 4 minutes on each side, basting frequently with the marinade. At this stage the meat should be crisp on the outside and slightly pink on the inside. If you prefer lamb well done, cook the kebabs for a little longer.

6 Sprinkle the kebabs with parsley and serve at once. Sprinkle the paprika over the sauce and serve chilled.

2

2

3

Lamb & Potato Moussaka

Minced (ground) lamb makes a very tasty and authentic moussaka. For a change, use minced (ground) beef.

NUTRITIONAL INFORMATION	
Calories 422	Sugars 8g
Protein 32g	Fat 18g
Carbohydrate ...35g	Saturates 8g

45 MINS — 1¼ HOURS

SERVES 4

INGREDIENTS

- 1 large aubergine (eggplant), sliced
- 1 tbsp olive or vegetable oil
- 1 onion, chopped finely
- 1 garlic clove, crushed
- 350 g/12 oz lean minced (ground) lamb
- 250 g/9 oz mushrooms, sliced
- 425 g/15 oz can chopped tomatoes with herbs
- 150 ml/¼ pint/⅔ cup lamb or vegetable stock
- 2 tbsp cornflour (cornstarch)
- 2 tbsp water
- 500 g/1 lb 2 oz potatoes, parboiled for 10 minutes and sliced
- 2 eggs
- 125 g/4½ oz/½ cup low-fat soft cheese
- 150 ml/¼ pint/⅔ cup low-fat natural yogurt
- 60 g/2 oz/½ cup grated low-fat mature (sharp) Cheddar cheese
- salt and pepper
- fresh flat-leaf parsley, to garnish
- green salad, to serve

1 Lay the aubergine (eggplant) slices on a clean surface and sprinkle liberally with salt, to extract the bitter juices. Leave for 10 minutes then turn the slices over and repeat. Put in a colander, rinse and drain well.

2 Meanwhile, heat the oil in a saucepan and fry the onion and garlic for 3–4 minutes. Add the lamb and mushrooms and cook for 5 minutes, until browned. Stir in the tomatoes and stock, bring to the boil and simmer for 10 minutes. Mix the cornflour (cornstarch) with the water and stir into the pan. Cook, stirring, until thickened.

3 Spoon half the mixture into an ovenproof dish. Cover with the aubergine (eggplant) slices, then the remaining lamb mixture. Arrange the sliced potatoes on top.

4 Beat together the eggs, soft cheese, yogurt and seasoning. Pour over the potatoes to cover them completely. Sprinkle with the grated cheese.

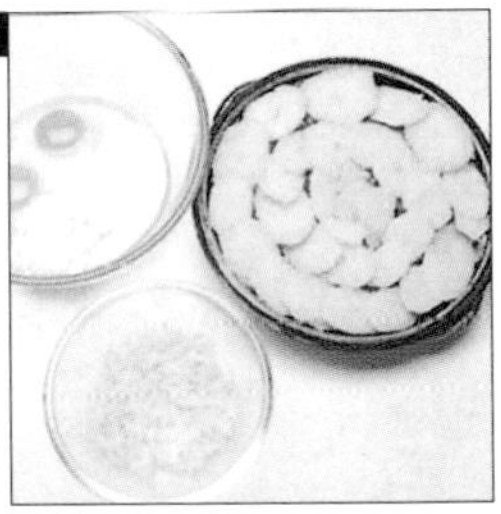

5 Bake in a preheated oven at 190°C/375°F/Gas Mark 5 for 45 minutes until the topping is set and golden brown. Garnish with flat-leaf parsley and serve with a green salad.

Masala Kebabs

Indian kebab dishes are not necessarily cooked on a skewer; they can also be served in a dish and are always dry dishes with no sauce.

NUTRITIONAL INFORMATION

Calories 294	Sugars 0g
Protein 35g	Fat 17g
Carbohydrate 0g	Saturates 7g

1¼ HOURS 20 MINS

SERVES 4

INGREDIENTS

- 1 dried bay leaf
- 2.5 cm/1 inch piece ginger root, chopped
- 2.5 cm/1 inch cinnamon stick
- 1 tsp coriander seeds
- ½ tsp salt
- 1 tsp fennel seeds
- 1 tsp chilli powder
- 1 tsp garam masala
- 1 tsp lemon juice
- 1 tsp ground turmeric
- 1 tbsp oil
- 750 g/1 lb 10 oz lamb neck fillet

TO GARNISH

- sprigs of fresh coriander (cilantro)
- lemon wedges

TO SERVE

- bread
- chutney

1

3
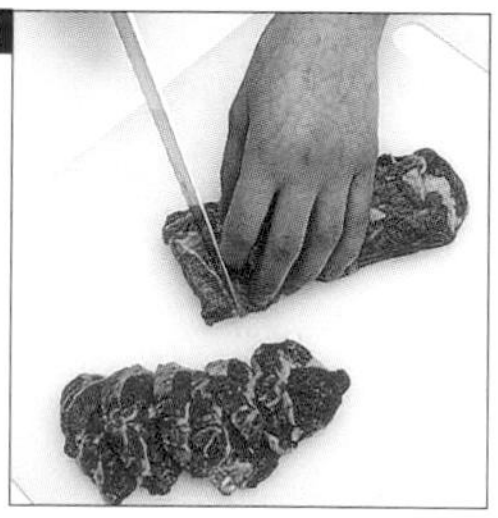

4

1 Use a food processor, blender or pestle and mortar to grind together the bay leaf, ginger, cinnamon, coriander seeds, salt, fennel seeds and chilli powder.

2 Combine this spice mix with the garam masala, lemon juice, turmeric and oil in a large bowl.

3 Cut the lamb into 5 mm/¼ inch slices. Add to the spice mix and leave to marinate at room temperature for about 1 hour, or in the refrigerator for 3 hours or overnight.

4 Spread out the pieces of lamb on a baking sheet and cook in a preheated oven, 200°C/400°F/Gas Mark 6, for 20 minutes until well done. Transfer the pieces of lamb to paper towels to drain any excess fat.

5 Thread 3 or 4 pieces of meat on to each skewer and garnish with sprigs of fresh coriander (cilantro) and lemon wedges.

6 Serve the masala kebabs hot with bread and chutney.

Lamb Couscous

Couscous is a dish that originated among the Berbers of North Africa. When steamed, it is a delicious plump grain, ideal for serving with stews.

NUTRITIONAL INFORMATION	
Calories 537	Sugars 11g
Protein 32g	Fat 14g
Carbohydrate . . .73g	Saturates 4g

15 MINS 35 MINS

SERVES 4

INGREDIENTS

- 2 medium red onions, sliced
- juice of 1 lemon
- 1 large red (bell) pepper, deseeded and thickly sliced
- 1 large green (bell) pepper, deseeded and thickly sliced
- 1 large orange (bell) pepper, deseeded and thickly sliced
- pinch of saffron strands
- cinnamon stick, broken
- 1 tbsp clear honey
- 300 ml/½ pint/1¼ cups vegetable stock
- 2 tsp olive oil
- 350 g/12 oz lean lamb fillet, trimmed and sliced
- 1 tsp Harissa paste
- 200 g/7 oz can chopped tomatoes
- 425 g/15 oz can chickpeas (garbanzo beans), drained
- 350 g/12 oz precooked couscous
- 2 tsp ground cinnamon
- salt and pepper

1 Toss the onions in the lemon juice and transfer to a saucepan. Mix in the (bell) peppers, saffron, cinnamon stick and honey. Pour in the stock, bring to the boil, cover and simmer for 5 minutes.

1

3

4

2 Meanwhile, heat the oil in a frying pan (skillet) and gently fry the lamb for 3–4 minutes until browned all over.

3 Using a slotted spoon, drain the lamb and transfer it to the pan with the onions and peppers. Season and stir in the Harissa paste, tomatoes and chickpeas (garbanzo beans). Mix well, bring back to the boil and simmer, uncovered, for 20 minutes.

4 Soak the couscous, following the packet instructions. Bring a saucepan of water to the boil. Put the couscous in a steamer or sieve (strainer) lined with muslin (cheese-cloth) over the pan of boiling water. Cover and steam.

5 Transfer the couscous to a serving platter and dust with ground cinnamon. Discard the cinnamon stick and spoon the stew over the couscous.

Lamb Dopiaza

Do Pyaza usually indicates a dish of meat cooked with plenty of onions, and in this recipe the onions are cooked in two different ways.

NUTRITIONAL INFORMATION	
Calories 433	Sugars 6g
Protein 42g	Fat 27g
Carbohydrate 7g	Saturates 8g

10 MINS — 1³/₄ HOURS

SERVES 4

INGREDIENTS

- 2 tbsp ghee or vegetable oil
- 2 large onions, sliced finely
- 4 garlic cloves, 2 of them crushed
- 750 g/1 lb 10 oz lean boneless lamb, cut into 2.5 cm/1 inch cubes
- 1 tsp chilli powder
- 2.5 cm/1 inch piece ginger root, grated
- 2 fresh green chillies, chopped
- ½ tsp ground turmeric
- 175 ml/6 fl oz/½ cup low-fat natural yogurt
- 2 cloves
- 2.5 cm/1 inch piece cinnamon stick
- 300 ml/½ pint/1¼ cups water
- 2 tbsp chopped fresh coriander (cilantro)
- 3 tbsp lemon juice
- salt and pepper
- naan bread, to serve

1

2

6

1 Heat the ghee or oil in a large saucepan and add 1 of the onions and all the garlic. Cook for 2–3 minutes, stirring constantly.

2 Add the lamb and brown all over. Remove and set aside. Add the chilli powder, ginger, chillies and turmeric and stir for a further 30 seconds.

3 Add plenty of salt and pepper, the yogurt, cloves, cinnamon and water.

4 Return the lamb to the pan. Bring to the boil then simmer for 10 minutes.

5 Transfer the mixture to an ovenproof dish and cook uncovered in a preheated oven, 180°C/350°F/Gas Mark 4, for 40 minutes.

6 Adjust the seasoning, if necessary, stir in the remaining onion and cook uncovered for a further 40 minutes.

7 Add the fresh coriander (cilantro) and lemon juice.

8 Transfer the lamb dopiaza to a warm serving dish and serve with naan bread.

Venison & Garlic Mash

Rich game is best served with a sweet fruit sauce. Here the venison steaks are cooked with sweet, juicy prunes and redcurrant jelly.

NUTRITIONAL INFORMATION

Calories	602	Sugars	18g
Protein	51g	Fat	14g
Carbohydrate	62g	Saturates	1g

10 MINS 35 MINS

SERVES 4

INGREDIENTS

- 8 medallions of venison, 75 g/2¾ oz each
- 1 tbsp vegetable oil
- 1 red onion, chopped
- 150 ml/5 fl oz/⅔ cup fresh beef stock
- 150 ml/5 fl oz/⅔ cup red wine
- 3 tbsp redcurrant jelly
- 100 g/3½ oz no-need-to-soak dried, pitted prunes
- 2 tsp cornflour (cornstarch)
- 2 tbsp brandy
- salt and pepper
- patty pans, to serve (optional)

GARLIC MASH

- 900 g/2 lb potatoes, peeled and diced
- ½ tsp garlic purée (paste)
- 2 tbsp low-fat natural fromage frais (unsweetened yogurt)
- 4 tbsp fresh parsley, chopped

1 Trim off any excess fat from the meat and season with salt and pepper on both sides. Heat the oil in a frying pan (skillet) and fry the lamb with the onions for 2 minutes on each side until brown.

2 Lower the heat and pour in the stock and wine. Add the redcurrant jelly and prunes and stir until the jelly melts. Cover and simmer for 10 minutes.

3 Meanwhile, make the garlic mash. Place the potatoes in a saucepan and cover with water. Bring to the boil and cook for 8–10 minutes. Drain well and mash until smooth. Add the garlic purée (paste), fromage frais (yogurt) and parsley and blend thoroughly. Season, set aside and keep warm.

4 Remove the medallions from the frying pan (skillet) with a slotted spoon and keep warm.

5 Blend the cornflour (cornstarch) with the brandy in a small bowl and add to the pan juices. Heat, stirring, until thickened. Season with salt and pepper to taste. Serve the venison with the redcurrant and prune sauce, garlic mash and patty pans (if using).

Poultry & Game

Chicken and turkey contain less fat than red meats, and even less if you remove the skin first. Duck is a rich meat with a distinctive flavour, and you only need a small amount

to create flavoursome dishes which are healthy too. Because chicken itself does not have a very strong flavour, it marries well with other ingredients and the recipes in this chapter exploit that quality. Fruit features heavily in low-fat diets and it works particularly well with chicken. In this chapter there are several examples. Grilling (broiling), or barbecuing, is a very healthy way to cook as it requires little or no fat, and it produces deliciously succulent meat with a cripsy coating,

Chicken with a Yogurt Crust

A spicy, Indian-style coating is baked around lean chicken to give a full flavour. Serve with a tomato, cucumber and coriander (cilantro) relish.

NUTRITIONAL INFORMATION

Calories	176	Sugars	5g
Protein	30g	Fat	4g
Carbohydrate	5g	Saturates	1g

10 MINS   35 MINS

SERVES 4

INGREDIENTS

- 1 garlic clove, crushed
- 2.5 cm/1 inch piece root (fresh) ginger, finely chopped
- 1 fresh green chilli, deseeded and finely chopped
- 6 tbsp low-fat natural (unsweetened) yogurt
- 1 tbsp tomato purée (paste)
- 1 tsp ground turmeric
- 1 tsp garam masala
- 1 tbsp lime juice
- 4 boneless, skinless chicken breasts, each 125 g/4½ oz
- salt and pepper
- wedges of lime or lemon, to serve

RELISH

- 4 medium tomatoes
- ¼ cucumber
- 1 small red onion
- 2 tbsp fresh coriander (cilantro), chopped

1 Preheat the oven to 190°C/375°F/Gas Mark 5.

2 Place the garlic, ginger, chilli, yogurt, tomato purée (paste), spices, lime juice and seasoning in a bowl and mix to combine all the ingredients.

3 Wash and pat dry the chicken breasts with absorbent kitchen paper (paper towels) and place them on a baking sheet.

4 Brush or spread the spicy yogurt mix over the chicken and bake in the oven for 30–35 minutes until the meat is tender and cooked through.

5 Meanwhile, make the relish. Finely chop the tomatoes, cucumber and onion and mix together with the coriander (cilantro). Season with salt and pepper to taste, cover and chill in the refrigerator until required.

6 Drain the cooked chicken on absorbent kitchen paper (paper towels) and serve hot with the relish and lemon or lime wedges. Alternatively, allow to cool, chill for at least 1 hour and serve sliced as part of a salad.

Chicken in Spicy Yogurt

Make sure the barbecue (grill) is really hot before you start cooking. The coals should be white and glow red when fanned.

NUTRITIONAL INFORMATION

Calories	74	Sugars	2g
Protein	9g	Fat	4g
Carbohydrate	2g	Saturates	1g

$4^3/_4$ HOURS 25 MINS

SERVES 6

INGREDIENTS

- 3 dried red chillies
- 2 tbsp coriander seeds
- 2 tsp turmeric
- 2 tsp garam masala
- 4 garlic cloves, crushed
- ½ onion, chopped
- 2.5 cm/1 inch piece fresh ginger root, grated
- 2 tbsp lime juice
- 1 tsp salt
- 125 ml/4 fl oz/½ cup low-fat natural (unsweetened) yogurt
- 1 tbsp oil
- 2 kg/4 lb 8 oz lean chicken, cut into 6 pieces, or 6 chicken portions

TO SERVE

- chopped tomatoes
- diced cucumber
- sliced red onion
- cucumber and yogurt

1 Grind together the chillies, coriander seed, turmeric, garam masala, garlic, onion, ginger, lime juice and salt with a pestle and mortar or grinder.

2 Gently heat a frying pan (skillet) and add the spice mixture. Stir until fragrant, about 2 minutes, and turn into a shallow non-porous dish.

3 Add the natural (unsweetened) yogurt and the oil to the spice paste and mix well to combine.

4 Remove the skin from the chicken portions and make three slashes in the flesh of each piece. Add the chicken to the dish containing the yogurt and spice mixture and coat the pieces completely in the marinade. Cover with cling film (plastic wrap) and chill for at least 4 hours. Remove the dish from the refrigerator and leave covered at room temperature for 30 minutes before cooking.

5 Wrap the chicken pieces in foil, sealing well so the juices cannot escape.

6 Cook the chicken pieces over a very hot barbecue (grill) for about 15 minutes, turning once.

7 Remove the foil, with tongs, and brown the chicken on the barbecue (grill) for 5 minutes.

8 Serve the chicken with the chopped tomatoes, diced cucumber, sliced red onion and the yogurt and cucumber mixture.

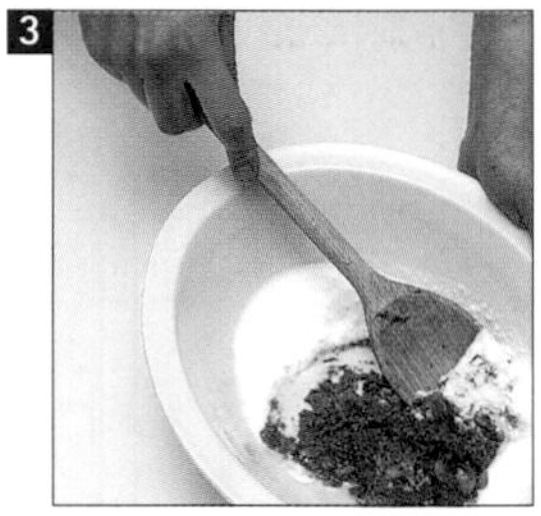

Spicy Tomato Chicken

These low-fat, spicy skewers are cooked in a matter of minutes – assemble ahead of time and store in the fridge until you need them.

NUTRITIONAL INFORMATION

Calories 195	Sugars 11g
Protein 28g	Fat 4g
Carbohydrate ...12g	Saturates 1g

10 MINS 10 MINS

SERVES 4

INGREDIENTS

- 500 g/1 lb 2 oz skinless, boneless chicken breasts
- 3 tbsp tomato purée (paste)
- 2 tbsp clear honey
- 2 tbsp Worcestershire sauce
- 1 tbsp chopped fresh rosemary
- 250 g/9 oz cherry tomatoes
- sprigs of rosemary, to garnish
- couscous or rice, to serve

1 Cut the chicken into 2.5 cm/1 inch chunks and place in a bowl.

2 Mix together the tomato purée (paste), honey, Worcestershire sauce and rosemary. Add to the chicken, stirring to coat evenly.

3 Alternating the chicken pieces and cherry tomatoes, thread them on to eight wooden skewers.

4 Spoon over any remaining glaze. Cook under a preheated hot grill (broiler) for 8–10 minutes, turning occasionally, until the chicken is thoroughly cooked.

5 Serve on a bed of couscous or rice and garnish with sprigs of rosemary.

COOK'S TIP

Couscous is made from semolina that has been made into separate grains. It usually just needs moistening or steaming before serving.

1

2

3

Karahi Chicken

A karahi is an extremely versatile two-handled metal pan, similar to a wok. Food is always cooked over a high heat in a karahi.

NUTRITIONAL INFORMATION

Calories	270	Sugars	1g
Protein	41g	Fat	11g
Carbohydrate	1g	Saturates	2g

5 MINS 20 MINS

SERVES 4

INGREDIENTS

- 2 tbsp ghee
- 3 garlic cloves, crushed
- 1 onion, chopped finely
- 2 tbsp garam masala
- 1 tsp coriander seeds, ground
- ½ tsp dried mint
- 1 bay leaf
- 750 g/1 lb 10 oz lean boneless chicken meat, diced
- 200 ml/7 fl oz/scant 1 cup chicken stock
- 1 tbsp fresh coriander (cilantro), chopped
- salt
- warm naan bread or chapatis, to serve

1

3

3

1 Heat the ghee in a karahi, wok or a large, heavy frying pan (skillet). Add the garlic and onion. Stir-fry for about 4 minutes until the onion is golden.

2 Stir in the garam masala, ground coriander, mint and bay leaf.

3 Add the chicken and cook over a high heat, stirring occasionally, for about 5 minutes. Add the stock and simmer for 10 minutes, until the sauce has thickened and the chicken juices run clear when the meat is tested with a sharp knife.

4 Stir in the fresh coriander (cilantro) and salt to taste, mix well and serve immediately with warm naan bread or chapatis.

COOK'S TIP

Always heat a karahi or wok before you add the oil to help maintain the high temperature.

Chicken Tikka

Traditionally, chicken tikka is cooked in a clay tandoori oven, but it works well on the barbecue (grill), too.

NUTRITIONAL INFORMATION

Calories	173	Sugars	6g
Protein	28g	Fat	4g
Carbohydrate	6g	Saturates	2g

2¹/₄ HOURS — 15 MINS

SERVES 4

INGREDIENTS

- 4 chicken breasts, skinned and boned
- ½ tsp salt
- 4 tbsp lemon or lime juice
- oil, for brushing

MARINADE

- 150 ml/5 fl oz/⅔ cup low-fat natural yogurt
- 2 cloves garlic, crushed
- 2.5 cm/1 inch piece root (fresh) ginger, peeled and grated
- 1 tsp ground cumin
- 1 tsp chilli powder
- ½ tsp ground coriander
- ½tsp ground turmeric

SAUCE

- 150 ml/5 fl oz/ ⅔ cup low-fat natural yogurt
- 1 tsp mint sauce

1

2

3

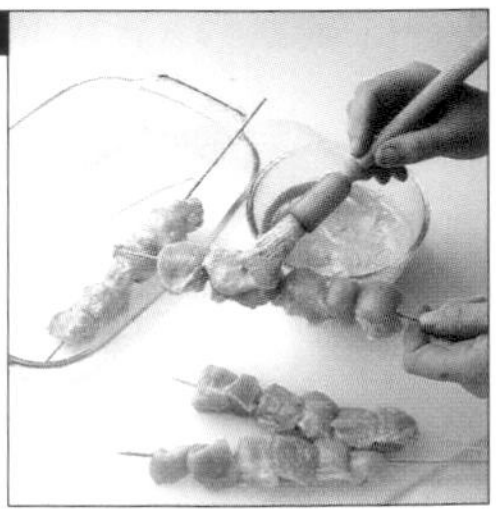

1 Cut the chicken into 2.5 cm/1 inch cubes. Sprinkle with the salt and the citrus juice. Set aside for 10 minutes.

2 To make the marinade, combine all the ingredients together in a small bowl until well mixed.

3 Thread the cubes of chicken on to skewers. Brush the marinade over the chicken. Cover and leave to marinate in the refrigerator for at least 2 hours, preferably overnight. Barbecue (grill) the chicken skewers over hot coals, brushing with oil and turning frequently, for 15 minutes or until cooked through.

4 Meanwhile, combine the yogurt and mint to make the sauce and serve with the chicken.

COOK'S TIP

Use the marinade to coat chicken portions, such as drumsticks, if you prefer. Barbecue (grill) over medium hot coals for 30–40 minutes, until the juices run clear when the chicken is pierced with a skewer.

Chicken Tikka Kebabs

Chicken tikka is a low-fat Indian dish. Recipes vary but you can try your own combination of spices to suit your personal taste.

NUTRITIONAL INFORMATION

Calories 191	Sugars 8g
Protein 30g	Fat 4g
Carbohydrate 8g	Saturates 2g

2¼ HOURS — 15 MINS

SERVES 4

INGREDIENTS

4 × 125 g/4½ oz boneless, skinless chicken breasts,

1 garlic clove, crushed

1 tsp grated ginger root

1 fresh green chilli, seeded and chopped finely

6 tbsp low-fat natural yogurt

1 tbsp tomato purée (paste)

1 tsp ground cumin

1 tsp ground coriander

1 tsp ground turmeric

1 large ripe mango

1 tbsp lime juice

salt and pepper

fresh coriander (cilantro) leaves, to garnish

TO SERVE

boiled white rice

lime wedges

mixed salad

warmed naan bread

1

2

3

1 Cut the chicken into 2.5 cm/1 inch cubes and place in a shallow dish.

2 Mix together the garlic, ginger, chilli, yogurt, tomato purée (paste), spices and seasoning. Spoon over the chicken, cover and chill for 2 hours.

3 Using a vegetable peeler, peel the skin from the mango. Slice down either side of the stone (pit) and cut the mango flesh into cubes. Toss in lime juice, cover and chill until required.

4 Thread the chicken and mango pieces alternately on to 8 skewers. Place the skewers on a grill (broiler) rack and brush the chicken with the yogurt marinade and the lime juice left from the mango.

5 Place under a preheated moderate grill (broiler) for 6–7 minutes. Turn over, brush again with the marinade and lime juice and cook for a further 6–7 minutes until the chicken juices run clear when pierced with a sharp knife.

6 Serve on a bed of rice on a warmed platter, garnished with fresh coriander (cilantro) leaves and accompanied by lime wedges, salad and naan bread.

Spiced Apricot Chicken

Spiced chicken legs are partially boned and packed with dried apricot. A golden, spiced, low-fat yogurt coating keeps the chicken moist.

NUTRITIONAL INFORMATION

Calories	305	Sugars	21g
Protein	15g	Fat	8g
Carbohydrate	45g	Saturates	1g

10 MINS   40 MINS

SERVES 4

INGREDIENTS

- 4 large, lean skinless chicken leg quarters
- finely grated rind of 1 lemon
- 200 g/7 oz/1 cup ready-to-eat dried apricots
- 1 tbsp ground cumin
- 1 tsp ground turmeric
- 125 g/4½ oz/½ cup low-fat natural yogurt
- salt and pepper

TO SERVE

- 250 g/9 oz/1½ cups brown rice
- 2 tbsp flaked hazelnuts, toasted
- 2 tbsp sunflower seeds, toasted

1 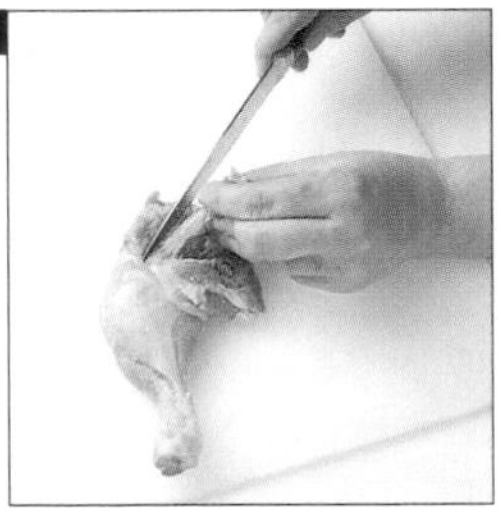

1 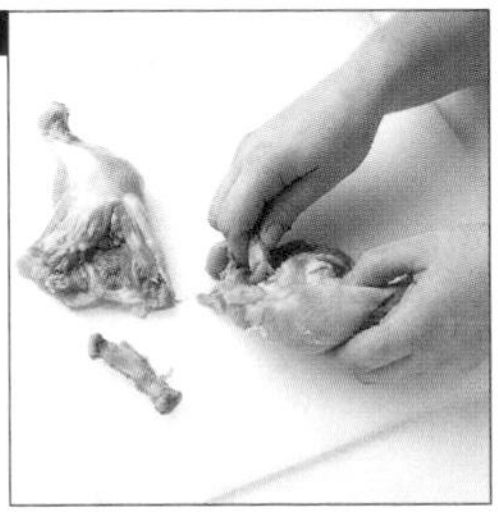

2 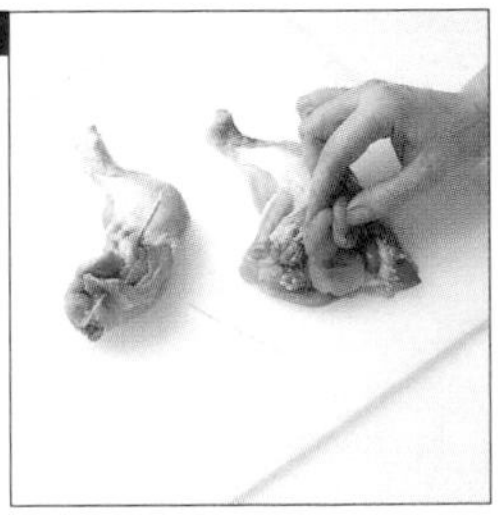

1 Remove any excess fat from the chicken legs. Use a small sharp knife to carefully cut the flesh away from the thigh bone. Scrape the meat away down as far as the knuckle. Grasp the thigh bone firmly and twist it to break it away from the drumstick.

2 Open out the boned part of the chicken and sprinkle with lemon rind and pepper. Pack the dried apricots into each piece of chicken.

3 Fold over to enclose, and secure with cocktail sticks. Mix together the cumin, turmeric, yogurt and salt and pepper, then brush this mixture over the chicken to coat evenly. Place the chicken in an ovenproof dishand bake in a preheated oven, 190°C/375°F/Gas Mark 5, for 35–40 minutes, or until the chicken juices run clear, not pink, when pierced through the thickest part with a skewer.

4 Meanwhile, cook the rice in boiling, lightly salted water until just tender, then drain well. Stir the hazelnuts and sunflower seeds into the rice and serve.

VARIATION

For a change use dried herbs instead of spices to flavour the coating. Use dried oregano, tarragon or rosemary – but remember dried herbs are more powerful than fresh, so you will only need a little.

Thai Red Chicken

This is a really colourful dish, the red of the tomatoes perfectly complementing the orange of the sweet potato.

NUTRITIONAL INFORMATION

Calories	249	Sugars	14g
Protein	26g	Fat	7g
Carbohydrate	22g	Saturates	2g

10 MINS   35 MINS

SERVES 4

INGREDIENTS

- 1 tbsp sunflower oil
- 450 g/1 lb lean boneless, skinless chicken
- 2 cloves garlic, crushed
- 2 tbsp Thai red curry paste
- 2 tbsp fresh grated galangal or root ginger
- 1 tbsp tamarind paste
- 4 lime leaves
- 225 g/8 oz sweet potato
- 600 ml/1 pint/2½ cups coconut milk
- 225 g/8 oz cherry tomatoes, halved
- 3 tbsp chopped fresh coriander (cilantro)
- cooked jasmine or Thai fragrant rice, to serve

3

4

4

1 Heat the sunflower oil in a large preheated wok.

2 Thinly slice the chicken. Add the chicken to the wok and stir-fry for 5 minutes.

3 Add the garlic, curry paste, galangal or root ginger, tamarind and lime leaves to the wok and stir-fry for about 1 minute.

4 Using a sharp knife, peel and dice the sweet potato. Add the coconut milk and sweet potato to the mixture in the wok and bring to the boil. Allow to bubble over a medium heat for 20 minutes, or until the juices start to thicken and reduce.

5 Add the cherry tomatoes and coriander (cilantro) to the curry and cook for a further 5 minutes, stirring occasionally. Transfer to serving plates and serve hot with cooked jasmine or Thai fragrant rice.

COOK'S TIP

Galangal is a spice very similar to ginger and is used to replace the latter in Thai cuisine. It can be bought fresh from Oriental food stores but is also available dried and as a powder. The fresh root, which is not as pungent as ginger, needs to be peeled before slicing to use.

Thai-Style Chicken Skewers

The chicken is marinated in an aromatic sauce before being cooked on the barbecue (grill). Use bay leaves if kaffir lime leaves are unavailable.

NUTRITIONAL INFORMATION

Calories	218	Sugars	4g
Protein	28g	Fat	10g
Carbohydrate	5g	Saturates	2g

2¼ HOURS   20 MINS

SERVES 4

INGREDIENTS

- 4 lean chicken breasts, skinned and boned
- 1 onion, peeled and cut into wedges
- 1 large red (bell) pepper, deseeded
- 1 large yellow (bell) pepper deseeded
- 12 kaffir lime leaves
- 2 tbsp sunflower oil
- 2 tbsp lime juice
- tomato halves, to serve

MARINADE

- 1 tbsp Thai red curry paste
- 150 ml/5 fl oz/⅔ cup canned coconut milk

1 To make the marinade, place the red curry paste in a small pan over medium heat and cook for 1 minute. Add half of the coconut milk to the pan and bring the mixture to the boil. Boil for 2–3 minutes until the liquid has reduced by about two-thirds.

2 Remove the pan from the heat and stir in the remaining coconut milk. Set aside to cool.

3 Cut the chicken into 2.5 cm/1 inch pieces. Stir the chicken into the cold marinade, cover and leave to chill for at least 2 hours.

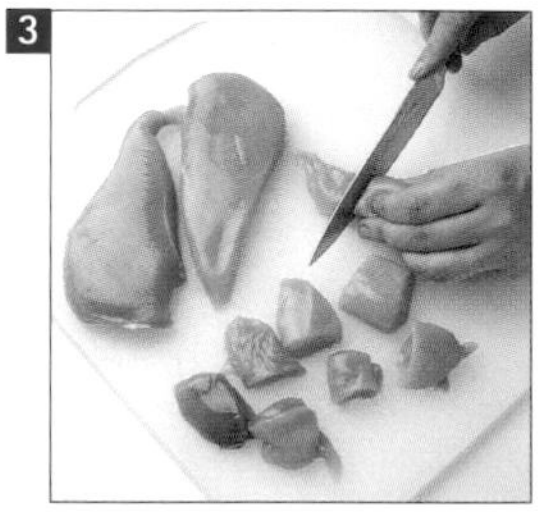

4 Cut the onion into wedges and the (bell) peppers into 2.5 cm/1 inch pieces.

5 Remove the chicken pieces from the marinade and thread them on to skewers, alternating the chicken with the vegetables and lime leaves.

6 Combine the oil and lime juice in a small bowl and brush the mixture over the kebabs. Barbecue (grill) the skewers over hot coals, turning and basting frequently for 10–15 minutes until the chicken is cooked through. Barbecue (grill) the tomato halves and serve with the chicken skewers.

COOK'S TIP

Cooking the marinade first intensifies the flavour. It is important to allow the marinade to cool before adding the chicken, or bacteria may breed in the warm temperature.

Ginger Chicken & Corn

Chicken wings and corn in a sticky ginger marinade are designed to be eaten with the fingers – there's no other way!

NUTRITIONAL INFORMATION

Calories	123	Sugars	3g
Protein	14g	Fat	6g
Carbohydrate	3g	Saturates	1g

10 MINS 20 MINS

SERVES 6

INGREDIENTS

- 3 cobs fresh sweetcorn (corn-on-the-cob)
- 12 chicken wings
- 2.5cm/1 inch piece fresh ginger root
- 6 tbsp lemon juice
- 4 tsp sunflower oil
- 1 tbsp golden caster (superfine) sugar
- jacket potatoes or salad, to serve

1 Remove the husks and silks from the corn. Using a sharp knife, cut each cob into 6 slices.

2 Place the corn in a large bowl with the chicken wings.

3 Peel and grate the ginger root or chop finely. Place in a bowl and add the lemon juice, sunflower oil and golden caster (superfine) sugar. Mix together until well combined.

4 Toss the corn and chicken in the ginger mixture to coat evely.

5 Thread the corn and chicken wings alternately on to metal or pre-soaked wooden skewers, to make turning easier.

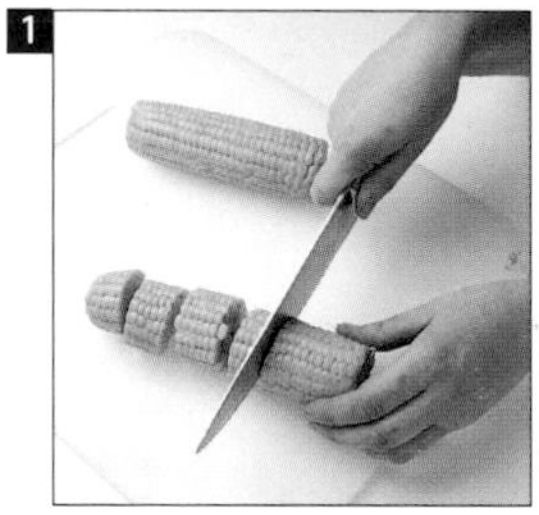

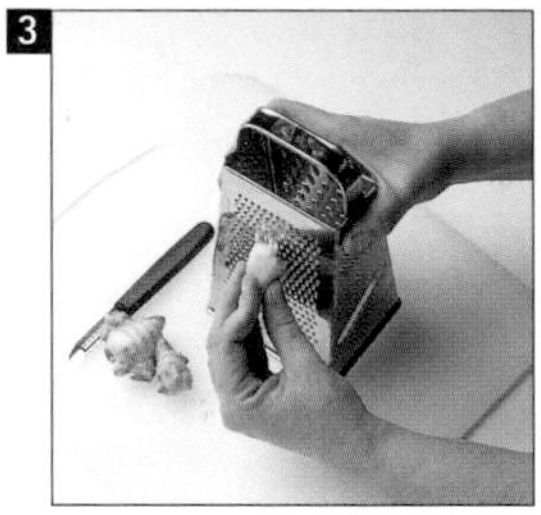

6 Cook under a preheated moderately hot grill (broiler) or barbecue (grill) for 15–20 minutes, basting with the gingery glaze and turning frequently until the corn is golden brown and tender and the chicken is cooked. Serve with jacket potatoes or salad.

COOK'S TIP

Cut off the wing tips before grilling (broiling) as they burn very easily. Or you can cover them with small pieces of foil.

Steamed Chicken Parcels

A healthy recipe with a delicate oriental flavour. Use large spinach leaves to wrap around the chicken, but make sure they are young leaves.

NUTRITIONAL INFORMATION

Calories	216	Sugars	7g
Protein	31g	Fat	7g
Carbohydrate	7g	Saturates	2g

20 MINS

30 MINS

SERVES 4

INGREDIENTS

- 4 lean boneless, skinless chicken breasts
- 1 tsp ground lemon grass
- 2 spring onions (scallions), chopped finely
- 250 g/9 oz/1 cup young carrots
- 250 g/9 oz/1¾ cups young courgettes (zucchini)
- 2 sticks (stalks) celery
- 1 tsp light soy sauce
- 250 g/9 oz/¾ cup spinach leaves
- 2 tsp sesame oil
- salt and pepper

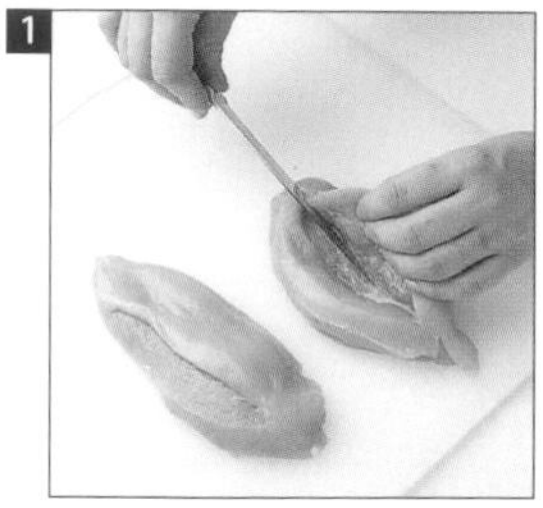

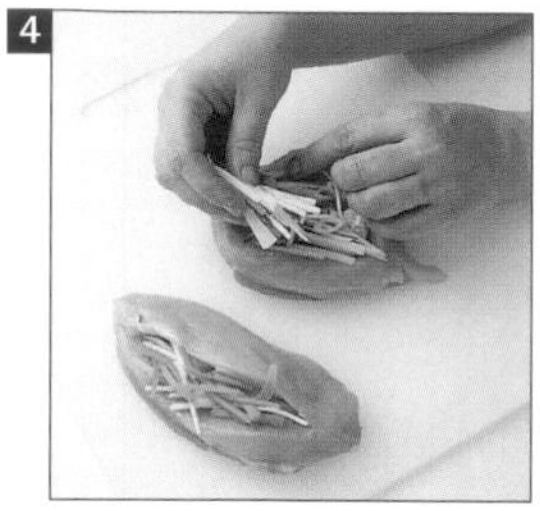

1 With a sharp knife, make a slit through one side of each chicken breast to open out a large pocket.

2 Sprinkle the inside of the pocket with lemon grass, salt and pepper. Tuck the spring onions (scallions) into the chicken pockets.

3 Trim the carrots, courgettes (zucchini) and celery, then cut into small matchsticks. Plunge them into a pan of boiling water for 1 minute, then drain and toss in the soy sauce.

4 Pack the mixture into the pockets in each chicken breast and fold over firmly to enclose. Reserve the remaining vegetables. Wash and dry the spinach leaves then wrap the chicken breasts firmly in the leaves to enclose completely. If the leaves are too firm, steam them for a few seconds until they are softened and more flexible.

5 Place the wrapped chicken in a steamer and steam over rapidly boiling water for 20–25 minutes, depending on size.

6 Stir-fry any leftover vegetable sticks and spinach for 1–2 minutes in the sesame oil and serve with the chicken.

Crispy Stuffed Chicken

An attractive main course of chicken breasts filled with mixed (bell) peppers and set on a sea of red (bell) peppers and tomato sauce.

NUTRITIONAL INFORMATION

Calories 196	Sugars 4g
Protein 29g	Fat 6g
Carbohydrate 6g	Saturates 2g

20 MINS 50 MINS

SERVES 4

INGREDIENTS

- 4 boneless chicken breasts, about 150 g/ 5½ oz each, skinned
- 4 sprigs fresh tarragon
- ½ small orange (bell) pepper, deseeded and sliced
- ½ small green (bell) pepper, deseeded and sliced
- 15 g/½ oz wholemeal breadcrumbs
- 1 tbsp sesame seeds
- 4 tbsp lemon juice
- 1 small red (bell) pepper, halved and deseeded
- 200 g/7 oz can chopped tomatoes
- 1 small red chilli, deseeded and chopped
- ¼ tsp celery salt
- salt and pepper
- fresh tarragon, to garnish

1

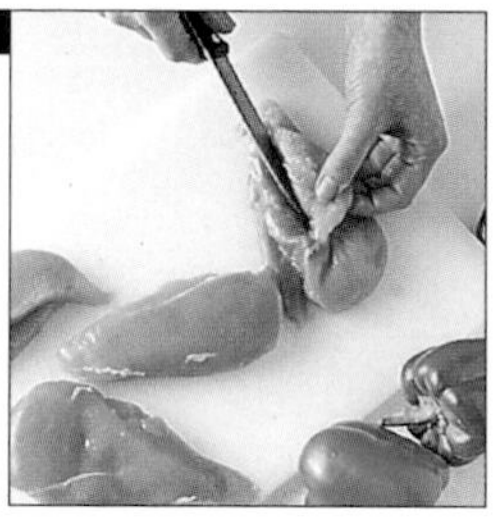

3

5

1 Preheat the oven to 200°C/400°F/Gas Mark 6. Slit the chicken breasts with a small, sharp knife to create a pocket in each. Season inside each pocket.

2 Place a sprig of tarragon and a few slices of orange and green (bell) peppers in each pocket. Place the chicken breasts on a non-stick baking tray (cookie sheet) and sprinkle over the breadcrumbs and sesame seeds.

3 Spoon 1 tablespoon lemon juice over each chicken breast and bake in the oven for 35–40 minutes until the chicken is tender and cooked through.

4 Meanwhile, preheat the grill (broiler) to hot. Arrange the red (bell) pepper halves, skin side up, on the rack and cook for 5–6 minutes until the skin blisters. Leave to cool for 10 minutes, then peel off the skins.

5 Put the red (bell) pepper in a blender, add the tomatoes, chilli and celery salt and process for a few seconds. Season to taste. Alternatively, finely chop the red (bell) pepper and press through a sieve with the tomatoes and chilli.

6 When the chicken is cooked, heat the sauce, spoon a little on to a warm plate and arrange a chicken breast in the centre. Garnish with tarragon and serve.

Teppanyaki

This simple, Japanese style of cooking is ideal for thinly-sliced breast of chicken. You can use thin turkey escalopes, if you prefer.

NUTRITIONAL INFORMATION

Calories	206	Sugars	4g
Protein	30g	Fat	7g
Carbohydrate	6g	Saturates	2g

5 MINS — 10 MINS

SERVES 4

INGREDIENTS

- 4 boneless chicken breasts
- 1 red (bell) pepper
- 1 green (bell) pepper
- 4 spring onions (scallions)
- 8 baby corn cobs (corn-on-the-cob)
- 100 g/3½ oz/½ cup bean sprouts
- 1 tbsp sesame or sunflower oil
- 4 tbsp soy sauce
- 4 tbsp mirin
- 1 tbsp grated fresh ginger root

1 Remove the skin from the chicken and slice at a slight angle, to a thickness of about 5 mm/¼ inch.

2 Deseed and thinly slice the (bell) peppers and trim and slice the spring onions (scallions) and corn cobs (corn-on-the-cob).

3 Arrange the (bell) peppers, spring onions (scallions), corn and bean sprouts on a plate with the sliced chicken.

4 Heat a large griddle or heavy frying pan then lightly brush with oil. Add the vegetables and chicken slices in small batches, allowing space between them so that they cook thoroughly.

5 Combine the soy sauce, mirin and ginger and serve as a dip with the chicken and vegetables.

COOK'S TIP

Mirin is a rich, sweet rice wine which you can buy in oriental shops, but if it is not available add one 1 tablespoon of soft light brown sugar to the sauce instead.

1

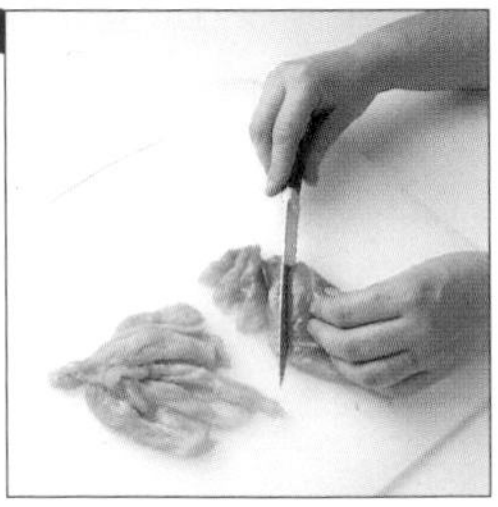

2

5

Sweet and Sour Chicken

This sweet-citrusy chicken is delicious hot or cold. Sesame-flavoured noodles are the ideal accompaniment for the hot version.

NUTRITIONAL INFORMATION

Calories	248	Sugars	8g
Protein	30g	Fat	8g
Carbohydrate	16g	Saturates	2g

5 MINS

25 MINS

SERVES 4

INGREDIENTS

- 4 boneless chicken breasts, about 125 g/ 4½ oz each
- 2 tbsp clear honey
- 1 tbsp dark soy sauce
- 1 tsp lemon rind, finely grated
- 1 tbsp lemon juice
- salt and pepper

TO GARNISH

- 1 tbsp fresh chives, chopped
- lemon rind, grated

NOODLES

- 225 g/8 oz rice noodles
- 2 tsp sesame oil
- 1 tbsp sesame seeds
- 1 tsp lemon rind, finely grated

1 Preheat the grill (broiler) to medium. Skin and trim the chicken breasts to remove any excess fat, then wash and pat them dry with absorbent kitchen paper. Using a sharp knife, score the chicken breasts with a criss-cross pattern on both sides (making sure that you do not cut all the way through the meat).

2 Mix together the honey, soy sauce, lemon rind and juice in a small bowl, and then season well with black pepper.

3 Arrange the chicken breasts on the grill (broiler) rack and brush with half the honey mixture. Cook for 10 minutes, turn over and brush with the remaining mixture. Cook for a further 8–10 minutes or until cooked through.

4 Meanwhile, prepare the noodles according to the instructions on the packet. Drain well and transfer to a warm serving bowl. Mix the noodles with the sesame oil, sesame seeds and the lemon rind. Season and keep warm.

5 Drain the chicken and serve with a small mound of noodles, garnished with chopped chives and grated lemon rind.

1

3

4

VARIATION

For a different flavour, replace the lemon with orange or lime. If you prefer, serve the chicken with boiled rice or pasta, which you can flavour with sesame seeds and citrus rind in the same way.

Chicken & Ginger Stir-Fry

The pomegranate seeds add a sharp Chinese flavour to this Indian stir-fry. Serve in the summer with a spicy rice salad or a mixed green salad.

NUTRITIONAL INFORMATION

Calories 291	Sugars 0g
Protein 41g	Fat 14g
Carbohydrate 0g	Saturates 3g

10 MINS 25 MINS

SERVES 4

INGREDIENTS

- 3 tbsp oil
- 700 g/1 lb 9 oz lean skinless, boneless chicken breasts, cut into 5 cm/2 inch strips
- 3 garlic cloves, crushed
- 3.5 cm/1½ inch piece fresh ginger root, cut into strips
- 1 tsp pomegranate seeds, crushed
- ½ tsp ground turmeric
- 1 tsp garam masala
- 2 fresh green chillies, sliced
- ½ tsp salt
- 4 tbsp lemon juice
- grated rind of 1 lemon
- 6 tbsp chopped fresh coriander (cilantro)
- 125 ml/4 fl oz/½ cup chicken stock
- naan bread, to serve

1

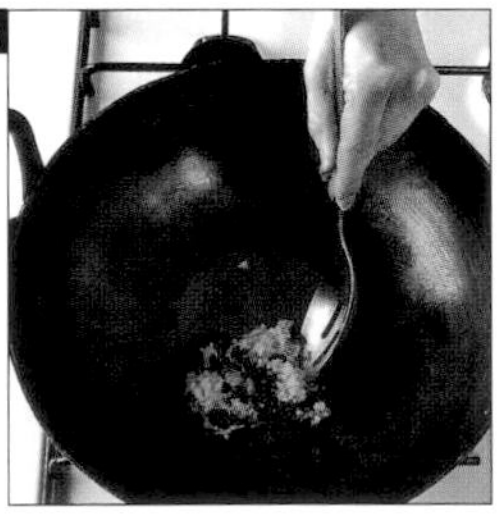
2

3

1 Heat the oil in a wok or large frying pan (skillet) and stir-fry the chicken until golden brown all over. Remove from the pan and set aside.

2 Add the garlic, ginger and pomegranate seeds to the pan and fry in the oil for 1 minute taking care not to let the garlic burn.

3 Stir in the turmeric, garam masala and chillies, and fry for 30 seconds.

4 Return the chicken to the pan and add the salt, lemon juice, lemon rind, coriander (cilantro) and stock. Stir the chicken well to make sure it is coated in the sauce.

5 Bring the mixture to the boil, then lower the heat and simmer for 10–15 minutes until the chicken is thoroughly cooked. Serve with warm naan bread.

COOK'S TIP

Stir-frying is perfect for low-fat diets as only a little oil is needed. Cooking the food over a high temperature ensures that food is sealed and cooked quickly to hold in the flavour.

Filipino Chicken

Tomato ketchup is a very popular ingredient in Asian dishes, as it imparts a zingy sweet-sour flavour.

NUTRITIONAL INFORMATION	
Calories 197	Sugars 7g
Protein 28g	Fat 4g
Carbohydrate 8g	Saturates 1g

2³/4 HOURS   20 MINS

SERVES 4

INGREDIENTS

- 1 can lemonade or lime-and-lemonade
- 2 tbsp gin
- 4 tbsp tomato ketchup
- 2 tsp garlic salt
- 2 tsp Worcestershire sauce
- 4 lean chicken suprêmes or breast fillets
- salt and pepper

TO SERVE

- thread egg noodles
- 1 green chilli, chopped finely
- 2 spring onions (scallions), sliced

1

2

4

1 Combine the lemonade or lime-and-lemonade, gin, tomato ketchup, garlic salt, Worcestershire sauce and seasoning in a large non-porous dish.

2 Put the chicken supremes into the dish and make sure that the marinade covers them completely.

3 Leave to marinate in the refrigerator for 2 hours. Remove and leave covered at room temperature for 30 minutes.

4 Place the chicken over a medium barbecue (grill) and cook for 20 minutes.

5 Turn the chicken once, halfway through the cooking time.

6 Remove from the barbecue (grill) and leave to rest for 3–4 minutes before serving.

7 Serve with egg noodles, tossed with a little green chilli and spring onions (scallions).

COOK'S TIP

Cooking the meat on the bone after it has reached room temperature means that it cooks in a shorter time, which ensures that the meat remains moist right through to the bone.

Poussin with Dried Fruits

Baby chickens are ideal for a one or two portion meal, and cook very easily and quickly for a special dinner – either in the oven or microwave.

NUTRITIONAL INFORMATION

Calories	316	Sugars	23g
Protein	23g	Fat	15g
Carbohydrate	23g	Saturates	2g

35 MINS 30 MINS

SERVES 2

INGREDIENTS

125 g/4½ oz/¾ cup dried apples, peaches and prunes

120 ml/4 floz/½ cup boiling water

2 baby chickens

25 g/1 oz/⅓ cup walnut halves

1 tbsp honey

1 tsp ground allspice

1 tbsp walnut oil

salt and pepper

vegetables and new potatoes, to serve

1 Place the fruits in a bowl, cover with the water and leave to stand for about 30 minutes.

2 Cut the chickens in half down the breastbone using a sharp knife, or leave whole.

3 Mix the fruit and any juices with the walnuts, honey and allspice and divide between two small roasting bags or squares of foil.

4 Brush the chickens with walnut oil and sprinkle with salt and pepper then place on top of the fruits.

5 Close the roasting bags or fold the foil over to enclose the chickens and bake on a baking sheet in a preheated oven, 190°C/375°F/Gas Mark 5, for 25–30 minutes or until the juices run clear. To cook in a microwave, use microwave roasting bags and cook on high/100% power for 6–7 minutes each, depending on size.

6 Transfer the poussin to a warm plate and serve hot with fresh vegetables and new potatoes.

1

3

4

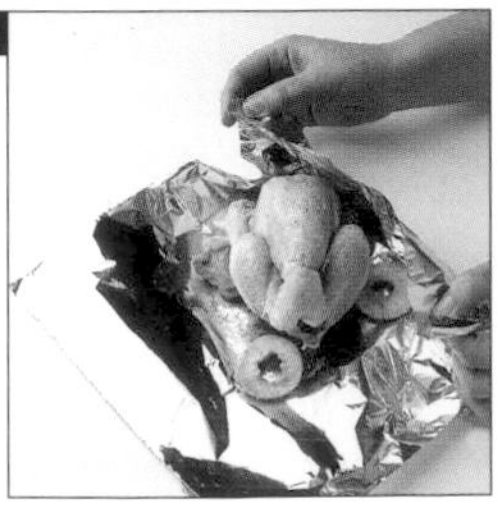

VARIATION

Alternative dried fruits that can be used in this recipe are cherries, mangoes or paw-paws (papayas).

Pot-Roast Orange Chicken

This colourful, nutritious pot-roast could be served for a family meal or for a special dinner. Add more vegetables if you're feeding a crowd.

NUTRITIONAL INFORMATION

Calories	302	Sugar	17g
Protein	29g	Fats	11g
Carbohydrates	22g	Saturates	2g

10 MINS

2 HOURS

SERVES 4

INGREDIENTS

- 2 tbsp sunflower oil
- 1 chicken, weighing about 1.5 kg/3 lb 5 oz
- 2 large oranges
- 2 small onions, quartered
- 500 g/1 lb 2 oz/2 cups small whole carrots or thin carrots, cut into 5 cm/2 inch lengths
- 150 ml/¼ pint/⅔ cup orange juice
- 2 tbsp brandy
- 2 tbsp sesame seeds
- 1 tbsp cornflour (cornstarch)
- salt and pepper

2
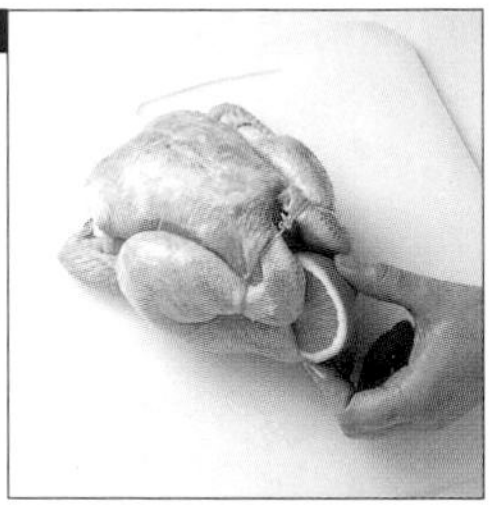

2

3

1 Heat the oil in a large flameproof casserole and fry the chicken, turning occasionally until evenly browned.

2 Cut one orange in half and place half inside the cavity of the chicken. Place the chicken in a large, deep casserole. Arrange the onions and carrots around the chicken. Season with salt and pepper and pour over the orange juice.

3 Cut the remaining oranges into thin wedges and tuck around the chicken, among the vegetables.

4 Cover and cook in a preheated oven, 180°C/350°F/Gas Mark 4, for about 1½ hours, or until the chicken juices run clear when pierced, and the vegetables are tender. Remove the lid and sprinkle with the brandy and sesame seeds. Return to the oven for 10 minutes.

5 To serve, lift the chicken on to a large platter and add the vegetables. Skim any excess fat from the juices. Blend the cornflour (cornstarch) with 1 tablespoon of cold water, then stir into the juices and bring to the boil, stirring. Season to taste, then serve the sauce with the chicken.

Harlequin Chicken

This colourful dish will tempt the appetites of all the family – it is ideal for toddlers, who enjoy the fun shapes of the multi-coloured peppers.

NUTRITIONAL INFORMATION

Calories	183	Sugar	8g
Protein	24g	Fats	6g
Carbohydrates	8g	Saturates	1g

5 MINS

25 MINS

SERVES 4

INGREDIENTS

- 10 skinless, boneless chicken thighs
- 1 medium onion
- 1 each medium red, green and yellow (bell) peppers
- 1 tbsp sunflower oil
- 400 g/14 oz can chopped tomatoes
- 2 tbsp chopped fresh parsley
- pepper
- wholemeal bread and salad, to serve

1

2

4

1 Using a sharp knife, cut the chicken thighs into bite-sized pieces.

2 Peel and thinly slice the onion. Halve and deseed the (bell) peppers and cut into small diamond shapes.

3 Heat the sunflower oil in a shallow pan then quickly fry the chicken and onion until golden.

4 Add the (bell) peppers, cook for 2–3 minutes, then stir in the tomatoes and chopped fresh parsley and season with pepper.

5 Cover tightly and simmer for about 15 minutes, until the chicken and vegetables are tender. Serve hot with wholemeal (whole wheat) bread and a green salad.

COOK'S TIP

If you are making this dish for small children, the chicken can be finely chopped or minced (ground) first.

Mediterranean Chicken

This recipe uses ingredients found in the Languedoc area of France, where cooking over hot embers is a way of life.

NUTRITIONAL INFORMATION

Calories	143	Sugars	4g
Protein	13g	Fat	8g
Carbohydrate	4g	Saturates	2g

2¾ HOURS

40 MINS

SERVES 4

INGREDIENTS

4 tbsp low-fat natural yogurt

3 tbsp sun-dried tomato paste

1 tbsp olive oil

15 g/½ oz/¼ cup fresh basil leaves, lightly crushed

2 garlic cloves, chopped roughly

4 chicken quarters

green salad, to serve

1

2

4

1 Combine the yogurt, tomato paste, olive oil, basil leaves and garlic in a small bowl and stir well to mix.

2 Put the marinade into a bowl large enough to hold the chicken quarters in a single layer. Add the chicken quarters. Make sure that the chicken pieces are thoroughly coated in the marinade.

3 Leave to marinate in the refrigerator for 2 hours. Remove and leave covered at room temperature for 30 minutes.

4 Place the chicken over a medium barbecue and cook for 30–40 minutes, turning frequently. Test for readiness by piercing the flesh at the thickest part – usually at the top of the drumstick. If the juices that run out are clear, it is cooked through.

5 Serve hot with a green salad. It is also delicious eaten cold.

VARIATION

For a marinade with an extra zingy flavour combine 2 garlic cloves, coarsely chopped, the juice of 2 lemons and 3 tbsp olive oil, and cook in the same way.

Chicken with Two Sauces

With its red and yellow (bell) pepper sauces, this quick and simple dish is colourful and healthy, and perfect for an impromptu lunch or supper.

NUTRITIONAL INFORMATION

Calories	257	Sugars	7g
Protein	29g	Fat	10g
Carbohydrate	8g	Saturates	2g

10 MINS

1½ HOURS

SERVES 4

INGREDIENTS

- 2 tbsp olive oil
- 2 medium onions, chopped finely
- 2 garlic cloves, crushed
- 2 red (bell) peppers, chopped
- good pinch cayenne pepper
- 2 tsp tomato purée (paste)
- 2 yellow (bell) peppers, chopped
- pinch of dried basil
- 4 lean skinless, boneless chicken breasts
- 150 ml/¼ pint/⅔ cup dry white wine
- 150 ml/¼ pint/⅔ cup chicken stock
- bouquet garni
- salt and pepper
- fresh herbs, to garnish

1 Heat 1 tablespoon of olive oil in each of two medium saucepans. Place half the chopped onions, 1 of the garlic cloves, the red (bell) peppers, the cayenne pepper and the tomato purée (paste) in one of the saucepans. Place the remaining onion, garlic, yellow (bell) peppers and basil in the other pan.

2 Cover each pan and cook over a very low heat for 1 hour until the (bell) peppers are very soft. If either mixture becomes dry, add a little water. Process then sieve the contents of each pan separately.

3 Return to the pans and season with salt and pepper. Gently reheat the two sauces while the chicken is cooking.

4 Put the chicken breasts into a frying pan and add the wine and stock. Add the bouquet garni and bring the liquid to simmer. Cook the chicken for about 20 minutes until tender.

5 To serve, put a pool of each sauce on to four serving plates, slice the chicken breasts and arrange on the plates. Garnish with fresh herbs.

1

3

4

Chicken with Whisky Sauce

After cooking with stock and vegetables, chicken breasts are served with a velvety sauce made from whisky and low-fat crème fraîche.

1

3

5

NUTRITIONAL INFORMATION

Calories	337	Sugars	6g
Protein	37g	Fat	15g
Carbohydrate	6g	Saturates	8g

5 MINS

30 MINS

SERVES 4

INGREDIENTS

- 25 g/1 oz/2 tbsp butter
- 60 g/2 oz/½ cup shredded leeks
- 60 g/2 oz/⅓ cup diced carrot
- 60 g/2 oz/¼ cup diced celery
- 4 shallots, sliccd
- 600 ml/1 pint/2½ cups chicken stock
- 6 chicken breasts
- 50 ml/2 fl oz/¼ cup whisky
- 200 ml/7 fl oz/1 cup low-fat crème fraîche
- 2 tbsp freshly grated horseradish
- 1 tsp honey, warmed
- 1 tsp chopped fresh parsley
- salt and pepper
- parsley, to garnish

TO SERVE

- vegetable patty
- mashed potato
- fresh vegetables

1 Melt the butter in a large saucepan and add the leeks, carrot, celery and shallots. Cook for 3 minutes, add half the chicken stock and cook for about 8 minutes.

2 Add the remaining chicken stock, and bring to the boil. Add the chicken breasts and cook for about 10 minutes or until tender.

3 Remove the chicken with a perforated spoon and cut into thin slices. Place on a large, hot serving dish and keep warm.

4 In another saucepan, heat the whisky until reduced by half. Strain the chicken stock through a fine sieve, add to the pan and heat until the liquid is reduced by half.

5 Add the crème fraîche, the horseradish and the honey. Heat gently and add the chopped fresh parsley and salt and pepper to taste.

6 Pour a little of the whisky sauce around the chicken and pour the remaining sauce into a sauceboat to serve.

7 Serve with a vegetable patty made from the leftover vegetables, mashed potato and fresh vegetables. Garnish with fresh parsley.

Two-in-One Chicken

Cook four chicken pieces and serve two hot, topped with a crunchy herb mixture. Serve the remainder as a salad in a delicious curry sauce.

NUTRITIONAL INFORMATION

Calories	421	Sugars	20g
Protein	31g	Fat	18g
Carbohydrate	34g	Saturates	4g

2½ HOURS 45 MINS

SERVES 2

INGREDIENTS

4 lean chicken thighs
oil for brushing
garlic powder
½ dessert (eating) apple, grated coarsely
1½ tbsp dry parsley and thyme stuffing mix
salt and pepper
pasta shapes, to serve

SAUCE

15 g/½ oz/1 tbsp butter or margarine
2 tsp plain (all-purpose) flour
5 tbsp skimmed milk
2 tbsp dry white wine or stock
½ tsp dried mustard powder
1 tsp capers or chopped gherkins

SPICED CHICKEN SALAD

½ small onion, chopped finely
1 tbsp oil
1 tsp tomato purée (paste)
½ tsp curry powder
1 tsp apricot jam
1 tsp lemon juice
2 tbsp low-fat mayonnaise
1 tbsp low-fat natural fromage frais
90 g/3 oz/¾ cup seedless grapes, halved
60 g/2 oz ¼ cup white long-grain rice, cooked, to serve

1 Place the chicken in a shallow ovenproof dish. Brush with oil, sprinkle with garlic powder and season with salt and pepper. Place in a preheated oven, 200°C/400°F/Gas Mark 6, for 25 minutes, or until almost cooked through. Combine the apple with the stuffing mix. Baste the chicken, then spoon the mixture over two of the pieces. Return all the chicken pieces to the oven for about 10 minutes until the chicken is cooked.

2 To make the sauce, melt the magarine in a pan, stir in the flour and cook for 1–2 minutes. Add the milk gradually, then the wine or stock, and bring to the boil. Stir in the mustard, capers or gherkins, and seasoning. Simmer for 1 minute. Serve the two crunchy-topped pieces of chicken with the sauce and pasta shapes.

3 For the salad, fry the onion gently in the oil until barely coloured. Add the tomato purée (paste), curry powder and jam, and cook for 1 minute. Leave the mixture to cool. Blend the mixture in a food processor, or press through a sieve (strainer). Beat in the lemon juice, mayonnaise and fromage frais. Season to taste with salt and pepper.

4 Cut the chicken into strips and add to the sauce with the grapes. Mix well, and chill. Serve with the rice.

Sticky Chicken Wings

These need to be eaten with your fingers so serve them at an informal supper.

NUTRITIONAL INFORMATION

Calories	165	Sugars	12g
Protein	14g	Fat	7g
Carbohydrate	12g	Saturates	1g

3 1/4 HOURS 1 HOUR

SERVES 4–6

INGREDIENTS

- 2 tbsp olive oil
- 1 small onion, finely chopped
- 2 garlic cloves, crushed
- 425 ml/¾ pint passata (sieved tomatoes)
- 2 tsp dried thyme
- 1 tsp dried oregano
- pinch fennel seeds
- 3 tbsp red wine vinegar
- 2 tbsp Dijon mustard
- pinch ground cinnamon
- 2 tbsp brown sugar
- 1 tsp chilli flakes
- 2 tbsp black treacle
- 16 chicken wings
- salt and pepper

TO GARNISH

- celery stalks
- cherry tomatoes

1 Heat the olive oil in a large frying pan (skillet) and fry the onion and garlic for about 10 minutes.

2 Add the passata (sieved tomatoes), dried herbs, fennel, red wine vinegar, mustard and cinnamon to the frying pan (skillet) along with the sugar, chilli flakes, treacle, and salt and pepper. Bring to the boil, then reduce the heat and simmer gently for about 15 minutes, until the sauce is slightly reduced.

3 Put the chicken wings in a large dish, and coat liberally with the sauce. Leave to marinate for 3 hours or as long as possible, turning the wings over often in the marinade.

4 Transfer the wings to a clean baking sheet (cookie sheet), and roast in a preheated oven, 220°C/425°F/ Gas Mark 7, for 10 minutes. Reduce the heat to 190°C/375°F/Gas Mark 5 and cook for 20 minutes, basting often.

5 Serve the wings piping hot, garnished with celery stalks and cherry tomatoes.

1

2

3

Jerk Chicken

This is perhaps one of the best-known Caribbean dishes. The 'jerk' in the name refers to the hot spicy coating.

NUTRITIONAL INFORMATION

Calories	158	Sugars	0.4g
Protein	29g	Fat	4g
Carbohydrate	2g	Saturates	1g

24 HOURS — 30 MINS

SERVES 4

INGREDIENTS

- 4 lean chicken portions
- 1 bunch spring onions (scallions), trimmed
- 1–2 Scotch Bonnet chillies, deseeded
- 1 garlic clove
- 5 cm/2 inch piece root (fresh) ginger, peeled and roughly chopped
- ½ tsp dried thyme
- ½ tsp paprika
- ¼ tsp ground allspice
- pinch ground cinnamon
- pinch ground cloves
- 4 tbsp white wine vinegar
- 3 tbsp light soy sauce
- pepper

2

3

5

1 Rinse the chicken portions and pat them dry on absorbent kitchen paper. Place them in a shallow dish.

2 Place the spring onions (scallions), chillies, garlic, ginger, thyme, paprika, allspice, cinnamon, cloves, wine vinegar, soy sauce and pepper to taste in a food processor and process until smooth.

3 Pour the spicy mixture over the chicken. Turn the chicken portions over so that they are well coated in the marinade.

4 Transfer the chicken portions to the refrigerator and leave to marinate for up to 24 hours.

5 Remove the chicken from the marinade and barbecue (grill) over medium hot coals for about 30 minutes, turning the chicken over and basting occasionally with any remaining marinade, until the chicken is browned and cooked through.

6 Transfer the chicken portions to individual serving plates and serve at once.

Lime Fricassée of Chicken

The addition of lime juice and lime rind adds a delicious tangy flavour to this chicken stew.

NUTRITIONAL INFORMATION	
Calories 235	Sugars 3g
Protein 20g	Fat 6g
Carbohydrate ...26g	Saturates 1g

15 MINS — $1^3/_4$ HOURS

SERVES 4

INGREDIENTS

- 2 tbsp oil
- 1 large chicken, cut into small portions
- 60 g/2 oz/½ cup flour, seasoned
- 500 g/1 lb 2 oz baby onions or shallots, sliced
- 1 each green and red (bell) pepper, sliced thinly
- 150 ml/¼ pint/⅔ cup chicken stock
- juice and rind of 2 limes
- 2 chillies, chopped
- 2 tbsp oyster sauce
- 1 tsp Worcestershire sauce
- salt and pepper

1 Heat the oil in a large frying pan (skillet). Coat the chicken pieces in the seasoned flour and cook for about 4 minutes until browned all over.

2 Transfer the chicken to a large casserole. Sprinkle with the onions.

3 Slowly fry the (bell) peppers in the juices in the frying pan.

4 Add the chicken stock, lime juice and rind and cook for a further 5 minutes.

5 Add the chillies, oyster sauce and Worcestershire sauce, mixing well.

6 Season to taste with salt and pepper, then pour the (bell) peppers and juices over the chicken and onions.

7 Cover the casserole with a lid or cooking foil.

8 Cook in the centre of a preheated oven, 190°C/375°F/Gas Mark 5, for 1½ hours until the chicken is very tender, then serve.

COOK'S TIP

Try this casserole with a cheese scone (biscuit) topping. About 30 minutes before the end of cooking time, simply top with rounds cut from .cheese scone (biscuit) pastry.

Mexican Chicken

Chilli, tomatoes and corn are typical ingredients in a Mexican dish. This is a quick and easy meal for unexpected guests.

NUTRITIONAL INFORMATION

Calories	207	Sugars	8g
Protein	18g	Fat	9g
Carbohydrate	13g	Saturates	2g

5 MINS

35 MINS

SERVES 4

INGREDIENTS

- 2 tbsp oil
- 8 chicken drumsticks
- 1 medium onion, finely chopped
- 1 tsp chilli powder
- 1 tsp ground coriander
- 425 g/15 oz can chopped tomatoes
- 2 tbsp tomato purée (paste)
- 125 g/4½ oz/⅔ cup frozen sweetcorn (corn-on-the-cob)
- salt and pepper

TO SERVE

- boiled rice
- mixed (bell) pepper salad

1 Heat the oil in a large frying pan (skillet), add the chicken drumsticks and cook over a medium heat until lightly browned on all sides. Remove from the pan and set aside.

2 Add the onion to the pan and cook for 3–4 minutes until soft, then stir in the chilli powder and coriander and cook for a few seconds.

3 Add the chopped tomatoes with their juice and the tomato purée (paste).

1

3

4

4 Return the chicken to the pan and simmer gently for 20 minutes until the chicken is tender and thoroughly cooked. Add the sweetcorn (corn-on-the-cob) and cook a further 3–4 minutes. Season to taste.

5 Serve with boiled rice and mixed (bell) pepper salad.

COOK'S TIP

If you dislike the heat of the chillies, just leave them out – the chicken will still taste delicious.

Barbecued (Grilled) Chicken

These chicken wings are brushed with a simple barbecue (grill) glaze, which can be made in minutes, but will be enjoyed by all.

NUTRITIONAL INFORMATION

Calories	143	Sugars	6g
Protein	14g	Fat	7g
Carbohydrate	6g	Saturates	1g

5 MINS — 20 MINS

SERVES 4

INGREDIENTS

- 8 chicken wings or 1 chicken cut into 8 portions
- 3 tbsp tomato purée (paste)
- 3 tbsp brown fruity sauce
- 1 tbsp white wine vinegar
- 1 tbsp clear honey
- 1 tbsp olive oil
- 1 clove garlic, crushed (optional)
- salad leaves, to serve

1 Remove the skin from the chicken if you want to reduce the fat in the dish.

2 To make the barbecue glaze, place the tomato purée (paste), brown fruity sauce, white wine vinegar, honey, oil and garlic in a small bowl. Stir all of the ingredients together until they are thoroughly blended.

3 Brush the barbecue (grill) glaze over the chicken and barbecue (grill) over hot coals for 15–20 minutes. Turn the chicken portions over occasionally and baste frequently with the barbecue (grill) glaze.

4 If the chicken begins to blacken before it is cooked, raise the rack if possible or move the chicken to a cooler part of the barbecue (grill) to slow down the cooking.

5 Transfer the barbecued (grilled) chicken to warm serving plates and serve with fresh salad leaves.

1

2

3

COOK'S TIP

When poultry is cooked over a very hot barbecue (grill) the heat immediately seals in all of the juices, leaving the meat succulent. For this reason make sure that the coals are hot enough before starting to barbecue (grill).

Festive Apple Chicken

The stuffing in this recipe is cooked under the breast skin so all the flavour sealed in, and the chicken stays really moist and succulent .

NUTRITIONAL INFORMATION

Calories	219	Sugars	7g
Protein	29g	Fat	8g
Carbohydrate	9g	Saturates	4g

10 MINS 2¼ HOURS

SERVES 6

INGREDIENTS

- 1 chicken, weighing 2 kg/4½ lb
- 2 dessert apples
- 15 g/½ oz/1 tbsp butter
- 1 tbsp redcurrant jelly
- parsley, to garnish

STUFFING

- 15 g/½ oz/1 tbsp butter
- 1 small onion, chopped finely
- 60 g/2 oz mushrooms, chopped finely
- 60 g/2 oz lean smoked ham, chopped finely
- 25 g/1 oz/½ cup fresh breadcrumbs
- 1 tbsp chopped fresh parsley
- 1 crisp eating apple
- 1 tbsp lemon juice
- oil, to brush
- salt and pepper

2

4

6

1 To make the stuffing, melt the butter and fry the onion gently, stirring until softened. Stir in the mushrooms and cook over a moderate heat for 2–3 minutes. Remove from the heat and stir in the ham, breadcrumbs and the chopped parsley.

2 Core the apple, leaving the skin on, and grate coarsely. Add the stuffing mixture to the apple with the lemon juice. Season to taste.

3 Loosen the breast skin of the chicken and carefully spoon the stuffing mixture under it, smoothing evenly with your hands.

4 Place the chicken in a roasting tin (pan) and brush lightly with oil.

5 Roast the chicken in a preheated oven, 190°C/375°F/Gas Mark 5, for 25 minutes per 500 g/1 lb 2 oz plus 25 minutes, or until there is no trace of pink in the juices when the chicken is pierced through the thickest part with a skewer. If the breast starts to brown too much, cover the chicken with foil.

6 Core and slice the remaining apples and sauté in the butter until golden. Stir in the redcurrant jelly and warm through until melted. Serve the chicken garnished with the apple and parsley.

Roast Duck with Apple

The richness of the duck meat contrasts well with the apricot sauce. If duckling portions are unavailable, use a whole bird cut into joints.

NUTRITIONAL INFORMATION

Calories	316	Sugars	38g
Protein	25g	Fat	6g
Carbohydrate	40g	Saturates	1g

10 MINS 1½ HOURS

SERVES 4

INGREDIENTS

- 4 duckling portions, 350 g/12 oz each
- 4 tbsp dark soy sauce
- 2 tbsp light muscovado sugar
- 2 red-skinned apples
- 2 green-skinned apples
- juice of 1 lemon
- 2 tbsp clear honey
- few bay leaves
- salt and pepper
- assorted fresh vegetables, to serve

SAUCE

- 400 g/14 oz can apricots, in natural juice
- 4 tbsp sweet sherry

1 Preheat the oven to 190°C/375°F/Gas Mark 5. Wash the duck and trim away any excess fat. Place on a wire rack over a roasting pan and prick all over with a fork.

2 Brush the duck with the soy sauce. Sprinkle over the sugar and season with pepper. Cook in the oven, basting occasionally, for 50–60 minutes until the meat is cooked through – the juices should run clear when a skewer is inserted into the thickest part of the meat.

3 Meanwhile, core the apples and cut each into 6 wedges. Place in a small roasting tin and mix with the lemon juice and honey. Add a few bay leaves and season. Cook alongside the duck, basting occasionally, for 20–25 minutes until tender. Discard the bay leaves.

4 To make the sauce, place the apricots in a blender or food processor together with the juice from the can and the sherry. Process for a few seconds until smooth. Alternatively, mash the apricots with a fork until smooth and mix with the juice and sherry.

5 Just before serving, heat the apricot purée (paste) in a small pan. Remove the skin from the duck and pat the flesh with kitchen paper to absorb any fat. Serve the duck with the apple wedges, apricot sauce and fresh vegetables.

1

3

4

VARIATION

Fruit complements duck perfectly. Use canned pineapple in natural juice for a delicious alternative.

Citrus Duckling Skewers

The tartness of citrus fruit goes well with the rich meat of duckling. Duckling makes a change from chicken for the barbecue (grill).

NUTRITIONAL INFORMATION

Calories	205	Sugars	5g
Protein	24g	Fat	10g
Carbohydrate	5g	Saturates	2g

45 MINS — 20 MINS

SERVES 12

INGREDIENTS

- 3 duckling breasts, skinned, boned and cut into bite-size pieces
- 1 small red onion, cut into wedges
- 1 small aubergine (eggplant), cut into cubes
- lime and lemon wedges, to garnish (optional)

MARINADE

- grated rind and juice of 1 lemon
- grated rind and juice of 1 lime
- grated rind and juice of 1 orange
- 1 clove garlic, crushed
- 1 tsp dried oregano
- 2 tbsp olive oil
- dash of Tabasco sauce

1 Cut the duckling into bite-sized pieces. Place in a non-metallic bowl together with the prepared vegetables.

2 To make the marinade, place the lemon, lime and orange rinds and juices, garlic, oregano, oil and Tabasco sauce in a screw-top jar and shake until well combined. Pour the marinade over the duckling and vegetables and toss to coat. Leave to marinate for 30 minutes.

3 Remove the duckling and vegetables from the marinade and thread them on to skewers, reserving the marinade.

4 Barbecue (grill) the skewers on an oiled rack over medium hot coals, turning and basting frequently with the reserved marinade, for 15-20 minutes until the meat is cooked through. Serve the kebabs garnished with lemon and lime wedges for squeezing (if using).

COOK'S TIP

For more zing add 1 teaspoon of chilli sauce to the marinade. The meat can be marinated for several hours, but it is best to marinate the vegetables separately for only about 30 minutes.

1

2

4

Turkey with Redcurrant

Prepare these steaks the day before they are needed and serve in toasted ciabatta bread, accompanied with crisp salad leaves.

NUTRITIONAL INFORMATION

Calories	219	Sugars	4g
Protein	28g	Fat	10g
Carbohydrate	4g	Saturates	1g

12 HOURS 15 MINS

SERVES 4

INGREDIENTS

- 100 g/ 3½ oz redcurrant jelly
- 2 tbsp lime juice
- 3 tbsp olive oil
- 2 tbsp dry white wine
- ¼ tsp ground ginger
- pinch grated nutmeg
- 4 turkey breast steaks
- salt and pepper

TO SERVE

- mixed salad leaves
- vinaigrette dressing
- 1 ciabatta loaf
- cherry tomatoes

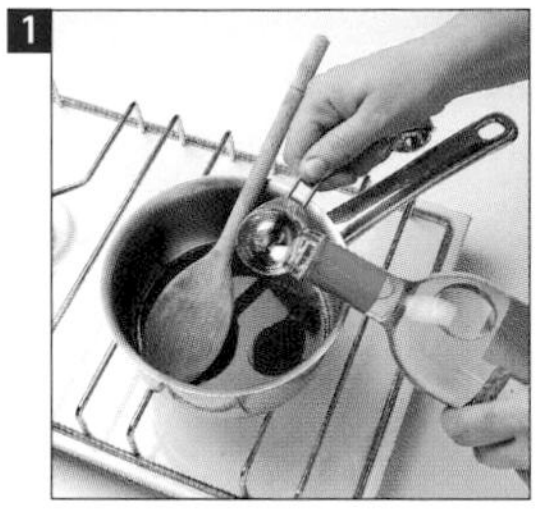

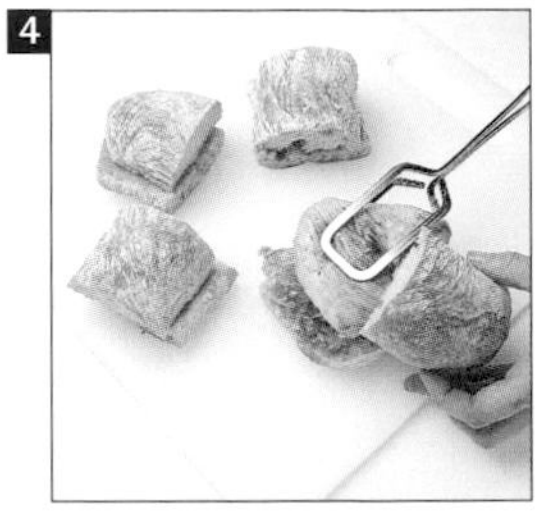

1 Place the redcurrant jelly and lime juice in a saucepan and heat gently until the jelly melts. Add the oil, wine, ginger and nutmeg.

2 Place the turkey steaks in a shallow, non-metallic dish and season with salt and pepper. Pour over the marinade, turning the meat so that it is well coated. Cover and refrigerate overnight.

3 Remove the turkey from the marinade, reserving the marinade for basting, and barbecue (grill) on an oiled rack over hot coals for about 4 minutes on each side. Baste the turkey steaks frequently with the reserved marinade.

4 Meanwhile, toss the salad leaves in the vinaigrette dressing. Cut the ciabatta loaf in half lengthwise and place, cut-side down, at the side of the barbecue. Barbecue (grill) until golden. Place each steak on top of a salad leaf, sandwich between 2 pieces of bread and serve with cherry tomatoes.

COOK'S TIP

Turkey and chicken escalopes are also ideal for cooking on the barbecue (grill). Because they are thin, they cook through without burning on the outside. Leave them overnight in a marinade of your choice and cook, basting with a little lemon juice and oil.

Fish & Seafood

Naturally low in fat yet rich in minerals and proteins, white fish and shellfish are ideal to include in a low-fat diet. There are so many different textures and flavours

available that they lend themselves to a wide range of cooking methods, as you will see from the recipes that follow. White fish such as cod, haddock, halibut, monkfish and mullet are readily available and easy to cook. Shellfish such as prawns (shrimp), oysters, crab and lobster may take a little longer to prepare but are well worth the effort. Oily fish – like salmon, trout, tuna and mackerel – are high in fat and should be eaten in moderation.

Oriental Shellfish Kebabs

These shellfish and vegetable kebabs are ideal for serving at parties. They are quick and easy to prepare and take next to no time to cook.

NUTRITIONAL INFORMATION

Calories	93	Sugars	1g
Protein	15g	Fat	2g
Carbohydrate	2g	Saturates	0.3g

2½ HOURS 5 MINS

MAKES 12

INGREDIENTS

- 350 g/12 oz raw tiger prawns (jumbo shrimp), peeled leaving tails intact
- 350 g/12 oz scallops, cleaned, trimmed and halved (quartered if large)
- 1 bunch spring onions (scallions), sliced into 2.5 cm/1 inch pieces
- 1 medium red (bell) pepper, deseeded and cubed
- 100 g/3½ oz baby corn cobs, trimmed and sliced into 1 cm/½ inch pieces
- 3 tbsp dark soy sauce
- ½ tsp hot chilli powder
- ½ tsp ground ginger
- 1 tbsp sunflower oil
- 1 red chilli, deseeded and sliced, to garnish

DIP

- 4 tbsp dark soy sauce
- 4 tbsp dry sherry
- 2 tsp clear honey
- 2.5 cm/1 inch piece root (fresh) ginger, peeled and grated
- 1 spring onion (scallion), trimmed and sliced very finely

1

2

2

1 Divide the prawns (shrimp), scallops, spring onions (scallions), (bell) pepper and baby corn into 12 portions and thread on to the skewers (soaked for 10 minutes in water to prevent them from burning). Cover the ends with foil so that they do not burn and place in a shallow dish.

2 Mix the soy sauce, chilli powder and ground ginger and coat the kebabs. Cover and chill for about 2 hours.

3 Preheat the grill (broiler) to hot. Arrange the kebabs on the rack, brush with oil and cook for 2–3 minutes on each side until the prawns (shrimp) turn pink, the scallops become opaque and the vegetables soften.

4 Mix together the dip ingredients.

5 Remove the foil and transfer the kebabs to a warm serving platter. Garnish with sliced chilli and serve with the dip.

Scallop Skewers

As the scallops are marinated, it is not essential that they are fresh; frozen shellfish are fine for a barbecue (grill).

NUTRITIONAL INFORMATION

Calories	182	Sugars	0g
Protein	29g	Fat	7g
Carbohydrate	0g	Saturates	1g

30 MINS 10 MINS

SERVES 4

INGREDIENTS

- grated zest and juice of 2 limes
- 2 tbsp finely chopped lemon grass or 1 tbsp lemon juice
- 2 garlic cloves, crushed
- 1 green chilli, deseeded and chopped
- 16 scallops, with corals
- 2 limes, each cut into 8 segments
- 2 tbsp sunflower oil
- 1 tbsp lemon juice
- salt and pepper

TO SERVE

- 60 g/2 oz/1 cup rocket (arugula) salad
- 200 g/7 oz/3 cups mixed salad leaves (greens)

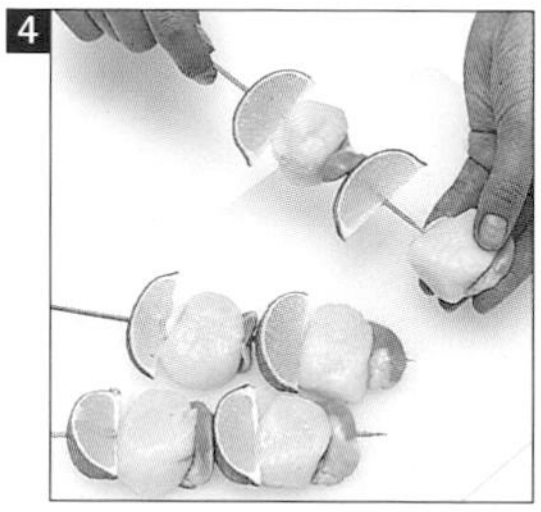
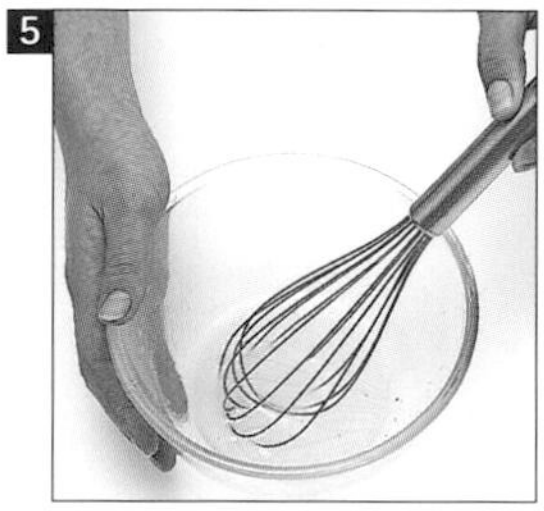

1 Soak 8 skewers in warm water for at least 10 minutes before you use them to prevent the food from sticking.

2 Combine the lime juice and zest, lemon grass, garlic and chilli together in a pestle and mortar or spice grinder to make a paste.

3 Thread 2 scallops on to each of the soaked skewers. Cover the ends with foil to prevent them from burning.

4 Alternate the scallops with the lime segments.

5 Whisk together the oil, lemon juice, salt and pepper to make the dressing.

6 Coat the scallops with the spice paste and place over a medium barbecue, basting occasionally.

7 Cook for 10 minutes, turning once.

8 Toss the rocket (arugula), mixed salad leaves (greens) and dressing together well. Put into a serving bowl.

9 Serve the scallops piping hot, 2 skewers on each plate, with the salad.

Salmon Yakitori

The Japanese sauce used here combines well with salmon, although it is usually served with chicken.

NUTRITIONAL INFORMATION

Calories	247	Sugars	10g
Protein	19g	Fat	11g
Carbohydrate	12g	Saturates	2g

20 MINS 15 MINS

SERVES 4

INGREDIENTS

- 350 g/12 oz chunky salmon fillet
- 8 baby leeks

YAKITORI SAUCE

- 5 tbsp light soy sauce
- 5 tbsp fish stock
- 2 tbsp caster (superfine) sugar
- 5 tbsp dry white wine
- 3 tbsp sweet sherry
- 1 clove garlic, crushed

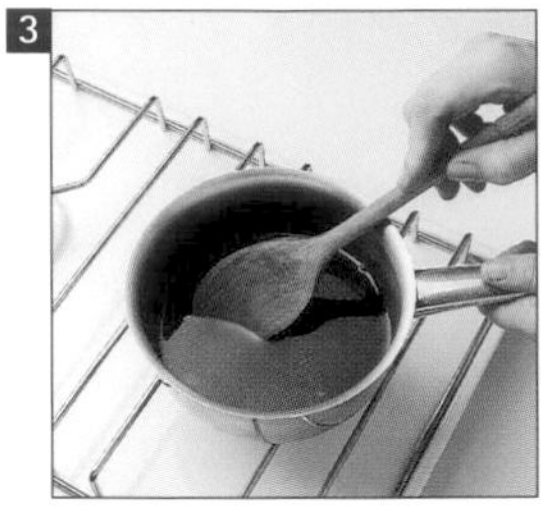

1 Skin the salmon and cut the flesh into 5 cm/2 inch chunks. Trim the leeks and cut them into 5 cm/2 inch lengths.

2 Thread the salmon and leeks alternately on to 8 pre-soaked wooden skewers. Leave to chill in the refrigerator until required.

3 To make the sauce, place all of the ingredients in a small pan and heat gently, stirring, until the sugar has dissolved.

4 Bring to the boil, then reduce the heat and simmer for 2 minutes. Strain the sauce through a fine sieve (strainer) and leave to cool until it is required.

5 Pour about one-third of the sauce into a small dish and set aside to serve with the kebabs.

6 Brush plenty of the remaining sauce over the skewers and cook directly on the rack.

7 If preferred, place a sheet of oiled kitchen foil on the rack and cook the salmon on that.

8 Barbecue (grill) the salmon and leek kebabs over hot coals for about 10 minutes or until cooked though, turning once.

9 Use a brush to baste frequently during cooking with the remaining sauce in order to prevent the fish and vegetables from drying out. Transfer the kebabs to a large serving platter and serve with a small bowl of the reserved sauce for dipping.

Butterfly Prawns (Shrimp)

These prawns (shrimp) look stunning when presented on the skewers, and they will certainly be an impressive prelude to the main meal.

NUTRITIONAL INFORMATION

Calories	183	Sugars	0g
Protein	28g	Fat	8g
Carbohydrate	0g	Saturates	1g

4½ HOURS — 10 MINS

SERVES 2–4

INGREDIENTS

- 500 g/1 lb 2 oz or 16 raw tiger prawns (shrimp), shelled, leaving tails intact
- juice of 2 limes
- 1 tsp cardamom seeds
- 2 tsp cumin seeds, ground
- 2 tsp coriander seeds, ground
- ½ tsp ground cinnamon
- 1 tsp ground turmeric
- 1 garlic clove, crushed
- 1 tsp cayenne pepper
- 2 tbsp oil
- cucumber slices, to garnish

1 Soak 8 wooden skewers in water for 20 minutes. Cut the prawns (shrimp) lengthways in half down to the tail and flatten out to form a symmetrical shape.

2 Thread a prawn (shrimp) on to 2 wooden skewers, with the tail between them, so that, when laid flat, the skewers hold the prawn (shrimp) in shape. Thread another 3 prawns (shrimp) on to these 2 skewers in the same way.

3 Repeat until you have 4 sets of 4 prawns (shrimp) each.

4 Lay the skewered prawns (shrimp) in a non-porous, non-metallic dish, and sprinkle over the lime juice.

5 Combine the spices and the oil, and coat the prawns (shrimp) well in the mixture. Cover the prawns (shrimp) and chill for 4 hours.

6 Cook over a hot barbecue (grill) or in a grill (broiler) pan lined with foil under a preheated grill (broiler) for 6 minutes, turning once.

7 Serve immediately, garnished with cucumber and accompanied by a sweet chutney – walnut chutney is ideal.

1

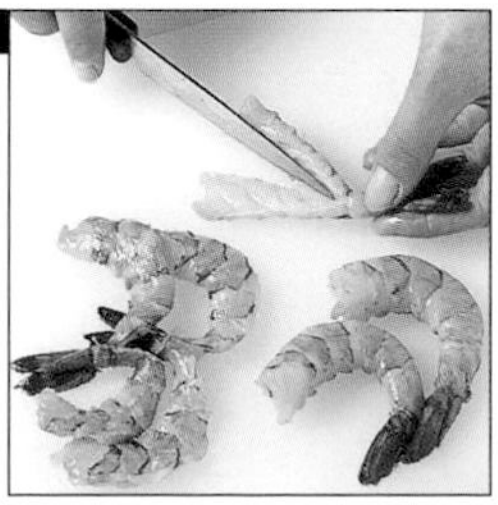

2

4

Monkfish with Coconut

This is a tasty kebab with a mild marinade. Allow the skewers to marinate for at least an hour before cooking.

NUTRITIONAL INFORMATION

Calories	193	Sugars	2g
Protein	39g	Fat	3g
Carbohydrate	2g	Saturates	1g

4 HOURS — 30 MINS

SERVES 4

INGREDIENTS

- 450 g/1 lb monkfish tails
- 225 g/8 oz uncooked peeled prawns (shrimp)
- desiccated (shredded) coconut, toasted, to garnish (optional)

MARINADE

- 1 tsp sunflower oil
- ½ small onion, finely grated
- 1 tsp root (fresh) ginger, grated
- 150 ml/5 fl oz/⅔ cup canned coconut milk
- 2 tbsp chopped, fresh coriander (cilantro)

1 To make the marinade, heat the oil in a wok or saucepan and fry the onion and ginger for 5 minutes until just softened but not browned.

2 Add the coconut milk to the pan and bring to the boil. Boil rapidly for about 5 minutes or until reduced to the consistency of single (light) cream.

3 Remove the pan from the heat and allow to cool completely.

4 When cooled, stir the coriander (cilantro) into the coconut milk and pour into a shallow dish.

5 Cut the fish into bite-sized chunks and stir gently into the coconut mixture together with the prawns (shrimp). Leave to chill for 1–4 hours.

6 Thread the fish and prawns (shrimp) on to skewers and discard any remaining marinade. Barbecue (grill) the skewers over hot coals for 10–15 minutes, turning frequently. Garnish with toasted coconut (if using).

COOK'S TIP

Look out for uncooked prawns (shrimp) in the freezer cabinet in large supermarkets. If you cannot obtain them, you can use cooked prawns (shrimp), but remember they only need heating through.

Caribbean Prawns (Shrimp)

This is an ideal recipe for cooks who have difficulty in finding raw prawns (shrimp).

NUTRITIONAL INFORMATION

Calories	110	Sugars	15g
Protein	5g	Fat	4g
Carbohydrate	15g	Saturates	3g

40 MINS 15 MINS

SERVES 4

INGREDIENTS

16 cooked king (tiger) prawns (shrimp)
1 small pineapple
flaked coconut, to garnish (optional)

MARINADE

150 ml/5 fl oz/⅔ cup pineapple juice
2 tbsp white wine vinegar
2 tbsp dark muscovado sugar
2 tbsp desiccated (shredded) coconut

1 If they are unpeeled, peel the prawns (shrimp), leaving the tails attached if preferred.

2 Peel the pineapple and cut it in half lengthways. Cut one pineapple half into wedges then into chunks.

3 To make the marinade, mix together half of the pineapple juice and the vinegar, sugar and coconut in a shallow, non-metallic dish. Add the peeled prawns (shrimp) and pineapple chunks and toss until well coated. Leave the prawns and pineapple to marinate for at least 30 minutes.

4 Remove the pineapple and prawns (shrimp) from the marinade and thread them on to skewers. Reserve the marinade.

1

2

5

5 Strain the marinade and place in a food processor. Roughly chop the remaining pineapple and add to the processor with the remaining pineapple juice. Process the pineapple for a few seconds to produce a thick sauce.

6 Pour the sauce into a small saucepan. Bring to the boil then simmer for about 5 minutes. If you prefer, you can heat up the sauce by the side of the barbecue (grill).

7 Transfer the kebabs to the barbecue (grill) and brush with some of the sauce. Barbecue (grill) for about 5 minutes until the kebabs are piping hot. Turn the kebabs, brushing occasionally with the sauce.

8 Serve the kebabs with extra sauce, sprinkled with flaked coconut (if using).

Lemony Monkfish Skewers

A simple basting sauce is brushed over these tasty kebabs. When served with crusty bread, they make a perfect light meal.

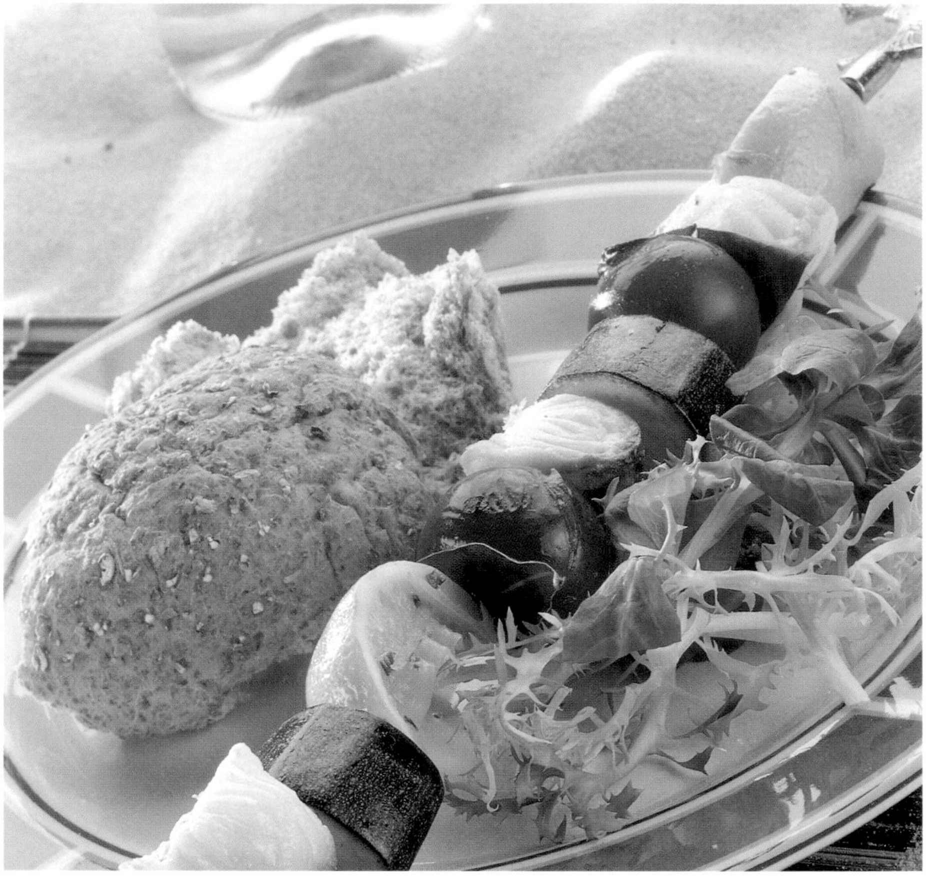

NUTRITIONAL INFORMATION

Calories 191	Sugars 2g
Protein 21g	Fat 11g
Carbohydrate 1g	Saturates 1g

10 MINS 15 MINS

SERVES 4

INGREDIENTS

- 450 g/1 lb monkfish tail
- 2 courgettes (zucchini)
- 1 lemon
- 12 cherry tomatoes
- 8 bay leaves

SAUCE

- 3 tbsp olive oil
- 2 tbsp lemon juice
- 1 tsp chopped, fresh thyme
- ½ tsp lemon pepper
- salt

TO SERVE

- green salad leaves
- fresh, crusty bread

1 Cut the monkfish into 5 cm/2 inch chunks.

3
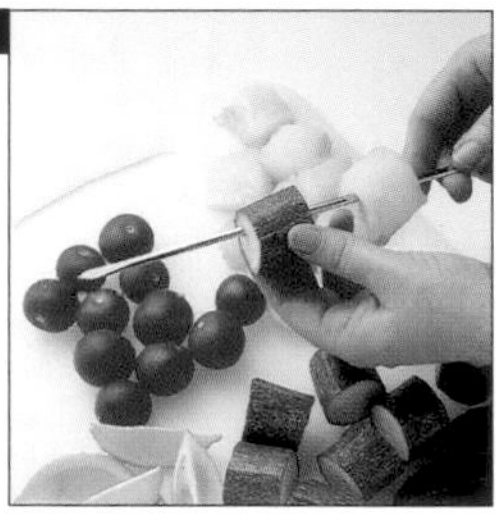

4

5

2 Cut the courgettes (zucchini) into thick slices and the lemon into wedges.

3 Thread the monkfish, courgettes (zucchini), lemon, tomatoes and bay leaves on to 4 skewers.

4 To make the basting sauce, combine the oil, lemon juice, thyme, lemon pepper and salt to taste in a small bowl.

5 Brush the basting sauce liberally all over the fish, lemon, tomatoes and bay leaves on the skewers.

6 Cook the skewers on the barbecue (grill) for about 15 minutes over medium-hot coals, basting them frequently with the sauce, until the fish is cooked through. Transfer the skewers to plates and serve with green salad leaves and wedges of crusty bread.

VARIATION

Use plaice (flounder) fillets instead of the monkfish, if you prefer. Allow two fillets per person, and skin and cut each fillet lengthways into two. Roll up each piece and thread them on to the skewers.

Balti Scallops

This is a wonderful recipe for a special occasion dish. Cooked with coriander (cilantro) and tomatoes, the scallops have a spicy flavour.

NUTRITIONAL INFORMATION

Calories	258	Sugars	2g
Protein	44g	Fat	8g
Carbohydrate	3g	Saturates	1g

1¼ HOURS — 15 MINS

SERVES 4

INGREDIENTS

- 750 g/1 lb 10 oz shelled scallops
- 2 tbsp oil
- 2 onions, chopped
- 3 tomatoes, quartered
- 2 fresh green chillies, sliced
- 4 lime wedges, to garnish

MARINADE

- 3 tbsp chopped fresh coriander (cilantro)
- 2.5 cm/1 inch piece ginger root, grated
- 1 tsp ground coriander
- 3 tbsp lemon juice
- grated rind of 1 lemon
- ¼ tsp ground black pepper
- ½ tsp salt
- ½ tsp ground cumin
- 1 garlic clove, crushed

1. To make the marinade, mix all the ingredients together in a bowl.
2. Put the scallops into a bowl. Add the marinade and turn the scallops until they are well coated.
3. Then cover and leave to marinate for 1 hour or overnight in the fridge.
4. Heat the oil in a Balti pan or wok, add the onions and stir-fry until softened.
5. Add the tomatoes and chillies and stir-fry for 1 minute.
6. Add the scallops and stir-fry for 6–8 minutes until the scallops are cooked through, but still succulent inside.
7. Serve garnished with lime wedges.

1

2

5

COOK'S TIP

It is best to buy the scallops fresh in the shell with the roe – you will need 1.5 kg/3 lb 5 oz – a fishmonger will clean them and remove the shell for you.

Seafood Stir-Fry

This combination of assorted seafood and tender vegetables flavoured with ginger makes an ideal light meal served with thread noodles.

NUTRITIONAL INFORMATION

Calories	226	Sugars	5g
Protein	35g	Fat	7g
Carbohydrate	6g	Saturates	1g

5 MINS | 15 MINS

SERVES 4

INGREDIENTS

- 100 g/3½ oz small, thin asparagus spears, trimmed
- 1 tbsp sunflower oil
- 2.5 cm/1 inch piece root (fresh) ginger, cut into thin strips
- 1 medium leek, shredded
- 2 medium carrots, julienned
- 100 g/3½ oz baby sweetcorn cobs, quartered lengthwise
- 2 tbsp light soy sauce
- 1 tbsp oyster sauce
- 1 tsp clear honey
- 450 g/1 lb cooked, assorted shellfish, thawed if frozen
- freshly cooked egg noodles, to serve

TO GARNISH

- 4 large cooked prawns
- small bunch fresh chives, freshly snipped

1

3

5

1 Bring a small saucepan of water to the boil and blanch the asparagus for 1–2 minutes.

2 Drain the asparagus, set aside and keep warm.

3 Heat the oil in a wok or large frying pan (skillet) and stir-fry the ginger, leek, carrot and sweetcorn for about 3 minutes. Do not allow the vegetables to brown.

4 Add the soy sauce, oyster sauce and honey to the wok or frying pan (skillet).

5 Stir in the cooked shellfish and continue to stir-fry for 2–3 minutes until the vegetables are just tender and the shellfish are thoroughly heated through. Add the blanched asparagus and stir-fry for about 2 minutes.

6 To serve, pile the cooked noodles on to 4 warm serving plates and spoon the seafood and vegetable stir fry over them.

7 Garnish with the cooked prawns and freshly snipped chives and serve immediately. Serve garnished with a large prawn and freshly snipped chives.

Provençale-Style Mussels

These delicious large mussels are served hot with a tasty tomato and vegetable sauce. Mop up the delicious sauce with some crusty bread.

NUTRITIONAL INFORMATION

Calories 253	Sugars 8g
Protein 31g	Fat 8g
Carbohydrate 9g	Saturates 1g

5 MINS   50 MINS

SERVES 4

INGREDIENTS

- 1 tbsp olive oil
- 1 large onion, finely chopped
- 1 garlic clove, finely chopped
- 1 small red (bell) pepper, deseeded and finely chopped
- sprig of rosemary
- 2 bay leaves
- 400 g/14 oz can chopped tomatoes
- 150 ml/5 fl oz/⅔ cup white wine
- 1 courgette (zucchini), diced finely
- 2 tbsp tomato purée (paste)
- 1 tsp caster (superfine) sugar
- 50 g/1¾ oz pitted black olives in brine, drained and chopped
- 675 g/1½ lb cooked New Zealand mussels in their shells
- 1 tsp orange rind
- salt and pepper
- crusty bread, to serve
- 2 tbsp chopped, fresh parsley, to garnish

1 Heat the olive oil in a large saucepan and gently fry the chopped onion, garlic and (bell) pepper for 3–4 minutes until just softened.

2 Add the rosemary and bay leaves to the saucepan with the tomatoes and 100 ml/3½ fl oz/⅓ cup wine. Season to taste, then bring to the boil and simmer for 15 minutes.

3 Stir in the courgette (zucchini), tomato purée (paste), sugar and olives. Simmer for 10 minutes.

4 Meanwhile, bring a pan of water to the boil. Arrange the mussels in a steamer or a large sieve (strainer) and place over the water. Sprinkle with the remaining wine and the orange rind. Cover and steam until the mussels open (discard any that remain closed).

5 Remove the mussels with a slotted spoon and arrange on a serving plate. Discard the herbs and spoon the sauce over the mussels. Garnish with chopped parsley and serve with crusty bread.

Yucatan Fish

Herbs, onion, green (bell) pepper and pumpkin seeds are used to flavour this baked fish dish, which is first marinated in lime juice.

NUTRITIONAL INFORMATION

Calories	248	Sugars	2g
Protein	33g	Fat	11g
Carbohydrate	3g	Saturates	1g

40 MINS 35 MINS

SERVES 4

INGREDIENTS

- 4 cod cutlets or steaks or hake cutlets (about 175 g/6 oz each)
- 2 tbsp lime juice
- salt and pepper
- 1 green (bell) pepper
- 1 tbsp olive oil
- 1 onion, chopped finely
- 1–2 garlic cloves, crushed
- 40 g/1½ oz green pumpkin seeds
- grated rind of ½ lime
- 1 tbsp chopped fresh coriander (cilantro) or parsley
- 1 tbsp chopped fresh mixed herbs
- 60 g/2 oz button mushrooms, sliced thinly
- 2–3 tbsp fresh orange juice or white wine

TO GARNISH

- lime wedges
- fresh mixed herbs

1 Wipe the fish, place in a shallow ovenproof dish and pour the lime juice over. Turn the fish in the juice, season with salt and pepper, cover and leave in a cool place for 15–30 minutes.

2 Halve the (bell) pepper, remove the seeds and place under a preheated moderate grill, skin-side upwards, until the skin burns and splits. Leave to cool slightly, then peel off the skin and chop the flesh.

3 Heat the oil in a pan and fry the onion, garlic, (bell) pepper and pumpkin seeds gently for a few minutes until the onion is soft.

4 Stir in the lime rind, coriander (cilantro) or parsley, mixed herbs, mushrooms and seasoning, and spoon over the fish.

5 Spoon or pour the orange juice or wine over the fish, cover with foil or a lid and place in a preheated oven at 180°C/350°F/Gas Mark 4 for about 30 minutes, or until the fish is just tender.

6 Garnish the fish with lime wedges and fresh herbs and serve.

1

2

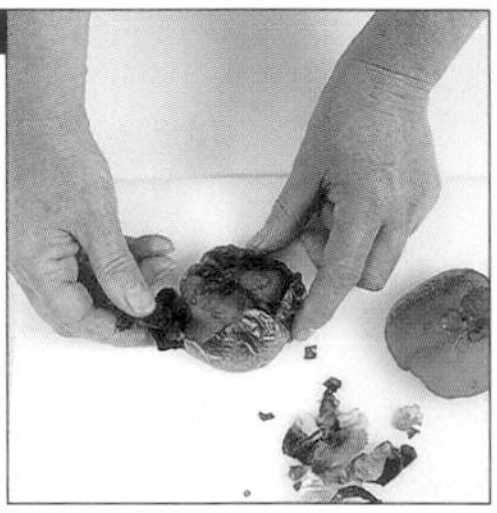

3

Prawn (Shrimp) Bhuna

This is a fiery recipe with subtle undertones. As the flavour of the prawns (shrimp) should be noticeable, the spices should not take over this dish.

NUTRITIONAL INFORMATION

Calories 141	Sugars 0.4g
Protein 19g	Fat 7g
Carbohydrate 1g	Saturates 1g

15 MINS — 20 MINS

SERVES 4–6

INGREDIENTS

- 2 dried red chillies, deseeded if liked
- 3 fresh green chillies, finely chopped
- 1 tsp ground turmeric
- 3 garlic cloves, crushed
- ½ tsp pepper
- 1 tsp paprika
- 2 tsp white wine vinegar
- ½ tsp salt
- 500 g/1 lb 2 oz uncooked peeled king prawns (shrimp)
- 3 tbsp oil
- 1 onion, chopped very finely
- 175 ml/6 fl oz/¾ cup water
- 2 tbsp lemon juice
- 2 tsp garam masala
- sprigs of fresh coriander (cilantro), to garnish

COOK'S TIP

Garam masala should be used sparingly and is generally added to foods towards the end of their cooking time. It is also used sprinkled over cooked meats, vegetables and pulses as a garnish.

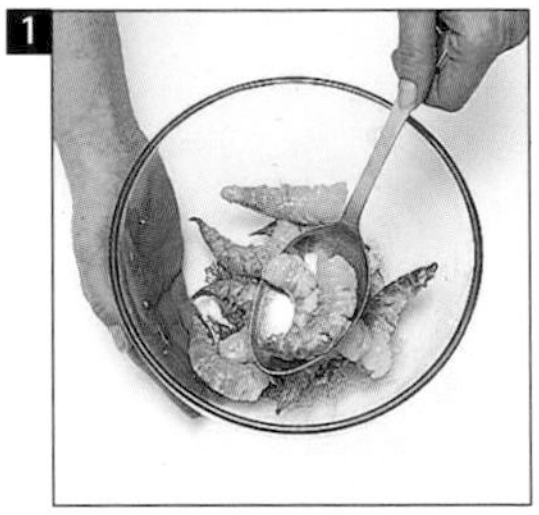

1 Combine the chillies, spices, vinegar and salt in a non-metallic bowl. Stir in the prawns (shrimp) and leave for 10 minutes.

2 Heat the oil in a large frying pan (skillet) or wok, add the onion and fry for 3–4 minutes until soft.

3 Add the prawns (shrimp) and the contents of the bowl to the pan and stir-fry over a high heat for 2 minutes. Reduce the heat, add the water and boil for 10 minutes, stirring occasionally, until the water is evaporated and the curry is fragrant.

4 Stir in the lemon juice and garam masala then transfer the mixture to a warm serving dish and garnish with fresh coriander (cilantro) sprigs.

5 Serve garnished with sprigs of fresh coriander (cilantro).

Charred Tuna Steaks

Tuna has a firm flesh, which is ideal for barbecuing (grilling), but it can be a little dry unless it is marinated first.

NUTRITIONAL INFORMATION

Calories	153	Sugars	1g
Protein	29g	Fat	3g
Carbohydrate	1g	Saturates	1g

2 HOURS · 15 MINS

SERVES 4

INGREDIENTS

- 4 tuna steaks
- 3 tbsp soy sauce
- 1 tbsp Worcestershire sauce
- 1 tsp wholegrain mustard
- 1 tsp caster (superfine) sugar
- 1 tbsp sunflower oil
- green salad, to serve

TO GARNISH

- flat-leaf parsley
- lemon wedges

3

4

6

1 Place the tuna steaks in a shallow dish.

2 Mix together the soy sauce, Worcestershire sauce, mustard, sugar and oil in a small bowl.

3 Pour the marinade over the tuna steaks.

4 Gently turn over the tuna steaks, using your fingers or a fork. Make sure that the fish steaks are well coated with the marinade.

5 Cover and place the tuna steaks in the refrigerator. Leave to chill for between 30 minutes and 2 hours.

6 Barbecue (grill) the marinated fish over hot coals for 10–15 minutes, turning once.

7 Baste frequently with any of the marinade that is left in the dish.

8 Garnish with flat-leaf parsley and lemon wedges. Serve with a fresh green salad.

COOK'S TIP

If a marinade contains soy sauce, the marinating time should be limited, usually to 2 hours. If allowed to marinate for too long, the fish will dry out and become tough.

Poached Salmon

Salmon steaks, poached in a well-flavoured stock and served with a piquant sauce, make a delicious summer lunch or supper dish.

NUTRITIONAL INFORMATION

Calories	712	Sugars	5g
Protein	66g	Fat	47g
Carbohydrate	6g	Saturates	9g

10 MINS 30 MINS

SERVES 4

INGREDIENTS

- 1 small onion, sliced
- 1 small carrot, sliced
- 1 stick celery, sliced
- 1 bay leaf
- pared rind and juice of ½ orange
- a few stalks of parsley
- salt
- 5-6 black peppercorns
- 700 ml/1¼ pints/3 cups water
- 4 salmon steaks, about 350 g/12 oz each
- salad leaves, to serve
- lemon twists, to garnish

SAUCE

- 1 large avocado, peeled, halved and stoned
- 125 ml/4 fl oz/½ cup low-fat natural yogurt
- grated zest and juice of ½ orange
- black pepper
- a few drops of hot red pepper sauce

1 Put the onion, carrot, celery, bay leaf, orange rind, orange juice, parsley stalks, salt and peppercorns in a pan just large enough to take the salmon steaks in a single layer. Pour on the water, cover the pan and bring to the boil. Simmer the stock for 20 minutes.

2 Arrange the salmon steaks in the pan, return the stock to the boil and simmer for 3 minutes. Cover the pan, remove from the heat and leave the salmon to cool in the stock.

3 Roughly chop the avocado and place it in a blender or food processor with the yogurt, orange zest and orange juice. Process until smooth, then season to taste with salt, pepper and hot pepper sauce.

4 Remove the salmon steaks from the stock (reserve it to make fish soup or a sauce), skin them and pat dry with kitchen paper (paper towels).

5 Cover the serving dish with salad leaves, arrange the salmon steaks on top and spoon a little of the sauce into the centre of each one. Garnish the fish with lemon twists, and serve the remaining sauce separately.

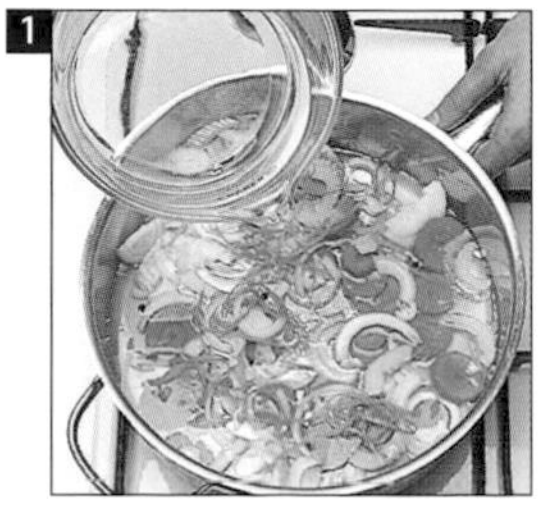

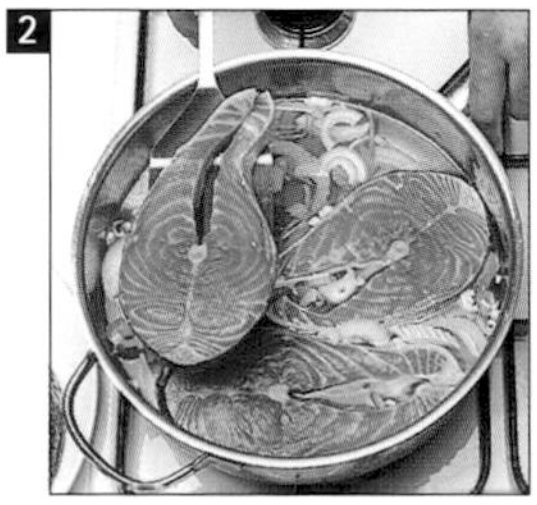

Salmon with Caper Sauce

The richness of salmon is beautifully balanced by the tangy capers in this creamy herb sauce.

NUTRITIONAL INFORMATION			
Calories	302	Sugars	0g
Protein	21g	Fat	24g
Carbohydrate	1g	Saturates	9g

5 MINS — 25 MINS

SERVES 4

INGREDIENTS

- 4 salmon fillets, skinned
- 1 fresh bay leaf
- few black peppercorns
- 1 tsp white wine vinegar
- 150 ml/¼ pint/⅔ cup fish stock
- 3 tbsp double (heavy) cream
- 1 tbsp capers
- 1 tbsp chopped fresh dill
- 1 tbsp chopped fresh chives
- 1 tsp cornflour (cornstarch)
- 2 tbsp skimmed milk
- salt and pepper
- new potatoes, to serve

TO GARNISH

- fresh dill sprigs
- chive flowers

1 Lay the salmon fillets in a shallow ovenproof dish. Add the bay leaf, peppercorns, vinegar and stock.

2 Cover with foil and bake in a preheated oven at 180°C/350°F/Gas Mark 4 for 15–20 minutes until the flesh is opaque and flakes easily when tested with a fork.

3 Transfer the fish to warmed serving plates, cover and keep warm.

4 Strain the cooking liquid into a saucepan. Stir in the cream, capers, dill and chives and seasoning to taste.

5 Blend the cornflour (cornstarch) with the milk. Add to the saucepan and heat, stirring, until thickened slightly. Boil for 1 minute.

6 Spoon the sauce over the salmon, garnish with dill sprigs and chive flowers.

7 Serve with new potatoes.

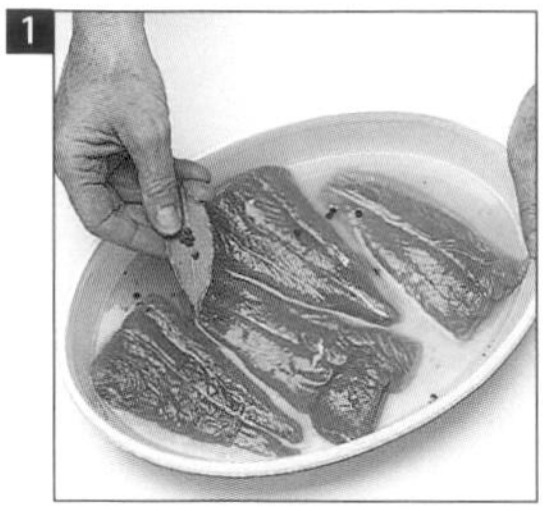

COOK'S TIP

Ask the fishmonger to skin the fillets for you. The cooking time for the salmon will depend on the thickness of the fish: the thin tail end of the salmon takes the least time to cook.

Mackerel with Lime

The secret of this dish lies in the simple, fresh flavours which perfectly complement the fish.

NUTRITIONAL INFORMATION

Calories	302	Sugars	0g
Protein	21g	Fat	24g
Carbohydrate	0g	Saturates	4g

10 MINS 10 MINS

SERVES 4

INGREDIENTS

- 4 small mackerel
- ¼ tsp ground coriander
- ¼ tsp ground cumin
- 4 sprigs fresh coriander (cilantro)
- 3 tbsp chopped, fresh coriander (cilantro)
- 1 red chilli, deseeded and chopped
- grated rind and juice of 1 lime
- 2 tbsp sunflower oil
- salt and pepper
- 1 lime, sliced, to garnish
- chilli flowers (optional), to garnish
- salad leaves, to serve

1 To make the chilli flowers (if using), cut the tip of a small chilli lengthways into thin strips, leaving the chilli intact at the stem end. Remove the seeds and place in iced water until curled.

1

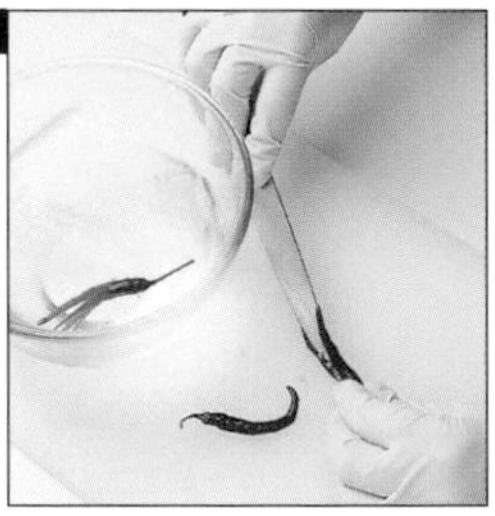

2

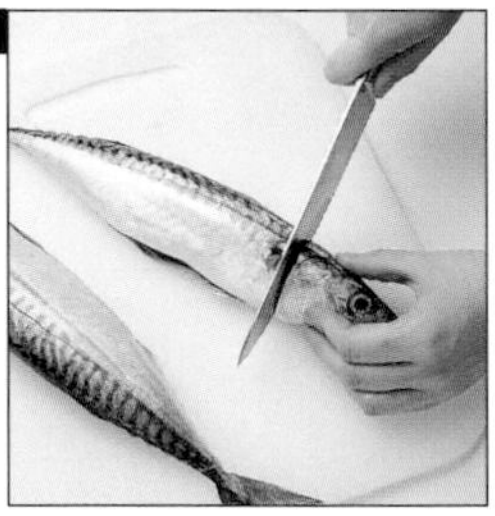

4

2 Clean and gut the mackerel, removing the heads if preferred. Transfer the mackerel to a chopping board.

3 Sprinkle the fish with the ground spices and salt and pepper to taste. Sprinkle 1 teaspoon of chopped coriander (cilantro) inside the cavity of each fish.

4 Mix together the chopped coriander (cilantro), chilli, lime rind and juice and the oil in a small bowl. Brush the mixture liberally over the fish.

5 Place the fish in a hinged rack if you have one. Barbecue (grill) the fish over hot coals for 3–4 minutes on each side, turning once. Brush the fish frequently with the remaining basting mixture. Transfer to plates and garnish with chilli flowers (if using) and lime slices, and serve with salad leaves.

COOK'S TIP

This recipe is suitable for other oily fish, such as trout, herring or sardines.

Delicately Spiced Trout

The firm, sweet flesh of the trout is enhanced by the sweet-spicy flavour of the marinade and cooking juices.

NUTRITIONAL INFORMATION

Calories	374	Sugars	13g
Protein	38g	Fat	19g
Carbohydrate	14g	Saturates	3g

45 MINS

20 MINS

SERVES 4

INGREDIENTS

- 4 trout, each weighing 175–250 g/ 6–9 oz, cleaned
- 3 tbsp oil
- 1 tsp fennel seeds
- 1tsp onion seeds
- 1 garlic clove, crushed
- 150 ml/¼ pint/⅔ cup coconut milk or fish stock
- 3 tbsp tomato purée (paste)
- 60 g/2 oz/⅓ cup sultanas (golden raisins)
- ½ tsp garam masala

TO GARNISH

- 25 g/1 oz/¼ cup chopped cashew nuts
- lemon wedges
- sprigs of fresh coriander (cilantro)

MARINADE

- 4 tbsp lemon juice
- 2 tbsp chopped fresh coriander (cilantro)
- 1 tsp ground cumin
- ½ tsp salt
- ½ tsp ground black pepper

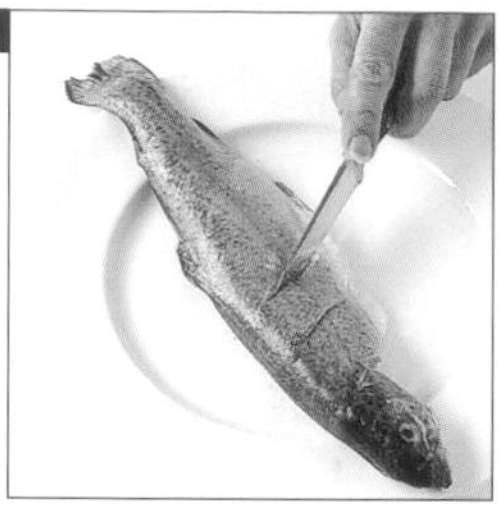

1 Slash the trout skin in several places on both sides with a sharp knife.

2 To make the marinade, mix all the ingredients together in a bowl.

3 Put the trout in a shallow dish and pour over the marinade. Leave to marinate for 30–40 minutes; turn the fish over during the marinating time.

4 Heat the oil in a Balti pan or wok and fry the fennel seeds and onion seeds until they start popping.

5 Add the crushed garlic, coconut milk or fish stock, and tomato purée (paste) and bring the mixture in the wok to the boil.

6 Add the sultanas (golden raisins), garam masala and trout with the juices from the marinade. Cover and simmer for 5 minutes. Turn the trout over and simmer for a further 10 minutes.

7 Serve garnished with the nuts, lemon and coriander (cilantro) sprigs.

Baked Sea Bass

Sea Bass is often paired with subtle oriental flavours. For a special occasion, you may like to bone the fish.

NUTRITIONAL INFORMATION

Calories	140	Sugars	0.1g
Protein	29g	Fat	1g
Carbohydrate	0.1g	Saturates	0.2g

10 MINS 15 MINS

SERVES 4–6

INGREDIENTS

2 sea bass, about 1 kg/2 lb 4 oz each, cleaned and scaled

2 spring onions (scallions), green part only, cut into strips

5 cm/2 inch piece ginger, peeled and cut into strips

2 garlic cloves, unpeeled, crushed lightly

2 tbsp mirin or dry sherry

salt and pepper

TO SERVE

pickled sushi ginger (optional)

soy sauce

1 For each fish lay out a double thickness of foil and oil the top piece well, or lay a piece of silicon paper over the foil.

2 Place the fish in the middle and expose the cavity.

3 Divide the spring onion (scallion) and ginger between each cavity. Put a garlic clove in each cavity.

4 Pour over the mirin or dry sherry. Season the fish well.

5 Close the cavities and lay each fish on its side. Bring over the foil and fold the edges together to seal securely. Fold each end neatly.

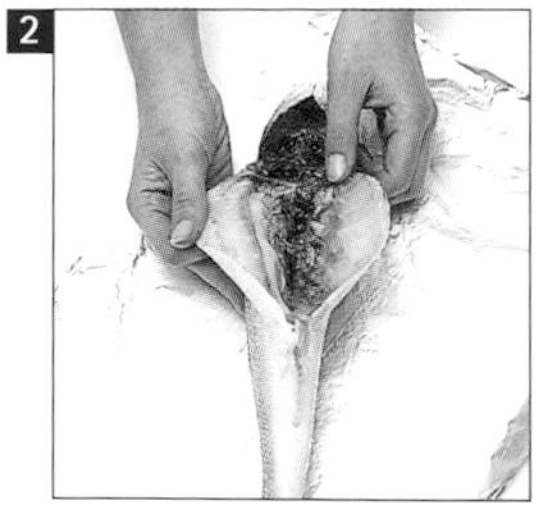

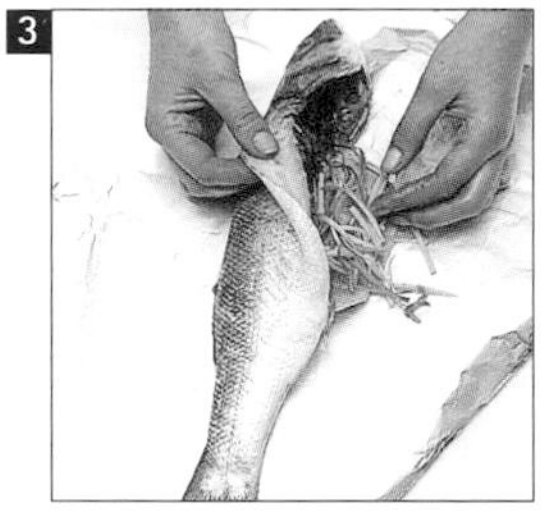

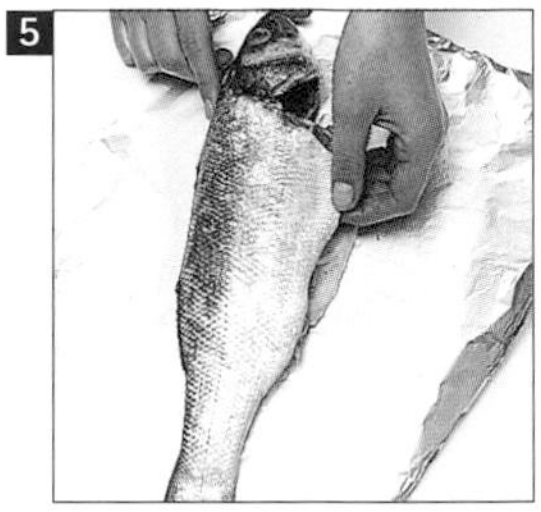

6 Cook over a medium barbecue (grill) for 15 minutes, turning once.

7 To serve, remove the foil and cut each fish into 2 or 3 pieces.

8 Serve with the pickled ginger (if using) accompanied by soy sauce.

COOK'S TIP

Fresh sea Bass is just as delicious when cooked very simply. Stuff the fish with garlic and chopped herbs, brush with olive oil and bake in the oven.

Indonesian-Style Spicy Cod

A delicious aromatic coating makes this dish rather special. Serve it with a crisp salad and crusty bread.

NUTRITIONAL INFORMATION

Calories	146	Sugars	2g
Protein	19g	Fat	7g
Carbohydrate	2g	Saturates	4g

10 MINS — 15 MINS

SERVES 4

INGREDIENTS

- 4 cod steaks
- 1 stalk lemon grass
- 1 small red onion, chopped
- 3 cloves garlic, chopped
- 2 fresh red chillies, deseeded and chopped
- 1 tsp grated root (fresh) ginger
- ¼ tsp turmeric
- 2 tbsp butter, cut into small cubes
- 8 tbsp canned coconut milk
- 2 tbsp lemon juice
- salt and pepper
- red chillies, to garnish (optional)

1 Rinse the cod steaks and pat them dry on absorbent kitchen paper (paper towels).

2 Remove and discard the outer leaves from the lemon grass and thinly slice the inner section.

3 Place the lemon grass, onion, garlic, chillies, ginger and turmeric in a food processor and blend until the ingredients are finely chopped. Season with salt and pepper to taste.

4 With the processor running, add the butter, coconut milk and lemon juice and process until well blended.

5 Place the fish in a shallow, non-metallic dish. Pour over the coconut mixture and turn the fish until well coated.

6 If you have one, place the fish steaks in a hinged basket, which will make them easier to turn. Barbecue (grill) over hot coals for 15 minutes or until the fish is cooked through, turning once. Serve garnished with red chillies (if using).

2

3

5

COOK'S TIP

If you prefer a milder flavour, omit the chillies altogether. For a hotter flavour do not remove the seeds from the chillies.

Japanese Plaice (Flounder)

The marinade for this dish has a distinctly Japanese flavour. Its subtle flavour goes well with any white fish.

NUTRITIONAL INFORMATION

Calories	207	Sugars	9g
Protein	22g	Fat	8g
Carbohydrate	10g	Saturates	1g

6 HOURS — 10 MINS

SERVES 4

INGREDIENTS

- 4 small plaice (flounders)
- 6 tbsp soy sauce
- 2 tbsp sake or dry white wine
- 2 tbsp sesame oil
- 1 tbsp lemon juice
- 2 tbsp light muscovado sugar
- 1 tsp root (fresh) ginger, grated
- 1 clove garlic, crushed

TO GARNISH

- 1 small carrot
- 4 spring onions (scallion)

2
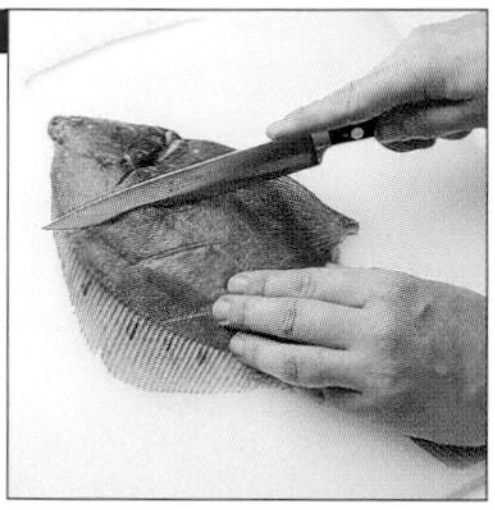
4
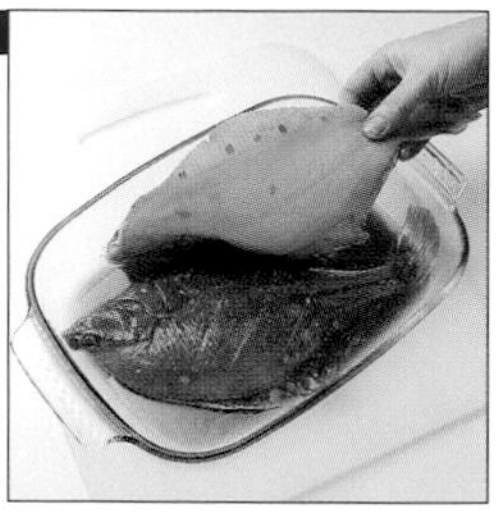
5
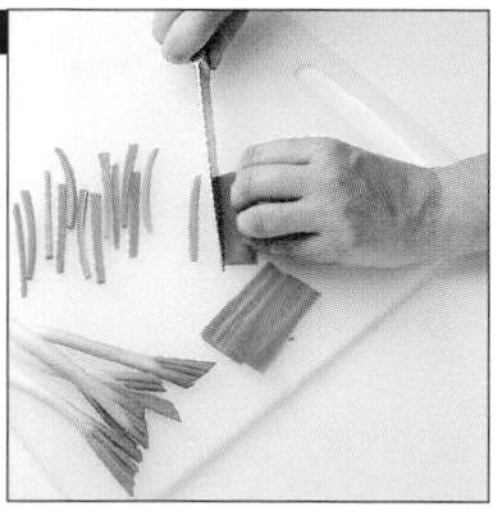

1 Rinse the fish and pat them dry on kitchen paper (paper towels).

2 Cut a few slashes into the sides of the fish so that they absorb the marinade.

3 Mix together the soy sauce, sake or wine, oil, lemon juice, sugar, ginger and garlic in a large, shallow dish.

4 Place the fish in the marinade and turn them over so that they are well coated on both sides. Leave to stand in the refrigerator for 1–6 hours.

5 Meanwhile, prepare the garnish. Cut the carrot into evenly-sized thin sticks and clean and shred the spring onions (scallions).

6 Barbecue (grill) the fish over hot coals for about 10 minutes, turning once.

7 Scatter the chopped spring onions (scallions) and carrot over the fish and transfer the fish to a serving dish. Serve immediately.

VARIATION

Use sole instead of the plaice (flounders) and scatter over some toasted sesame seeds instead of the carrot and spring onions (scallions), if you prefer.

Herrings with Tarragon

The fish are filled with an orange-flavoured stuffing and are wrapped in kitchen foil before being baked on the barbecue (grill).

NUTRITIONAL INFORMATION

Calories	332	Sugars	4g
Protein	21g	Fat	24g
Carbohydrate	9g	Saturates	6g

15 MINS 35 MINS

SERVES 4

INGREDIENTS

1 orange
4 spring onions (scallions)
50 g/1¾ oz fresh wholemeal breadcrumbs
1 tbsp fresh tarragon, chopped
4 herrings, cleaned and gutted
salt and pepper
green salad, to serve

TO GARNISH

2 oranges
1 tbsp light brown sugar
1 tbsp olive oil
sprigs of fresh tarragon

1 To make the stuffing, grate the rind from half of the orange, using a zester.

2 Peel and chop all of the orange flesh on a plate in order to catch all of the juice.

3 Mix together the orange flesh, juice, rind, spring onions (scallions), breadcrumbs and tarragon in a bowl. Season with salt and pepper to taste.

4 Divide the stuffing into 4 equal portions and use it to fill the body cavities of the fish.

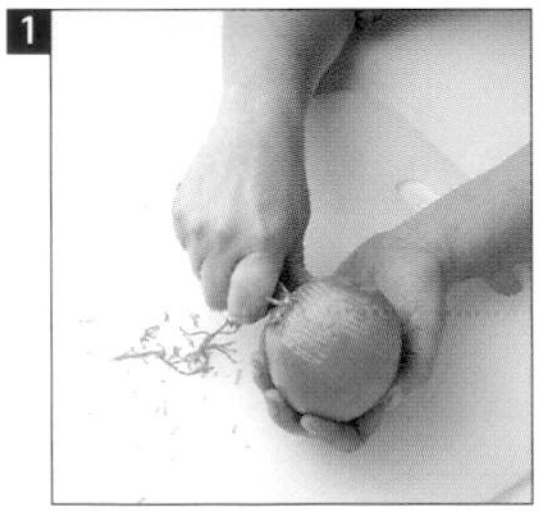

5 Place each fish on to a square of lightly greased kitchen foil and wrap the foil around the fish so that it is completely enclosed. Barbecue (grill) over hot coals for 20–30 minutes until the fish are cooked through – the flesh should be white and firm to the touch.

6 Meanwhile make the garnish. Peel and thickly slice the 2 oranges and sprinkle over the sugar.

7 Just before the fish is cooked, drizzle a little oil over the orange slices and place them on the barbecue for about 5 minutes to heat through.

8 Transfer the fish to serving plates and garnish with the barbecued (grilled) orange slices and sprigs of fresh tarragon.

9 Serve the fish with a fresh green salad.

Steamed Stuffed Snapper

Red mullet may be used instead of the snapper, although they are a little more difficult to stuff because of their size. Use one mullet per person.

NUTRITIONAL INFORMATION

Calories	406	Sugar	4g
Protein	68g	Fat	9g
Carbohydrate	9g	Saturates	0g

20 MINS   10 MINS

SERVES 4

INGREDIENTS

- 1.4 kg/3 lb whole snapper, cleaned and scaled
- 175 g/6 oz spinach
- orange slices and shredded spring onion (scallion), to garnish

STUFFING

- 60 g/2 oz/2 cups cooked long-grain rice
- 1 tsp grated fresh root ginger
- 2 spring onions (scallions), finely chopped
- 2 tsp light soy sauce
- 1 tsp sesame oil
- ½ tsp ground star anise
- 1 orange, segmented and chopped

1 Rinse the fish inside and out under cold running water and pat dry with kitchen paper (paper towels).

2 Blanch the spinach for 40 seconds, rinse in cold water and drain well, pressing out as much moisture as possible.

3 Arrange the spinach on a heatproof plate and place the fish on top.

4 To make the stuffing, mix together the cooked rice, grated ginger, spring onions (scallions), soy sauce, sesame oil, star anise and orange in a bowl.

5 Spoon the stuffing into the body cavity of the fish, pressing it in well with a spoon.

6 Cover the plate and cook in a steamer for 10 minutes, or until the fish is cooked through.

7 Transfer the fish to a warmed serving dish, garnish with orange slices and shredded spring onion (scallion) and serve.

COOK'S TIP

The name snapper covers a family of tropical and subtropical fish that vary in colour. They may be red, orange, pink, grey or blue-green. Some are striped or spotted and they range in size from about 15 cm/6 inches to 90 cm/3 ft.

Crab-Stuffed Red Snapper

This popular fish is pinkish-red in colour and has moist, tender flesh. For this recipe it is steamed, but it can also be baked or braised.

NUTRITIONAL INFORMATION

Calories	205	Sugars	0.1g
Protein	36g	Fat	6g
Carbohydrate	0.1g	Saturates	1g

10 MINS 25 MINS

SERVES 4

INGREDIENTS

4 red snappers, cleaned and scaled, about 175 g/6 oz each

2 tbsp dry sherry

salt and pepper

wedges of lime, to garnish

red chilli strips, to garnish

stir-fried shredded vegetables, to serve

STUFFING

1 small red chilli

1 garlic clove

1 spring onion (scallion)

½ tsp finely grated lime rind

1 tbsp lime juice

100 g/3½ oz white crab meat, flaked

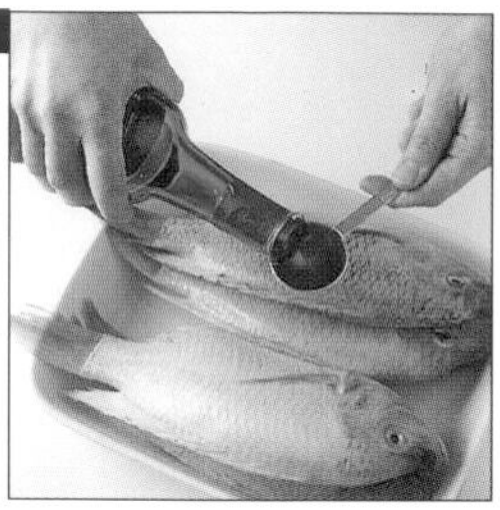
1

3

5

1 Rinse the fish and pat dry on kitchen paper (paper towels). Season inside and out and place in a shallow dish. Spoon over the sherry and set aside.

2 Meanwhile, make the stuffing. Carefully halve, deseed and finely chop the chilli. Place in a small bowl.

3 Peel and finely chop the garlic. Trim and finely chop the spring onion (scallion). Add to the chilli together with the grated lime rind, lime juice and the flaked crab meat.

4 Season with salt and pepper to taste and combine.

5 Spoon some of the stuffing into the cavity of each fish.

6 Bring a large saucepan of water to the boil. Arrange the fish in a steamer lined with baking parchment or in a large sieve (strainer) and place over the boiling water.

7 Cover and steam for 10 minutes. Turn the fish over and steam for a further 10 minutes or until the fish is cooked through.

8 Drain the fish and transfer to serving plates.

9 Garnish with wedges of lime and strips of chili, and serve the fish on a bed of stir-fried vegetables.

Pan-Seared Halibut

Liven up firm steaks of white fish with a spicy, colourful relish. Use red onions for a slightly sweeter flavour.

NUTRITIONAL INFORMATION

Calories	197	Sugars	1g
Protein	31g	Fat	7g
Carbohydrate	2g	Saturates	1g

55 MINS 30 MINS

SERVES 4

INGREDIENTS

- 1 tsp olive oil
- 4 halibut steaks, skinned, 175 g/6 oz each
- ½ tsp cornflour (cornstarch) mixed with 2 tsp cold water
- salt and pepper
- 2 tbsp fresh chives, snipped, to garnish

RED ONION RELISH

- 2 tsp olive oil
- 2 medium red onions
- 6 shallots
- 1 tbsp lemon juice
- 2 tbsp red wine vinegar
- 2 tsp caster (superfine) sugar
- 150 ml/5 fl oz/⅔ cup Fresh Fish Stock (see page 15)

1 To make the relish, peel and thinly shred the onions and shallots. Place in a small bowl and toss in the lemon juice.

2 Heat the oil in a pan and fry the onions and shallots for 3–4 minutes until just softened.

3 Add the vinegar and sugar and continue to cook for a further 2 minutes over a high heat. Pour in the stock and season well. Bring to the boil and simmer gently for a further 8–9 minutes until the sauce has thickened and is slightly reduced.

4 Brush a non-stick, ridged frying pan (skillet) with oil and heat until hot. Press the fish steaks into the pan to seal, lower the heat and cook for 4 minutes. Turn the fish over and cook for 4–5 minutes until cooked through. Drain on kitchen paper (paper towels) and keep warm.

5 Stir the cornflour (cornstarch) paste into the onion sauce and heat through, stirring, until thickened. Season to taste.

6 Pile the relish on to 4 warm serving plates and place a halibut steak on top of each. Garnish with chives.

1

3

4

COOK'S TIP

If raw onions make your eyes water, try peeling them under cold, running water. Alternatively, stand or sit well back from the onion so that your face isn't directly over it.

Sole Paupiettes

A delicate dish of sole fillets rolled up with spinach and prawns, (shrimp), and served in a creamy ginger sauce.

NUTRITIONAL INFORMATION			
Calories	253	Sugars	7g
Protein	24g	Fat	14g
Carbohydrate	9g	Saturates	5g

10 MINS

45 MINS

SERVES 4

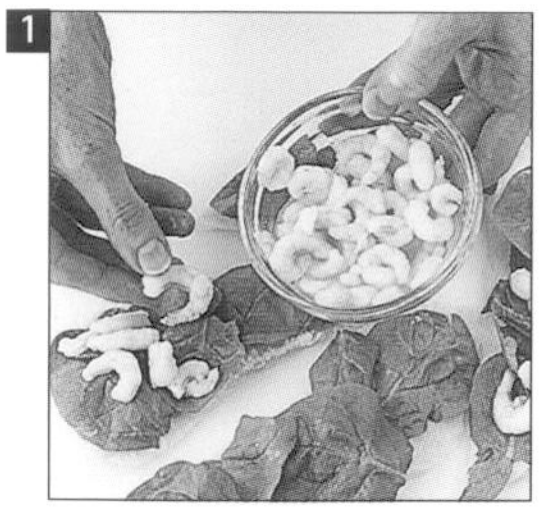

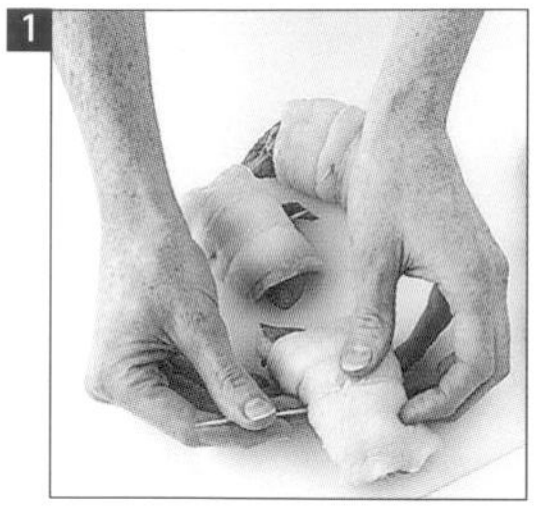

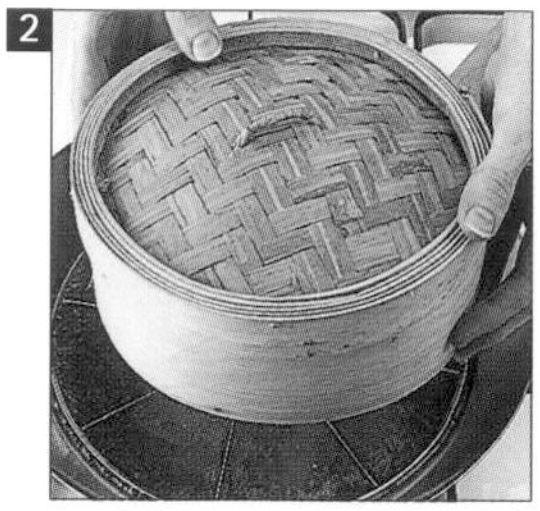

INGREDIENTS

- 125 g/4½ oz fresh young spinach leaves
- 2 Dover soles or large lemon soles or plaice, filleted
- 125 g/4½ oz peeled prawns (shrimp), defrosted if frozen
- 2 tsp sunflower oil
- 2-4 spring onions (scallions), finely sliced diagonally
- 2 thin slices ginger root, finely chopped
- 150 ml/¼ pint/⅔ cup fish stock or water
- 2 tsp cornflour (cornstarch)
- 4 tbsp single cream
- 6 tbsp low-fat natural yogurt
- salt and pepper
- whole prawns (shrimp), to garnish (optional)

1 Strip the stalks off the spinach, wash and dry on kitchen paper (paper towels). Divide the spinach between the seasoned fish fillets, laying the leaves on the skin side. Divide half the prawns (shrimp) between them. Roll up the fillets from head to tail and secure with wooden cocktail sticks. Arrange the rolls on a plate in the base of a bamboo steamer.

2 Stand a low metal trivet in the wok and add enough water to come almost to the top of it. Bring to the boil. Place the bamboo steamer on the trivet, cover with the steamer lid and then the wok lid, or cover tightly with a domed piece of foil. Steam gently for 30 minutes until the fish is tender and cooked through.

3 Remove the fish rolls and keep warm. Empty the wok and wipe dry with kitchen paper (paper towels). Heat the oil in the wok, swirling it around until really hot. Add the spring onions (scallions) and ginger and stir-fry for 1-2 minutes.

4 Add the stock to the wok and bring to the boil. Blend the cornflour (cornstarch) with the cream. Add the yogurt and remaining prawns (shrimp) to the wok and heat gently until boiling. Add a little sauce to the blended cream and return it all to the wok. Heat gently until thickened and season to taste. Serve the paupiettes with the sauce spooned over and garnished with whole prawns (shrimp), if using.

Smoky Fish Pie

This flavoursome and colourful fish pie is perfect for a light supper. The addition of smoked salmon gives it a touch of luxury.

NUTRITIONAL INFORMATION

Calories	523	Sugars	15g
Protein	58g	Fat	6g
Carbohydrate	63g	Saturates	2g

15 MINS — 1 HOUR

SERVES 4

INGREDIENTS

- 900 g/2 lb smoked haddock or cod fillets
- 600 ml/1 pint/2½ cups skimmed milk
- 2 bay leaves
- 115 g/4 oz button mushrooms, quartered
- 115 g/4 oz frozen peas
- 115 g/4 oz frozen sweetcorn kernels
- 675 g/1½ lb potatoes, diced
- 5 tbsp low-fat natural (unsweetened) yogurt
- 4 tbsp chopped fresh parsley
- 60 g/2 oz smoked salmon, sliced into thin strips
- 3 tbsp cornflour (cornstarch)
- 25 g/1 oz smoked cheese, grated
- salt and pepper

1 Preheat the oven to 200°C/400°F/Gas Mark 6. Place the fish in a pan and add the milk and bay leaves. Bring to the boil, cover and then simmer for 5 minutes.

2 Add the mushrooms, peas and sweetcorn, bring back to a simmer, cover and cook for 5–7 minutes. Leave to cool.

3 Place the potatoes in a saucepan, cover with water, boil and cook for 8 minutes. Drain well and mash with a fork or a potato masher. Stir in the yogurt, parsley and seasoning. Set aside.

4 Using a slotted spoon, remove the fish from the pan. Flake the cooked fish away from the skin and place in an ovenproof gratin dish. Reserve the cooking liquid.

5 Drain the vegetables, reserving the cooking liquid, and gently stir into the fish with the salmon strips.

6 Blend a little cooking liquid into the cornflour (cornstarch) to make a paste. Transfer the rest of the liquid to a saucepan and add the paste. Heat through, stirring, until thickened. Discard the bay leaves and season to taste. Pour the sauce over the fish and vegetables and mix. Spoon over the mashed potato so that the fish is covered, sprinkle with cheese and bake for 25–30 minutes.

1

3

6

COOK'S TIP

If possible, use smoked haddock or cod that has not been dyed bright yellow or artificially flavoured to give the illusion of having been smoked.

Seafood Pizza

Make a change from the standard pizza toppings – this dish is piled high with seafood baked with a red (bell) pepper and tomato sauce.

NUTRITIONAL INFORMATION

Calories 248	Sugars 7g
Protein 27g	Fat 6g
Carbohydrate ...22g	Saturates 2g

25 MINS 55 MINS

SERVES 4

INGREDIENTS

- 145 g/5 oz standard pizza base mix
- 4 tbsp chopped fresh dill or 2 tbsp dried dill
- fresh dill, to garnish

SAUCE

- 1 large red (bell) pepper
- 400 g/14 oz can chopped tomatoes with onion and herbs
- 3 tbsp tomato purée (paste)
- salt and pepper

TOPPING

- 350 g/12 oz assorted cooked seafood, thawed if frozen
- 1 tbsp capers in brine, drained
- 25 g/1 oz pitted black olives in brine, drained
- 25 g/1 oz low-fat Mozzarella cheese, grated
- 1 tbsp grated, fresh Parmesan cheese

2

3

5

1 Preheat the oven to 200°C/400°F/Gas Mark 6. Place the pizza base mix in a bowl and stir in the dill. Make the dough according to the instructions on the packet.

2 Press the dough into a round measuring 25.5 cm/10 inches across on a baking sheet lined with baking parchment. Set aside to prove (rise).

3 Preheat the grill (broiler) to hot. To make the sauce, halve and deseed the (bell) pepper and arrange on a grill (broiler) rack. Cook for 8–10 minutes until softened and charred. Leave to cool slightly, peel off the skin and chop the flesh.

4 Place the tomatoes and (bell) pepper in a saucepan. Bring to the boil and simmer for 10 minutes. Stir in the tomato purée (paste) and season to taste.

5 Spread the sauce over the pizza base and top with the seafood. Sprinkle over the capers and olives, top with the cheeses and bake for 25–30 minutes.

6 Garnish with sprigs of dill and serve hot.

Green Fish Curry

This dish has a wonderful fresh, hot, exotic taste resulting from the generous amount of fresh herbs, sharp fresh chillies and coconut milk.

NUTRITIONAL INFORMATION

Calories	223	Sugars	2g
Protein	44g	Fat	5g
Carbohydrate	2g	Saturates	1g

5 MINS — 20 MINS

SERVES 4

INGREDIENTS

1 tbsp oil
2 spring onions (scallions), sliced
1 tsp cumin seeds, ground
2 fresh green chillies, chopped
1 tsp coriander seeds, ground
4 tbsp chopped fresh coriander (cilantro)
4 tbsp chopped fresh mint
1 tbsp chopped chives
150 ml/¼ pint/⅔ cup coconut milk
4 white fish fillets, about 225 g/8 oz each
salt and pepper
basmati rice, to serve
1 mint sprig, to garnish

1 Heat the oil in a large frying pan (skillet) or shallow saucepan and add the spring onions (scallions).

2 Stir-fry the spring onions (scallions) over a medium heat until they are softened but not coloured.

3 Stir in the cumin, chillies and ground coriander, and cook until fragrant.

4 Add the fresh coriander (cilantro), mint, chives and coconut milk and season liberally.

5 Carefully place the fish in the pan and poach for 10–15 minutes until the flesh flakes when tested with a fork.

6 Serve the fish fillets in the sauce with the rice. Garnish with a mint sprig.

COOK'S TIP

Never overcook fish – it is surprising how little time it takes compared to meat. It will continue to cook slightly while keeping warm in the oven and while being dished up and brought to the table.

3

4

5

Vegetables & Salads

There is more to the vegetarian diet than lentil roast and nut cutlets. For those of you who have cut out meat and fish completely from your diet or if you just want to reduce your intake of these ingredients, this chapter offers an exciting assortment of vegetarian dishes, ranging from pizzas to curries and bakes. The advantage of vegetable dishes is that very often the ingredients can be varied according to personal preference or seasonal availability, but always remember to buy the freshest vegetables available to ensure maximum flavour.

Stuffed Tomatoes

These barbecued (grilled) tomato cups are filled with a delicious Greek-style combination of herbs, nuts and raisins.

NUTRITIONAL INFORMATION

Calories	156	Sugars	10g
Protein	3g	Fat	7g
Carbohydrate	22g	Saturates	0.7g

25 MINS 10 MINS

SERVES 4

INGREDIENTS

- 4 beefsteak tomatoes
- 300 g/10½ oz/4½ cups cooked rice
- 8 spring onions (scallions), chopped
- 3 tbsp chopped, fresh mint
- 2 tbsp chopped, fresh parsley
- 3 tbsp pine nuts
- 3 tbsp raisins
- 2 tsp olive oil
- salt and pepper

1 Cut the tomatoes in half, then scoop out the seeds and discard.

2 Stand the tomatoes upside down on absorbent kitchen paper (paper towels) for a few moments in order for the juices to drain out.

3 Turn the tomatoes the right way up and sprinkle the insides with salt and pepper.

4 Mix together the rice, spring onions (scallions), mint, parsley, pine nuts and raisins.

5 Spoon the mixture into the tomato cups.

1

5

6

6 Drizzle over a little olive oil, then barbecue (grill) the tomatoes on an oiled rack over medium hot coals for about 10 minutes until they are tender and cooked through.

7 Transfer the tomatoes to serving plates and serve immediately while still hot.

COOK'S TIP

Tomatoes are a popular barbecue (grill) vegetable. Try grilling (broiling) slices of beefsteak tomato and slices of onion, brushed with a little oil and topped with sprigs of fresh herbs. Or thread cherry tomatoes on to skewers and barbecue (grill) for 5–10 minutes.

Risotto Verde

Risotto is an Italian dish which is easy to make and uses arborio rice, onion and garlic as a base for a range of savoury recipes.

NUTRITIONAL INFORMATION

Calories	374	Sugars	5g
Protein	10g	Fat	9g
Carbohydrate	55g	Saturates	2g

5 MINS   45 MINS

SERVES 4

INGREDIENTS

- 1.75 litres/3 pints/7½ cups vegetable stock
- 2 tbsp olive oil
- 2 garlic cloves, crushed
- 2 leeks, shredded
- 225 g/8 oz/1¼ cups arborio rice
- 300 ml/½ pint/1¼ cups dry white wine
- 4 tbsp chopped mixed herbs
- 225 g/8 oz baby spinach
- 3 tbsp low-fat natural (unsweetened) yogurt
- salt and pepper
- shredded leek, to garnish

1 Pour the stock into a large saucepan and bring to the boil. Reduce the heat to a simmer.

2 Meanwhile, heat the oil in a separate pan and sauté the garlic and leeks for 2–3 minutes until softened.

3 Stir in the rice and cook for 2 minutes, stirring until well coated.

4 Pour in half of the wine and a little of the hot stock. Cook over a gentle heat until all of the liquid has been absorbed.

5 Add the remaining stock and wine and cook over a low heat for 25 minutes or until the rice is creamy.

6 Stir in the chopped mixed herbs and baby spinach, season well with salt and pepper and cook for 2 minutes.

7 Stir in the natural (unsweetened) yogurt, garnish with the shredded leek and serve immediately.

3

4

6

COOK'S TIP

Do not hurry the process of cooking the risotto as the rice must absorb the liquid slowly in order for it to reach the correct consistency.

Fragrant Asparagus Risotto

Soft, creamy rice combines with the flavours of citrus and light aniseed to make this a delicious supper for four or a substantial starter for six.

NUTRITIONAL INFORMATION

Calories	223	Sugars	9g
Protein	6g	Fat	6g
Carbohydrate	40g	Saturates	1g

10 MINS 45 MINS

SERVES 4

INGREDIENTS

- 115 g/4 oz fine asparagus spears, trimmed
- 1.2 litres/2 pints/5 cups vegetable stock
- 2 bulbs fennel
- 25 g/1 oz low-fat spread
- 1 tsp olive oil
- 2 sticks celery, trimmed and chopped
- 2 medium leeks, trimmed and shredded
- 350 g/12 oz/2 cups arborio rice
- 3 medium oranges
- salt and pepper

1 Bring a small saucepan of water to the boil and cook the asparagus for 1 minute. Drain the asparagus and set aside until required.

2 Pour the stock into a saucepan and bring to the boil. Reduce the heat to maintain a gentle simmer.

3 Meanwhile, trim the fennel, reserving the fronds. Use a sharp knife to cut into thin slices.

4 Carefully melt the low-fat spread with the oil in a large saucepan, taking care that the water in the low-fat spread does not evaporate, and gently fry the fennel, celery and leeks for 3–4 minutes until just softened. Add the rice and cook, stirring, for a further 2 minutes until mixed.

4

5

7

5 Add a ladleful of stock to the pan and cook gently, stirring, until absorbed.

6 Continue ladling the stock into the rice until the rice becomes creamy, thick and tender. This process will take about 25 minutes and should not be hurried.

7 Finely grate the rind and extract the juice from 1 orange and mix in to the rice. Carefully remove the peel and pith from the remaining oranges. Holding the fruit over the saucepan, cut out the orange segments and add to the rice, along with any juice that falls.

8 Stir the orange into the rice along with the asparagus spears. Season to taste and garnish with the fennel fronds.

Mexican-Style Pizzas

Ready-made pizza bases are topped with a chilli-flavoured tomato sauce and topped with kidney beans, cheese and jalapeño chillies.

NUTRITIONAL INFORMATION

Calories	350	Sugars	8g
Protein	18g	Fat	10g
Carbohydrate	49g	Saturates	3g

10 MINS 20 MINS

SERVES 4

INGREDIENTS

- 4 x ready-made individual pizza bases
- 1 tbsp olive oil
- 200 g/7 oz can chopped tomatoes with garlic and herbs
- 2 tbsp tomato purée (paste)
- 200 g/7 oz can kidney beans, drained and rinsed
- 115 g/4 oz sweetcorn kernels, thawed if frozen
- 1–2 tsp chilli sauce
- 1 large red onion, shredded
- 100 g/3½ oz reduced-fat mature (sharp) Cheddar cheese, grated
- 1 large green chilli, sliced into rings
- salt and pepper

1 Preheat the oven to 220°C/425°F/Gas Mark 7. Arrange the pizza bases on a baking tray (cookie sheet) and brush them lightly with the oil.

2 In a bowl, mix together the chopped tomatoes, tomato purée (paste), kidney beans and sweetcorn, and add chilli sauce to taste. Season with salt and pepper.

3 Spread the tomato and kidney bean mixture evenly over each pizza base to cover.

4 Top each pizza with shredded onion and sprinkle with some grated cheese and a few slices of green chilli to taste.

5 Bake in the oven for about 20 minutes until the vegetables are tender, the cheese has melted and the base is crisp and golden.

6 Remove the pizzas from the baking tray (cookie sheet) and transfer to serving plates. Serve immediately.

1

3

4

COOK'S TIP

Serve a Mexican-style salad with this pizza. Arrange sliced tomatoes, fresh coriander (cilantro) leaves and a few slices of a small, ripe avocado on a platter. Sprinkle with fresh lime juice and coarse sea salt.

Potato & Tomato Calzone

These pizza dough Italian pasties are best served hot with a salad for a delicious lunch or supper dish.

NUTRITIONAL INFORMATION

Calories	524	Sugars	8g
Protein	17g	Fat	8g
Carbohydrate	103g	Saturates	2g

1½ HOURS — 35 MINS

SERVES 4

INGREDIENTS

DOUGH

- 450 g/1 lb/4 cups white bread flour
- 1 tsp easy blend dried yeast
- 300 ml/½ pint/1¼ cups vegetable stock
- 1 tbsp clear honey
- 1 tsp caraway seeds
- simmed milk, for glazing

FILLING

- 1 tbsp vegetable oil
- 225 g/8 oz waxy potatoes, diced
- 1 onion, halved and sliced
- 2 garlic cloves, crushed
- 40 g/1½ oz sun-dried tomatoes
- 2 tbsp chopped fresh basil
- 2 tbsp tomato purée (paste)
- 2 celery sticks, sliced
- 50 g/1¾ oz Mozzarella cheese, grated

1 To make the dough, sift the flour into a large mixing bowl and stir in the yeast. Make a well in the centre of the mixture. Stir in the vegetable stock, honey and caraway seeds and bring the mixture together to form a dough.

2 Turn the dough out on to a lightly floured surface and knead for 8 minutes until smooth. Place the dough in a lightly oiled mixing bowl, cover and leave to rise in a warm place for 1 hour or until it has doubled in size.

3 Meanwhile, make the filling. Heat the oil in a frying pan (skillet) and add all the remaining ingredients except for the cheese. Cook for about 5 minutes, stirring.

4 Divide the risen dough into 4 pieces. On a lightly floured surface, roll them out to form four 18 cm/7 inch circles. Spoon equal amounts of the filling on to one half of each circle. Sprinkle the cheese over the filling. Brush the edge of the dough with milk and fold the dough over to form 4 semi-circles, pressing to seal the edges.

5 Place on a non-stick baking tray (cookie sheet) and brush with milk. Cook in a preheated oven, 220°C/425°F/Gas Mark 7, for 30 minutes until golden and risen.

1

3

4

Potato Hash

This is a variation of the American dish, beef hash, which was made with salt beef and leftovers, and served to seagoing New Englanders.

NUTRITIONAL INFORMATION

Calories 302	Sugars 5g
Protein 15g	Fat 10g
Carbohydrate . . .40g	Saturates 4g

5 MINS 30 MINS

SERVES 4

INGREDIENTS

- 25 g/1 oz/2 tbsp butter
- 1 red onion, halved and sliced
- 1 carrot, diced
- 25 g/1 oz French (green) beans, halved
- 3 large waxy potatoes, diced
- 2 tbsp plain (all purpose) flour
- 600 ml/1 pint/1¼ cups vegetable stock
- 225 g/8 oz tofu (bean curd), diced
- salt and pepper
- chopped fresh parsley, to garnish

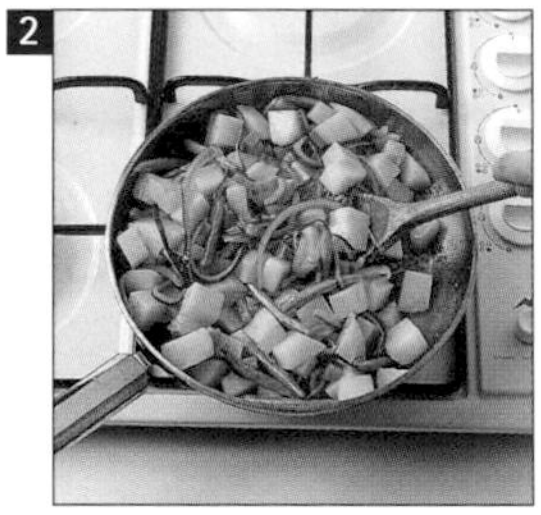

1 Melt the butter in a frying pan (skillet).

2 Add the onion, carrot, French (green) beans and potatoes and fry gently, stirring, for 5-7 minutes or until the vegetables begin to brown.

3 Add the flour to the frying pan (skillet) and cook for 1 minute, stirring constantly.

4 Gradually pour in the stock.

5 Reduce the heat and leave the mixture to simmer for 15 minutes or until the potatoes are tender.

6 Add the diced tofu (bean curd) to the mixture and cook for a further 5 minutes.

7 Season to taste with salt and pepper.

8 Sprinkle the chopped parsley over the top of the potato hash to garnish, then serve hot from the pan (skillet).

COOK'S TIP

Hash is an American term meaning to chop food into small pieces. Therefore a traditional hash dish is made from chopped fresh ingredients, such as roast beef or corned beef, (bell) peppers, onion and celery, often served with gravy.

Chinese Vegetable Pancakes

Chinese pancakes are made with hardly any fat – they are simply flattened white flour dough.

NUTRITIONAL INFORMATION

Calories 312	Sugars 5g
Protein 13g	Fat 19g
Carbohydrate . . .25g	Saturates 7g

5 MINS

10 MINS

SERVES 4

INGREDIENTS

- 1 tbsp vegetable oil
- 1 garlic clove, crushed
- 2.5 cm/1 inch piece root (fresh) ginger, grated
- 1 bunch spring onions (scallions), trimmed and shredded lengthwise
- 100 g/3½ oz mangetout (snow peas), topped, tailed and shredded
- 225 g/8 oz tofu (bean curd), drained and cut into 1 cm/½ inch pieces
- 2 tbsp dark soy sauce, plus extra to serve
- 2 tbsp hoisin sauce, plus extra to serve
- 60 g/2 oz canned bamboo shoots, drained
- 60 g/2 oz canned water chestnuts, drained and sliced
- 100 g/3½ oz bean sprouts
- 1 small red chilli, deseeded and sliced thinly
- 1 small bunch fresh chives
- 12 soft Chinese pancakes

TO SERVE

- shredded Chinese leaves (cabbage)
- 1 cucumber, sliced
- strips of red chilli

1 Heat the oil in a non-stick wok or a large frying pan (skillet) and stir-fry the garlic and ginger for 1 minute.

2 Add the spring onions (scallions), mangetout (snow peas), tofu (bean curd), soy and hoisin sauces. Stir-fry for 2 minutes.

3 Add the bamboo shoots, water chestnuts, bean sprouts and sliced red chilli to the pan.

4 Stir-fry gently for a further 2 minutes until the vegetables are just tender.

5 Snip the chives into 2.5 cm/1 inch lengths and stir into the mixture.

6 Heat the pancakes according to the packet instructions and keep warm.

7 Divide the vegetables and tofu (bean curd) among the pancakes. Roll up and serve with the Chinese leaves (cabbage), cucumber, chilli and extra sauce for dipping.

Oriental Vegetable Noodles

This dish has a mild, nutty flavour from the peanut butter and dry-roasted peanuts.

NUTRITIONAL INFORMATION

Calories	193	Sugars	5g
Protein	7g	Fat	12g
Carbohydrate	14g	Saturates	2g

10 MINS 15 MINS

SERVES 4

INGREDIENTS

- 175 g/6 oz/1½ cups green thread noodles or multi-coloured spaghetti
- 1 tsp sesame oil
- 2 tbsp crunchy peanut butter
- 2 tbsp light soy sauce
- 1 tbsp white wine vinegar
- 1 tsp clear honey
- 125 g/4½ oz daikon (mooli), grated
- 125 g/4½ oz/1 large carrot, grated
- 125 g/4½ oz cucumber, shredded finely
- 1 bunch spring onions (scallions), shredded finely
- 1 tbsp dry-roasted peanuts, crushed

TO GARNISH

- carrot flowers
- spring onion (scallion) tassels

1

2

3

1 Bring a large saucepan of water to the boil, add the noodles or spaghetti and cook according to the packet instructions. Drain well and rinse in cold water. Leave in a bowl of cold water until required.

2 To make the peanut butter sauce, put the sesame oil, peanut butter, soy sauce, vinegar, honey and seasoning into a small screw-top jar. Seal and shake well to mix thoroughly.

3 Drain the noodles or spaghetti well, place in a large serving bowl and mix in half the peanut sauce.

4 Using 2 forks, toss in the daikon (mooli), carrot, cucumber and spring onions (scallions). Sprinkle with crushed peanuts and garnish with carrot flowers and spring onion (scallion) tassels. Serve the noodles with the remaining peanut sauce.

COOK'S TIP

There are many varieties of oriental noodles available from oriental markets, delicatessens and supermarkets. Try rice noodles, which contain very little fat and require little cooking; usually soaking in boiling water is sufficient.

Biryani with Onions

An assortment of vegetables cooked with tender rice, is flavoured and coloured with bright yellow turmeric and other warming Indian spices.

NUTRITIONAL INFORMATION

Calories 223	Sugars 18g
Protein 8g	Fat 4g
Carbohydrate ...42g	Saturates 1g

1¼ HOURS 25 MINS

SERVES 4

INGREDIENTS

- 175 g/6 oz/1 cup Basmati rice, rinsed
- 60 g/2 oz/⅓ cup red lentils, rinsed
- 1 bay leaf
- 6 cardamom pods, split
- 1 tsp ground turmeric
- 6 cloves
- 1 tsp cumin seeds
- 1 cinnamon stick, broken
- 1 onion, chopped
- 225 g/8 oz cauliflower, broken into small florets
- 1 large carrot, diced
- 100 g/3½ oz frozen peas
- 60 g/2 oz sultanas (golden raisins)
- 600 ml/1 pint/2½ cups Fresh Vegetable Stock (see page 14)
- salt and pepper
- naan bread, to serve

CARAMELIZED ONIONS

- 2 tsp vegetable oil
- 1 medium red onion, shredded
- 1 medium onion, shredded
- 2 tsp caster (superfine) sugar

1

2

3

1 Place the rice, lentils, bay leaf, spices, onion, cauliflower, carrot, peas and sultanas (golden raisins) in a large saucepan. Season with salt and pepper and mix well.

2 Pour in the stock, bring to the boil, cover and simmer for 15 minutes, stirring occasionally, until the rice is tender. Remove from the heat and leave to stand, covered, for 10 minutes to allow the stock to be absorbed. Discard the bay leaf, cardamom pods, cloves and cinnamon stick.

3 Heat the oil in a frying pan (skillet) and fry the onions over a medium heat for 3–4 minutes until just softened. Add the caster (superfine) sugar, raise the heat and cook, stirring, for a further 2–3 minutes until the onions are golden.

4 Gently mix the rice and vegetables and transfer to warm serving plates. Spoon over the caramelized onions and serve with plain, warmed naan bread.

Balti Dhal

Chang dhal is the husked, split, black chickpea (garbanzo bean), which is yellow on the inside and has a nutty taste.

NUTRITIONAL INFORMATION			
Calories	132	Sugars	2g
Protein	6g	Fat	6g
Carbohydrate	15g	Saturates	1g

5 MINS

1¼ HOURS

SERVES 4

INGREDIENTS

- 225 g/8 oz/1 cup chang dhal or yellow split peas, washed
- ½ tsp ground turmeric
- 1 tsp ground coriander
- 1 tsp salt
- 4 curry leaves
- 2 tbsp oil
- ½ tsp asafoetida powder (optional)
- 1 tsp cumin seeds
- 2 onions, chopped
- 2 garlic cloves, crushed
- 1 cm/½ inch piece ginger root, grated
- ½ tsp garam masala

2

6

7

1 Put the chang dhal in a large saucepan. Pour in enough water to cover by 2.5 cm/1 inch.

2 Bring to the boil and use a spoon to remove the scum that has formed.

3 Add the turmeric, ground coriander, salt and curry leaves. Simmer for 1 hour. The chang dhal should be tender, but not mushy.

4 Heat the oil in a Balti pan or wok, Add the asafoetida (if using) and fry for 30 seconds.

5 Add the cumin seeds and fry until they start popping.

6 Add the onions and stir-fry until golden brown.

7 Add the garlic, ginger, garam masala and chang dhal to the pan or wok and stir-fry for 2 minutes. Serve the balti hot as a side dish with a curry meal or store in the refrigerator for later use.

COOK'S TIP

Dhal keeps well so it is a good idea to make a large amount and store it in the refrigerator or freezer in small portions. Reheat before serving.

Vegetable Curry

Vegetables are cooked in a mildly spiced curry sauce with yogurt and fresh coriander (cilantro) stirred in just before serving.

NUTRITIONAL INFORMATION

Calories	423	Sugars	24g
Protein	16g	Fat	19g
Carbohydrate	50g	Saturates	7g

10 MINS 30 MINS

SERVES 4

INGREDIENTS

- 2 tbsp sunflower oil
- 1 onion, sliced
- 2 tsp cumin seeds
- 2 tbsp ground coriander
- 1 tsp ground turmeric
- 2 tsp ground ginger
- 1 tsp chopped fresh red chilli
- 2 garlic cloves, chopped
- 400 g/14 oz can chopped tomatoes
- 3 tbsp powdered coconut mixed with 300 ml/½ pint/1¼ cups boiling water
- 1 small cauliflower, broken into florets
- 2 courgettes (zucchini), sliced
- 2 carrots, sliced
- 1 potato, diced
- 400 g/14 oz can chickpeas (garbanzo beans), drained and rinsed
- 150 ml/¼ pint/⅔ cup thick yogurt
- 2 tbsp mango chutney
- 3 tbsp chopped fresh coriander (cilantro)
- salt and pepper
- fresh coriander (cilantro) sprigs to garnish

TO SERVE

- onion relish
- banana raita
- basmati rice and naan bread

1

2

3

1 Heat the oil in a saucepan and fry the onion until softened. Add the cumin, ground coriander, turmeric, ginger, chilli and garlic and fry for 1 minute.

2 Add the tomatoes and coconut mixture and mix well.

3 Add the cauliflower, courgettes (zucchini), carrots, potato, chickpeas (garbanzo beans) and seasoning. Cover and simmer for 20 minutes until the vegetables are tender.

4 Stir in the yogurt, mango chutney and fresh coriander (cilantro) and heat through gently, but do not boil.

5 Garnish the curry with coriander (cilantro) sprigs and serve with onion relish, banana raita, basmati rice and naan bread.

Aubergine (Eggplant) Cake

This dish would make a stunning dinner party dish, yet it contains simple ingredients and is easy to make.

NUTRITIONAL INFORMATION

Calories	201	Sugars	4g
Protein	14g	Fat	7g
Carbohydrate	22g	Saturates	4g

55 MINS 35 MINS

SERVES 4

INGREDIENTS

- 1 medium aubergine (eggplant)
- 300 g/10½ oz tricolour pasta shapes
- 125 g/4½ oz low-fat soft cheese with garlic and herbs
- 350ml/12 fl oz/1⅓ cups passata (sieved tomatoes)
- 4 tbsp grated Parmesan cheese
- 1½ tsp dried oregano
- 2 tbsp dry white breadcrumbs
- salt and pepper

1 Preheat the oven to 190°C/375°F/Gas Mark 5. Grease and line a 20.5 cm/ 8 inch round spring-form cake tin (pan).

2 Trim the aubergine (eggplant) and slice lengthwise into slices about 5 mm/¼ inch thick. Place in a bowl, sprinkle with salt, and set aside for 30 minutes to remove any bitter juices. Rinse well under cold running water and drain.

3 Bring a saucepan of water to the boil and blanch the aubergine (eggplant) slices for 1 minute. Drain and pat dry with kitchen paper (paper towels). Set aside.

4 Cook the pasta shapes according to the instructions on the packet; for best results, the pasta should be slightly undercooked. Drain well and return to the saucepan. Add the soft cheese and allow it to melt over the pasta.

5 Stir in the passata (sieved tomatoes), Parmesan cheese, oregano and salt and pepper. Set aside.

6 Arrange the aubergine (eggplant) over the base and sides of the tin, overlapping the slices and making sure there are no gaps.

7 Pile the pasta mixture into the tin (pan), packing down well, and sprinkle with the breadcrumbs. Bake for 20 minutes and leave to stand for 15 minutes.

8 Loosen the cake round the edge with a palette knife (spatula) and release from the tin. Turn out the pasta cake, aubergine (eggplant)-side uppermost, and serve hot.

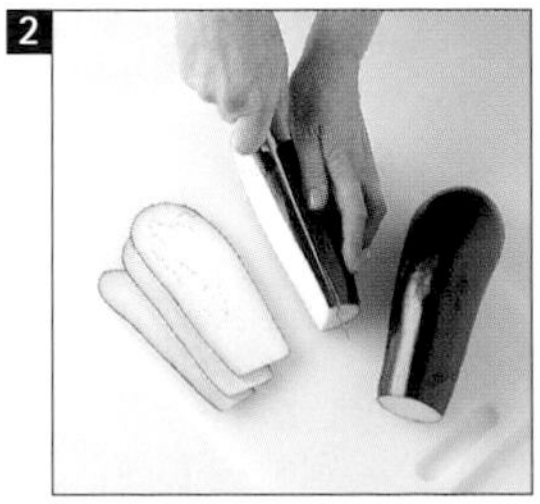

Spicy Mexican Beans

These stewed beans form the basis of many Mexican recipes. Don't add salt until the beans are tender – it prevents them from softening.

NUTRITIONAL INFORMATION

Calories	234	Sugars	6g
Protein	11g	Fat	13g
Carbohydrate	20g	Saturates	2g

12 HOURS 4 HOURS

SERVES 4

INGREDIENTS

225 g/8 oz pinto beans or cannellini beans
1 large onion, sliced
2 garlic cloves, crushed
1 litre /1¾ pints water
salt
chopped fresh coriander (cilantro) or parsley, to garnish

BEAN STEW

1 large onion, sliced
2 garlic cloves, crushed
8 rashers lean streaky bacon, diced
2 tbsp oil
400 g/14 oz can chopped tomatoes
1 tsp ground cumin
1 tbsp sweet chilli sauce

REFRIED BEANS

1 onion, chopped
2 garlic cloves, crushed
2 tbsp oil

1 Soak the beans in a saucepan of cold water overnight. Drain the beans and put into a saucepan with the onion, garlic and water, bring to the boil, cover and simmer gently for 1½ hours. Stir well, add more boiling water if necessary, and simmer, covered, for a further 1–1½ hours, or until the beans are tender.

2 When the beans are tender, add salt to taste (about 1 tsp) and continue to cook, uncovered, for about 15 minutes to allow most of the liquor to evaporate to form a thick sauce. Serve the basic beans hot sprinkled with chopped coriander (cilantro) or parsley; or cool then store in the refrigerator for up to 1 week.

3 To make a bean stew, fry the onion, garlic and bacon for 3–4 minutes in the oil, add the other ingredients and bring to the boil. Cover and simmer very gently for 30 minutes, then season.

4 To make refried beans, fry the onion and garlic in the oil until golden brown. Add a quarter of the basic beans with a little of their liquor and mash. Continue adding and mashing the beans, while simmering gently until thick. Adjust the seasoning and serve hot.

Mixed Bean Stir-Fry

Any type of canned beans can be used – butter beans, black-eyed beans etc – but rinse under cold water and drain well before use.

NUTRITIONAL INFORMATION

Calories	326	Sugars	16g
Protein	18g	Fat	7g
Carbohydrate	51g	Saturates	1g

10 MINS   10 MINS

SERVES 4

INGREDIENTS

- 1 x 400 g/14 oz can red kidney beans
- 1 x 400 g/14 oz can cannellini beans
- 6 spring onions (scallions)
- 1 x 200 g/7 oz can pineapple rings or pieces in natural juice, chopped
- 2 tbsp pineapple juice
- 3-4 pieces stem ginger
- 2 tbsp ginger syrup from the jar
- thinly pared rind of ½ lime or lemon, cut into julienne strips
- 2 tbsp lime or lemon juice
- 2 tbsp soy sauce
- 1 tsp cornflour (cornstarch)
- 1 tbsp sesame oil
- 125 g/4½ oz French beans, cut into 4 cm/ 1½ inch lengths
- 1 x 225 g/8 oz can bamboo shoots
- salt and pepper

COOK'S TIP

Be sure to drain and rinse the beans before using, as they are usually canned in salty water, which will spoil the flavour of the finished dish.

1 Drain all the beans, rinse under cold water and drain again very thoroughly.

2 Cut 4 spring onions (scallions) into narrow slanting slices. Thinly slice the remainder and reserve for garnish.

3 Combine the pineapple and juice, ginger and syrup, lime rind and juice, soy sauce and cornflour (cornstarch) in a bowl.

4 Heat the oil in the wok, swirling it around until really hot. Add the spring onions (scallions) and stir-fry for about a minute, then add the French beans. Drain and thinly slice the bamboo shoots, add to the pan and continue to stir-fry for 2 minutes.

5 Add the pineapple and ginger mixture and bring just to the boil. Add the canned beans and stir until very hot – for about a minute.

6 Season to taste, sprinkled with the reserved chopped spring onions (scallions); or serve as a vegetable accompaniment.

2

3

4

Lemony Spaghetti

Steaming vegetables helps to preserve their nutritional content and allows them to retain their bright, natural colours and crunchy texture.

NUTRITIONAL INFORMATION

Calories	133	Sugars	8g
Protein	8g	Fat	1g
Carbohydrate	25g	Saturates	0.2g

10 MINS

25 MINS

SERVES 4

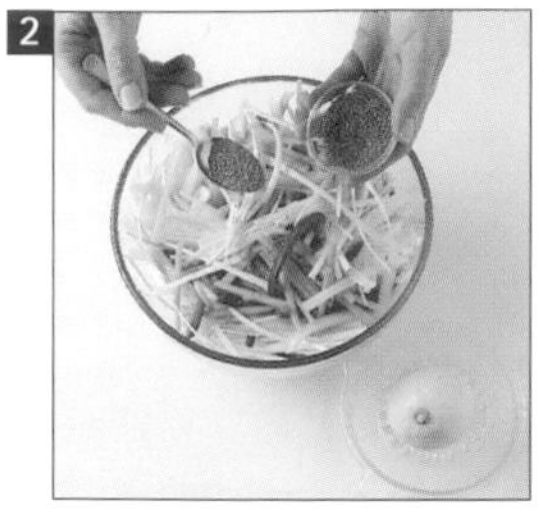

INGREDIENTS

225 g/8 oz celeriac
2 medium carrots
2 medium leeks
1 small red (bell) pepper
1 small yellow (bell) pepper
2 garlic cloves
1 tsp celery seeds
1 tbsp lemon juice
300 g/10½ oz spaghetti
celery leaves, chopped, to garnish

LEMON DRESSING

1 tsp finely grated lemon rind
1 tbsp lemon juice
4 tbsp low-fat natural fromage frais (unsweetened yogurt)
salt and pepper
2 tbsp snipped fresh chives

1 Peel the celeriac and carrots, cut into thin matchsticks and place in a bowl. Trim and slice the leeks, rinse under running water to flush out any trapped dirt, then shred finely. Halve, deseed and slice the (bell) peppers. Peel and thinly slice the garlic.

2 Add all of the vegetables to the bowl with the celeriac and the carrots. Toss the vegetables with the celery seeds and lemon juice.

3 Bring a large saucepan of water to the boil and cook the spaghetti according to the instructions on the packet. Drain and keep warm.

4 Meanwhile, bring another large saucepan of water to the boil, put the vegetables in a steamer or sieve (strainer) and place over the boiling water. Cover and steam for 6–7 minutes or until tender.

5 While the spaghetti and vegetables are cooking, mix the ingredients for the lemon dressing together.

6 Transfer the spaghetti and vegetables to a warm serving bowl and mix with the dressing. Garnish with chopped celery leaves and serve.

Basil & Tomato Pasta

Roasting the tomatoes gives a sweeter and smoother flavour to this sauce. Italian tomatoes, such as plum or flavia, have the best flavour.

NUTRITIONAL INFORMATION

Calories	177	Sugars	4g
Protein	5g	Fat	4g
Carbohydrate	31g	Saturates	1g

10 MINS 35 MINS

SERVES 4

INGREDIENTS

- 1 tbsp olive oil
- 2 sprigs rosemary
- 2 cloves garlic, unpeeled
- 450 g/1 lb tomatoes, halved
- 1 tbsp sun-dried tomato paste
- 12 fresh basil leaves, plus extra to garnish
- salt and pepper
- 675 g/1½ lb fresh farfalle or 350 g/12 oz dried farfalle

1 Place the oil, rosemary, garlic and tomatoes, skin side up, in a shallow roasting tin (pan).

2 Drizzle with a little oil and cook under a preheated grill (broiler) for 20 minutes or until the tomato skins are slightly charred.

3 Peel the skin from the tomatoes. Roughly chop the tomato flesh and place in a pan.

4 Squeeze the pulp from the garlic cloves and mix with the tomato flesh and sun-dried tomato paste.

5 Roughly tear the fresh basil leaves into smaller pieces and then stir them into the sauce. Season with a little salt and pepper to taste.

2

3
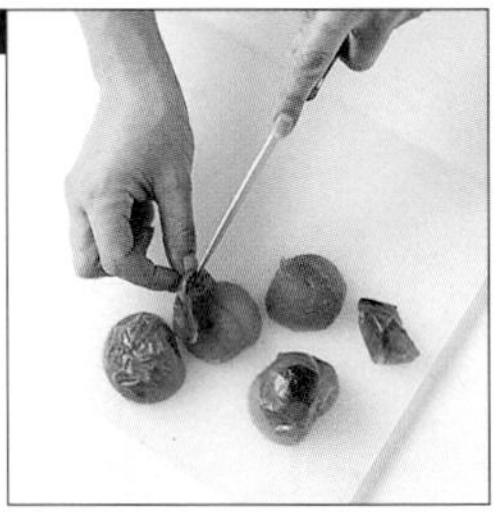

4

6 Cook the farfalle in a saucepan of boiling water according to the instructions on the packet or until it is just cooked through. Drain

7 Gently heat the tomato and basil sauce.

8 Transfer the farfalle to serving plates and garnish with the basil. Serve with the tomato sauce.

COOK'S TIP

This sauce tastes just as good when mixed in with the pasta and served cold as a salad. Sprinkle some chopped parsley on top for added flavour and colour.

Pesto Pasta

Italian pesto is usually laden with fat. This version has just as much flavour but is much healthier.

NUTRITIONAL INFORMATION

Calories	283	Sugars	5g
Protein	14g	Fat	3g
Carbohydrate	37g	Saturates	1g

1 HOUR — 30 MINS

SERVES 4

INGREDIENTS

- 225 g/8 oz chestnut mushrooms, sliced
- 150 ml/5 fl oz/¾ cup fresh vegetable stock
- 175 g/6 oz asparagus, trimmed and cut into 5 cm/2 inch lengths
- 300 g/10½ oz green and white tagliatelle
- 400 g/14 oz canned artichoke hearts, drained and halved
- Grissini (bread sticks), to serve

TO GARNISH

- basil leaves, shredded
- Parmesan shavings

PESTO

- 2 large garlic cloves, crushed
- 15 g/½ oz fresh basil leaves, washed
- 6 tbsp low-fat natural fromage frais (unsweetened yogurt)
- 2 tbsp freshly grated Parmesan cheese
- salt and pepper

1 Place the mushrooms in a saucepan with the stock. Bring to the boil, cover and simmer for 3–4 minutes until just tender. Drain and set aside, reserving the liquor to use in soups if wished.

2 Bring a small saucepan of water to the boil and cook the asparagus for 3–4 minutes until just tender. Drain and set aside until required.

3 Bring a large pan of lightly salted water to the boil and cook the tagliatelle according to the instructions on the packet. Drain, return to the pan and keep warm.

4 Meanwhile, make the pesto. Place all of the ingredients in a blender or food processor and process for a few seconds until smooth. Alternatively, finely chop the basil and mix all the ingredients together.

5 Add the mushrooms, asparagus and artichoke hearts to the pasta and cook, stirring, over a low heat for 2–3 minutes.

6 Remove from the heat and mix with the pesto.

7 Transfer to a warm bowl. Garnish with shredded basil leaves and Parmesan shavings and serve.

Mushroom Cannelloni

Thick pasta tubes are filled with a mixture of seasoned chopped mushrooms, and baked in a rich fragrant tomato sauce.

NUTRITIONAL INFORMATION

Calories	156	Sugar	8g
Protein	6g	Fats	1g
Carbohydrates	21g	Saturates	0.2g

35 MINS — 1½ HOURS

SERVES 4

INGREDIENTS

- 350 g/12 oz chestnut mushrooms
- 1 medium onion, chopped finely
- 1 garlic clove, crushed
- 1 tbsp chopped fresh thyme
- ½ tsp ground nutmeg
- 4 tbsp dry white wine
- 4 tbsp fresh white breadcrumbs
- 12 dried 'quick-cook' cannelloni
- Parmesan shavings, to garnish (optional)

TOMATO SAUCE

- 1 large red (bell) pepper
- 200 ml/7 fl oz/¾ cup dry white wine
- 450 ml/16 fl oz/2 cups passata (sieved tomatoes)
- 2 tbsp tomato purée (paste)
- 2 bay leaves
- 1 tsp caster (superfine) sugar

1 Preheat the oven to 200°C/400°F/Gas Mark 6. Finely chop the mushrooms and place in a pan with the onion and garlic. Stir in the thyme, nutmeg and 4 tbsp wine. Bring to the boil, cover and simmer for 10 minutes.

2 Stir in the breadcrumbs to bind the mixture together and season. Cool for 10 minutes.

3 Preheat the grill (broiler) to hot. To make the sauce, halve and deseed the (bell) pepper, place on the grill (broiler) rack and cook for 8–10 minutes until charred. Leave to cool for 10 minutes.

4 Once the (bell) pepper has cooled, peel off the charred skin. Chop the flesh and place in a food processor with the wine. Blend until smooth, and pour into a pan.

5 Mix the remaining sauce ingredients with the (bell) pepper and wine. Bring to the boil and simmer for 10 minutes. Discard the bay leaves.

6 Cover the base of an ovenproof dish with a thin layer of sauce. Fill the cannelloni with the mushroom mixture and place in the dish. Spoon over the remaining sauce, cover with foil and bake for 35–40 minutes.

1

5

6

COOK'S TIP

For a more filling meal, add some flaked tuna or diced cooked chicken or ham to the stuffing mixture.

Beetroot & Orange Salad

Use freshly cooked beetroot in this unusual combination of colours and flavours, as beetroot soaked in vinegar will spoil the delicate balance.

NUTRITIONAL INFORMATION

Calories 240	Sugars 29g
Protein 10g	Fat 2g
Carbohydrate ...49g	Saturates 0.3g

2¼ HOURS   1 HOUR

SERVES 4

INGREDIENTS

- 225 g/8 oz/1⅓ cups long-grain and wild rices
- 4 large oranges
- 450 g/1 lb cooked beetroot, peeled and drained (if necessary)
- 2 heads of chicory
- salt and pepper
- fresh snipped chives, to garnish

DRESSING

- 4 tbsp low-fat natural fromage frais (unsweetened yogurt)
- 1 garlic clove, crushed
- 1 tbsp wholegrain mustard
- ½ tsp finely grated orange rind
- 2 tsp clear honey

1 Cook the rices according to the packet instructions. Drain and set aside to cool.

2 Meanwhile, slice the top and bottom off each orange. Using a sharp knife, remove the skin and pith. Holding the orange over a bowl to catch the juice, carefully slice between each segment. Place the segments in a separate bowl. Cover the juice and leave to chill.

3 Dice the beetroot into small cubes. Mix with the orange segments, cover and chill.

4 When the rice has cooled, mix in the reserved orange juice until thoroughly incorporated and season with salt and pepper to taste.

5 Line 4 bowls or plates with the chicory leaves. Spoon over the rice and top with the beetroot and orange.

6 Mix all the dressing ingredients together and spoon over the salad, or serve separately in a bowl, if preferred. Garnish with fresh snipped chives.

Mexican Potato Salad

This dish is full of Mexican flavours, where potato slices are topped with tomatoes, chillies and ham, and served with a guacamole dressing.

NUTRITIONAL INFORMATION

Calories	260	Sugars	6g
Protein	6g	Fat	9g
Carbohydrate	41g	Saturates	2g

10 MINS 15 MINS

SERVES 4

INGREDIENTS

- 4 large waxy potatoes, sliced
- 1 ripe avocado
- 1 tsp olive oil
- 1 tsp lemon juice
- 1 garlic clove, crushed
- 1 onion, chopped
- 2 large tomatoes, sliced
- 1 green chilli, chopped
- 1 yellow (bell) pepper, sliced
- 2 tbsp chopped fresh coriander (cilantro)
- salt and pepper
- lemon wedges, to garnish

1 Cook the potato slices in a saucepan of boiling water for 10-15 minutes or until tender. Drain and leave to cool.

2 Meanwhile, cut the avocado in half and remove the stone. Using a spoon, scoop the avocado flesh from the 2 halves and place in a mixing bowl.

3 Mash the avocado flesh with a fork and stir in the olive oil, lemon juice, garlic and chopped onion. Cover the bowl and set aside.

4 Mix the tomatoes, chilli and yellow (bell) pepper together and transfer to a salad bowl with the potato slices.

5 Spoon the avocado mixture on top and sprinkle with the coriander (cilantro). Season to taste and serve garnished with lemon wedges.

COOK'S TIP

Mixing the avocado flesh with lemon juice prevents it from turning brown once exposed to the air.

Grapefruit & Coconut Salad

This salad is deceptively light – although it is, in fact, quite filling. Reserve the grapefruit juices and add to the coconut dressing.

NUTRITIONAL INFORMATION

Calories	201	Sugars	13g
Protein	3g	Fat	15g
Carbohydrate	14g	Saturates	9g

15 MINS 5 MINS

SERVES 4

INGREDIENTS

- 125 g/4½ oz/1 cup grated coconut
- 2 tsp light soy sauce
- 2 tbsp lime juice
- 2 tbsp water
- 2 tsp sunflower oil
- 1 garlic clove, halved
- 1 onion, chopped finely
- 2 large ruby grapefruits, peeled and segmented
- 90 g/3 oz/1½ cups alfalfa sprouts

1 Toast the coconut in a dry frying pan (skillet), stirring constantly, until golden brown, about 3 minutes. Transfer to a bowl.

2 Add the light soy sauce, lime juice and water.

3 Heat the oil in a saucepan and fry the garlic and onion until soft. Remove the garlic. Stir the onion into the coconut mixture.

4 Divide the grapefruit segments between 4 plates.

5 Sprinkle each with a quarter of the alfalfa sprouts and spoon over a quarter of the coconut mixture.

1

2

4
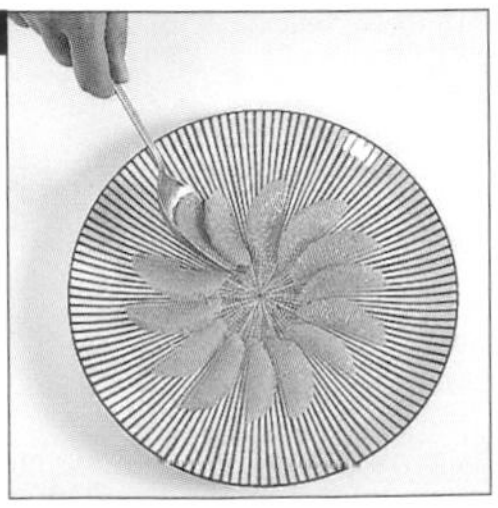

VARIATION

Try replacing the grapefruit with other citrus fruits belonging to the grapefruit family, such as pomelos, ugli fruit and mineolas.

Hot & Spicy Rice Salad

Serve this spicy Indian-style dish with a low-fat natural yogurt salad for a refreshing contrast.

NUTRITIONAL INFORMATION

Calories	329	Sugars	27g
Protein	8g	Fat	8g
Carbohydrate	59g	Saturates	1g

30 MINS 25 MINS

SERVES 4

INGREDIENTS

- 2 tsp vegetable oil
- 1 onion, chopped finely
- 1 fresh red chilli, deseeded and chopped finely
- 8 cardamom pods
- 1 tsp ground turmeric
- 1 tsp garam masala
- 350 g/12 oz/1¾ cups basmati rice, rinsed
- 700 ml/1¼ pints/3 cups boiling water
- 1 orange bell pepper, chopped
- 225 g/8 oz cauliflower florets, divided into small sprigs
- 4 ripe tomatoes, skinned, deseeded, and chopped
- 125 g/4½ oz/¾ cup seedless raisins
- 25 g/1 oz/¼ cup toasted flaked (slivered) almonds
- salt and pepper
- salad of low-fat natural yogurt, onion, cucumber and mint, to serve

1 Heat the oil in a large non-stick saucepan, add the onion, chilli, cardamom pods, turmeric and garam masala and fry gently for 2–3 minutes until the vegetables are just softened.

2 Stir in the rice, boiling water, seasoning, (bell) pepper and cauliflower.

3 Cover with a tight-fitting lid, bring to the boil, then cook over a low heat for 15 minutes without lifting the lid.

4 Uncover, fork through and stir in the tomatoes and raisins.

5 Cover again, turn off the heat and leave for 15 minutes. Discard the cardamom pods.

6 Pile on to a warmed serving platter and sprinkle over the toasted flaked (slivered) almonds.

7 Serve the rice salad with the yogurt salad.

1

2

4

Melon and Mango Salad

A little freshly grated root ginger mixed with creamy yogurt and clear honey makes a perfect dressing for this refreshing salad.

NUTRITIONAL INFORMATION

Calories 189	Sugars 30g
Protein 5g	Fat 7g
Carbohydrate ...30g	Saturates 1g

15 MINS   0 MINS

SERVES 4

INGREDIENTS

- 1 cantaloupe melon
- 60 g/2 oz/½ cup black grapes, halved and pipped
- 60 g/2 oz/½ cup green grapes
- 1 large mango
- 1 bunch of watercress, trimmed
- iceberg lettuce leaves, shredded
- 2 tbsp olive oil
- 1 tbsp cider vinegar
- 1 passion fruit
- salt and pepper

DRESSING

- 150 ml/¼ pint/⅔ cup low-fat thick natural yogurt
- 1 tbsp clear honey
- 1 tsp grated fresh root ginger

2

3

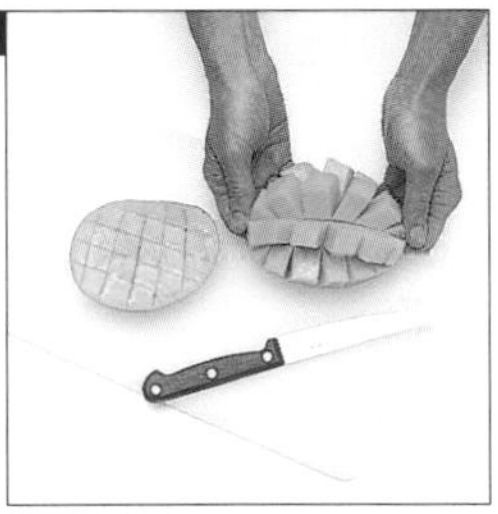

7

1 To make the dressing for the melon, mix together the yogurt, honey and ginger.

2 Halve the melon and scoop out the seeds. Slice, peel and cut into chunks. Mix with the grapes.

3 Slice the mango on each side of its large flat stone (pit). On each mango half, slash the flesh into a criss-cross pattern down to, but not through, the skin. Push the skin from underneath to turn the mango halves inside out. Now remove the flesh and add to the melon mixture.

4 Arrange the watercress and lettuce on 4 serving plates.

5 Make the dressing for the salad leaves (greens) by mixing together the olive oil and cider vinegar with a little salt and pepper. Drizzle over the watercress and lettuce.

6 Divide the melon mixture between the 4 plates and spoon over the yogurt dressing.

7 Scoop the seeds out of the passion fruit and sprinkle them over the salads. Serve immediately or chill in the refrigerator until required.

Cool Cucumber Salad

This cooling salad is another good foil for a highly spiced meal. Omit the green chilli, if preferred.

NUTRITIONAL INFORMATION

Calories	11	Sugars	2g
Protein	0.4g	Fat	0g
Carbohydrate	2g	Saturates	0g

1¼ HOURS — 0 MINS

SERVES 4

INGREDIENTS

- 225 g/8 oz cucumber
- 1 green chilli (optional)
- fresh coriander (cilantro) leaves, finely chopped
- 2 tbsp lemon juice
- ½ tsp salt
- 1 tsp sugar
- fresh mint leaves and red (bell) pepper strips, to garnish

1 Using a sharp knife, slice the cucumber thinly. Arrange the cucumber slices on a round serving plate.

2 Using a sharp knife, chop the green chilli (if using). Scatter the chopped chilli over the cucumber.

3 To make the dressing, mix together the coriander (cilantro), lemon juice, salt and sugar.

4 Place the cucumber in the refrigerator and leave to chill for at least 1 hour, or until required.

5 When ready to serve, transfer the cucumber to a serving dish. Pour the salad dressing over the cucumber just before serving and garnish with mint and red (bell) pepper.

1

2

3

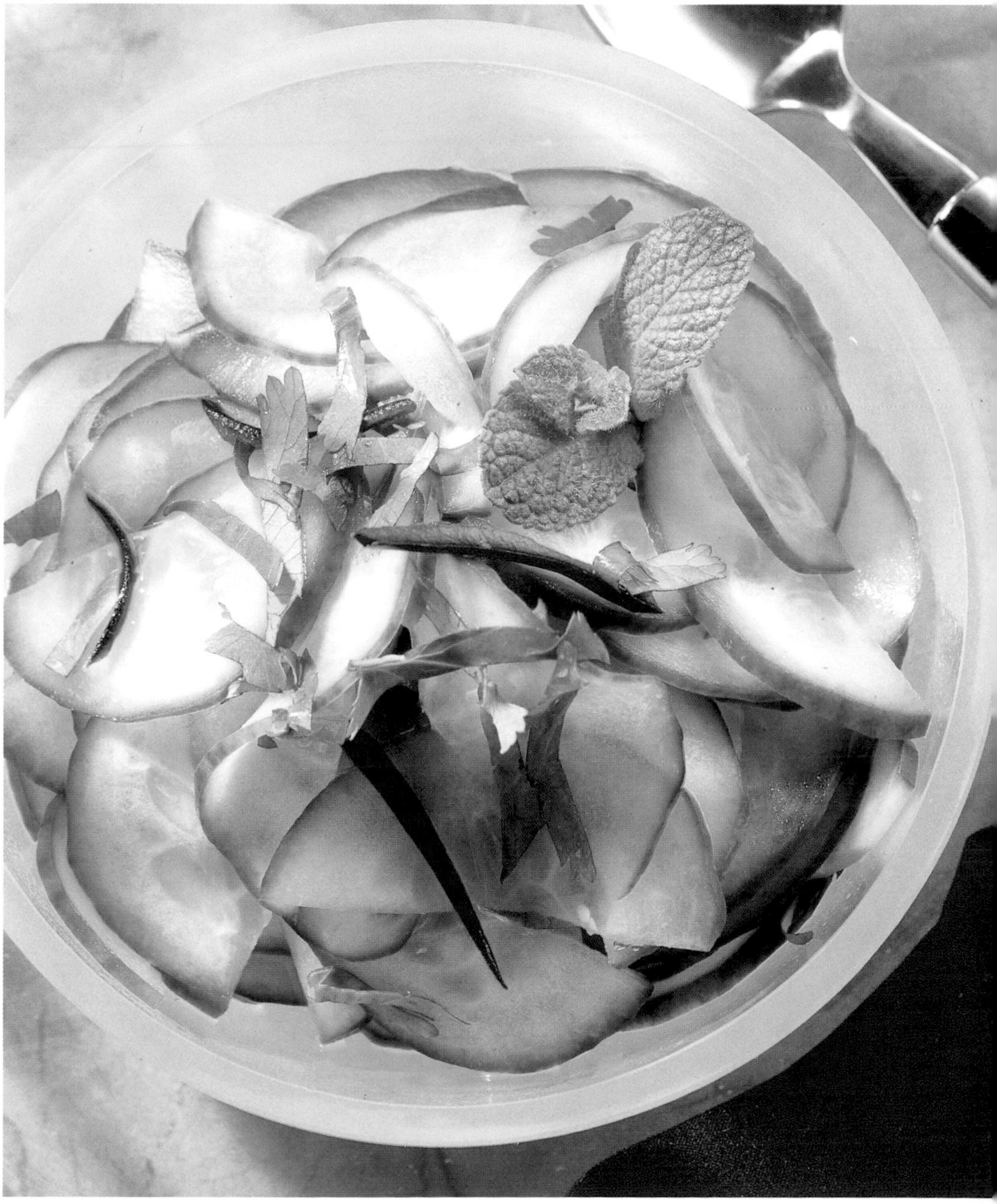

Moroccan Couscous Salad

Couscous is a type of semolina made from durum wheat. It is wonderful in salads as it readily takes up the flavour of the dressing.

NUTRITIONAL INFORMATION

Calories	195	Sugars	15g
Protein	8g	Fat	2g
Carbohydrate	40g	Saturates	0.3g

15 MINS   15 MINS

SERVES 6

INGREDIENTS

- 2 cups couscous
- 1 bunch spring onions (scallions), trimmed and chopped finely
- 1 small green (bell) pepper, cored,deseeded, and chopped
- 10 cm/4 inch piece cucumber, chopped
- 200 g/7 oz can chickpeas (garbanzo beans), rinsed and drained
- ⅔ cup sultanas (golden raisins)
- 2 oranges
- salt and pepper
- lettuce leaves, to serve
- sprigs of fresh mint, to garnish

DRESSING

- finely grated rind of 1 orange
- 1 tbsp chopped fresh mint
- ⅔ cup low-fat natural (unsweetened) yogurt

1 Put the couscous into a bowl and cover with boiling water. Leave it to soak for about 15 minutes to swell the grains, then stir with a fork to separate them.

2 Add the spring onions (scallions), green (bell) pepper, cucumber, chickpeas (garbanzo beans) and sultanas (golden raisins) to the couscous, stirring to combine. Season well with salt and pepper.

3 To make the dressing, mix the orange rind, mint, and yogurt. Pour over the couscous mixture and stir well.

4 Using a sharp serrated knife, remove the peel and pith from the oranges. Cut the flesh into segments, removing all the membrane.

5 Arrange the lettuce leaves on serving plates. Divide the couscous mixture between the plates and arrange the orange segments on top.

6 Garnish with sprigs of fresh mint and serve.

1

2

4

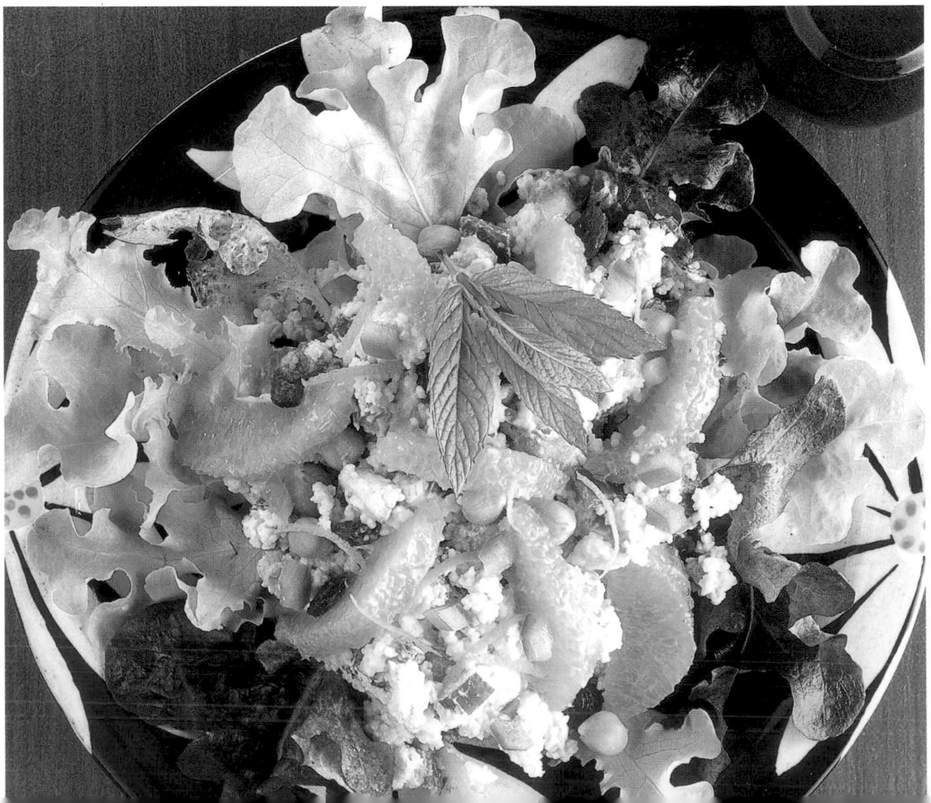

VARIATION

As an alternative, use bulgar (cracked) wheat instead of the couscous. Rinse thoroughly until the water runs clear, then soak in boiling water for 1 hour. Sieve if necessary.

Coleslaw

Home-made coleslaw tastes far superior to any that you can buy. If you make it in advance, add the sunflower seeds just before serving.

NUTRITIONAL INFORMATION

Calories	224	Sugars	8g
Protein	3g	Fat	20g
Carbohydrate	8g	Saturates	3g

10 MINS 5 MINS

SERVES 4

INGREDIENTS

- 150 ml/5 fl oz/⅔ cup low-fat mayonnaise
- 150 ml/5 fl oz/⅔ cup low-fat natural yogurt
- dash of Tabasco sauce
- 1 medium head white cabbage
- 4 carrots
- 1 green (bell) pepper
- 2 tbsp sunflower seeds
- salt and pepper

1 To make the dressing, combine the mayonnaise, yogurt, Tabasco sauce and salt and pepper to taste in a small bowl. Leave to chill until required.

2 Cut the cabbage in half and then into quarters. Remove and discard the tough centre stalk. Shred the cabbage leaves finely. Wash the leaves and dry them thoroughly.

1

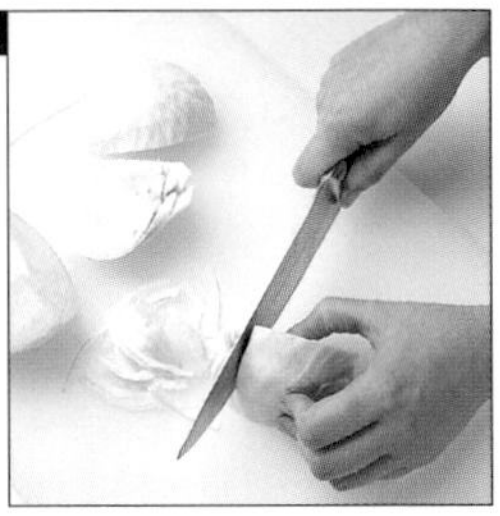

2

5

3 Peel the carrots and shred using a food processor or mandolin. Alternatively, coarsely grate the carrot.

4 Quarter and deseed the (bell) pepper and cut the flesh into thin strips.

5 Combine the vegetables in a large mixing bowl and toss to mix. Pour over the dressing and toss until the vegetables are well coated. Leave to chill in the refrigerator until required.

6 Just before serving, place the sunflower seeds on a baking tray (cookie sheet) and toast them in the oven or under the grill (broiler) until golden brown. Transfer the salad to a large serving dish, scatter with sunflower seeds and serve.

VARIATION

For a slightly different taste, add one or more of the following ingredients to the coleslaw: raisins, grapes, grated apple, chopped walnuts, cubes of cheese or roasted peanuts.

Green Bean & Carrot Salad

This colourful salad of crisp vegetables is tossed in a delicious sun-dried tomato dressing.

NUTRITIONAL INFORMATION

Calories	104	Sugars	9g
Protein	2g	Fat	6g
Carbohydrate	10g	Saturates	1g

10 MINS 5 MINS

SERVES 4

INGREDIENTS

- 350 g/12 oz green (French) beans
- 225 g/8 oz carrots
- 1 red (bell) pepper
- 1 red onion

DRESSING

- 2 tbsp extra virgin olive oil
- 1 tbsp red wine vinegar
- 2 tsp sun-dried tomato paste
- ¼ tsp caster (superfine) sugar
- salt and pepper

1 Top and tail the green (French) beans and blanch them in boiling water for 4 minutes, until just tender. Drain the beans and rinse them under cold water until they are cool. Drain again thoroughly.

2 Transfer the beans to a large salad bowl.

3 Peel the carrots and cut them into thin matchsticks, using a mandolin if you have one.

4 Halve and deseed the (bell) pepper and cut the flesh into thin strips.

5 Peel the onion and cut it into thin slices.

3

4

7

6 Add the carrot, (bell) pepper and onion to the beans and toss to mix.

7 To make the dressing, place the oil, wine vinegar, sun-dried tomato paste, sugar and salt and pepper to taste in a small screw-top jar and shake well.

8 Pour the dressing over the vegetables and serve immediately or leave to chill in the refrigerator until required.

COOK'S TIP

Use canned beans if fresh ones are unavailable. Rinse off the salty liquid and drain well. There is no need to blanch canned beans.

Spinach & Orange Salad

This is a refreshing and very nutritious salad. Add the dressing just before serving so that the leaves do not become soggy.

NUTRITIONAL INFORMATION

Calories	126	Sugars	10g
Protein	3g	Fat	9g
Carbohydrate	10g	Saturates	1g

10 MINS 0 MINS

SERVES 4

INGREDIENTS

- 225 g/8 oz baby spinach leaves
- 2 large oranges
- ½ red onion

DRESSING

- 3 tbsp extra virgin olive oil
- 2 tbsp freshly squeezed orange juice
- 2 tsp lemon juice
- 1 tsp clear honey
- ½ tsp wholegrain mustard
- salt and pepper

1 Wash the spinach leaves under cold running water and then dry them thoroughly on absorbent kitchen paper. Remove any tough stalks and tear the larger leaves into smaller pieces.

2 Slice the top and bottom off each orange with a sharp knife, then remove the peel. Carefully slice between the membranes of the orange to remove the segments. Reserve any juices for the salad dressing.

3 Using a sharp knife, finely chop the onion.

4 Mix together the salad leaves and orange segments and arrange in a serving dish.

1

2
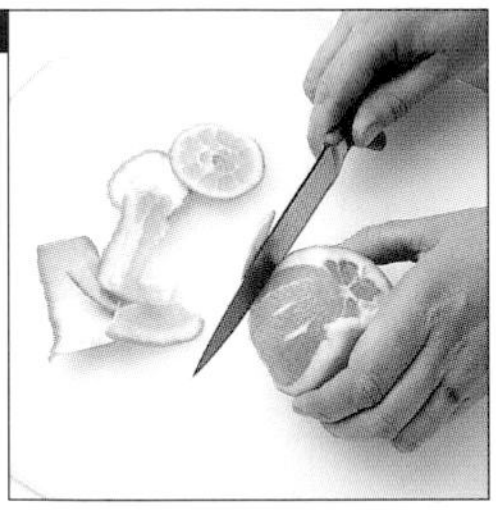

2

5 Scatter the chopped onion over the salad.

6 To make the dressing, whisk together the olive oil, orange juice, lemon juice, honey, mustard and salt and pepper to taste in a small bowl.

7 Pour the dressing over the salad just before serving. Toss the salad well to coat the leaves with the dressing.

VARIATION

Use a mixture of spinach and watercress leaves, if you prefer a slightly more peppery flavour.

Minted Fennel Salad

This is a very refreshing salad. The subtle liquorice flavour of fennel combines well with the cucumber and mint.

NUTRITIONAL INFORMATION

Calories	90	Sugars	7g
Protein	4g	Fat	5g
Carbohydrate	7g	Saturates	1g

25 MINS 0 MINS

SERVES 4

INGREDIENTS

1 bulb fennel

2 small oranges

1 small or ½ large cucumber

1 tbsp chopped mint

1 tbsp virgin olive oil

2 eggs, hard boiled (cooked)

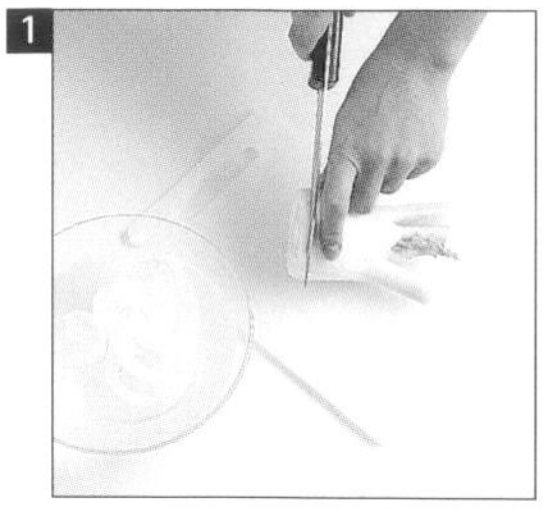

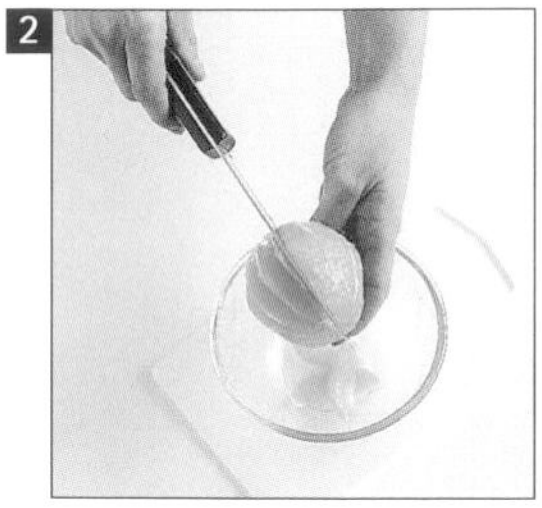

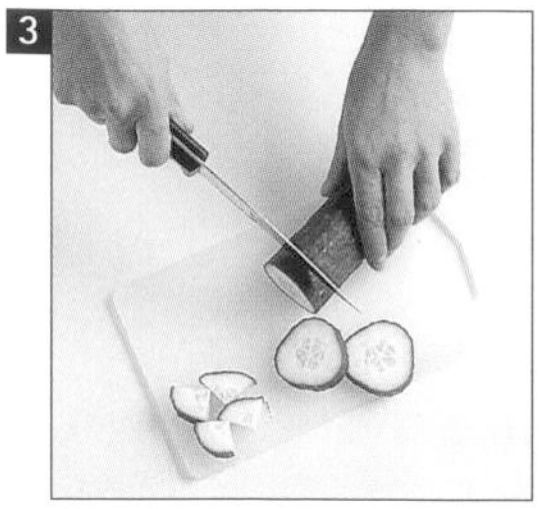

1 Using a sharp knife, trim the outer leaves from the fennel. Slice the fennel bulb thinly into a bowl of water and then sprinkle with lemon juice (see Cook's Tip).

2 Grate the rind of the oranges over a bowl. Using a sharp knife, pare away the orange peel, then segment the orange by carefully slicing between each line of pith. Do this over the bowl in order to retain the juice.

3 Using a sharp knife, cut the cucumber into 12 mm/½ inch rounds and then cut each round into quarters.

4 Add the cucumber to the fennel and orange mixture together with the mint.

5 Pour the olive oil over the fennel and cucumber salad and toss well.

6 Peel and quarter the eggs and use these to decorate the top of the salad. Serve at once.

COOK'S TIP

Fennel will discolour if it is left for any length of time without a dressing. To prevent any discoloration, place it in a bowl of water and sprinkle with lemon juice.

Pear & Roquefort Salad

The sweetness of the pear is a perfect partner to the 'bite' of the radicchio.

NUTRITIONAL INFORMATION

Calories	94	Sugars	10g
Protein	5g	Fat	4g
Carbohydrate	10g	Saturates	3g

10 MINS 0 MINS

SERVES 4

INGREDIENTS

- 50 g/1¾ oz Roquefort cheese
- 150 ml/5 fl oz/⅔ cup low-fat natural yogurt
- 2 tbsp snipped chives
- few leaves of lollo rosso
- few leaves of radicchio
- few leaves of lamb's lettuce (corn salad)
- 2 ripe pears
- pepper
- whole chives, to garnish

1 Place the cheese in a bowl and mash with a fork. Gradually blend the yogurt into the cheese to make a smooth dressing Add the chives and season with pepper to taste.

2 Tear the lollo rosso, radicchio and lamb's lettuce leaves into manageable pieces. Arrange the salad leaves on a serving platter or on individual serving plates.

3 Quarter and core the pears and then cut them into slices.

1

2

4

4 Arrange the pear slices over the salad leaves.

5 Drizzle the dressing over the pears and garnish with a few whole chives.

COOK'S TIP

Look out for bags of mixed salad leaves as these are generally more economical than buying lots of different leaves separately.

Desserts

The healthiest ending to a meal would be fresh fruit topped with low-fat yogurt or fromage frais. Fruit contains no fat and is naturally rich in sugar, vitamins and fibre – perfect for the low-fat diet. However, there are many other ways to use fruit as the basis for a range of delicious desserts. Experiment with the unusual and exotic

fruits that are increasingly available in our supermarkets. In this chapter there is a mouthwatering range of hot and cold fruit desserts, sophisticated mousses and fools and satisfying cakes, as well as variations on the traditional fruit salad. There are also a number of non-fruit based desserts and some low-fat treats for chocoholics.

Summer Pudding

Use whatever summer fruit you have available. Avoid strawberries as they do not give a good result, but cherries are delicious.

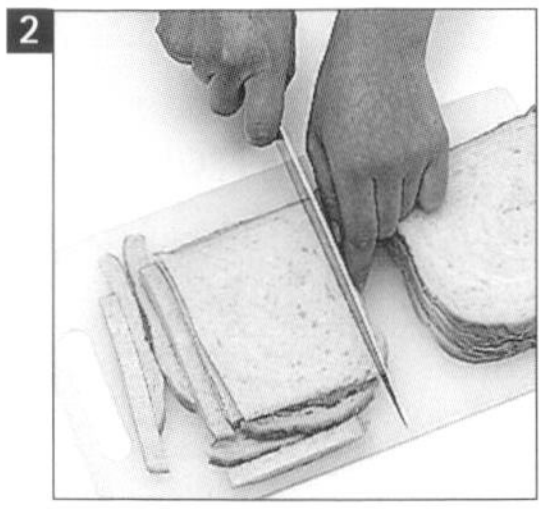

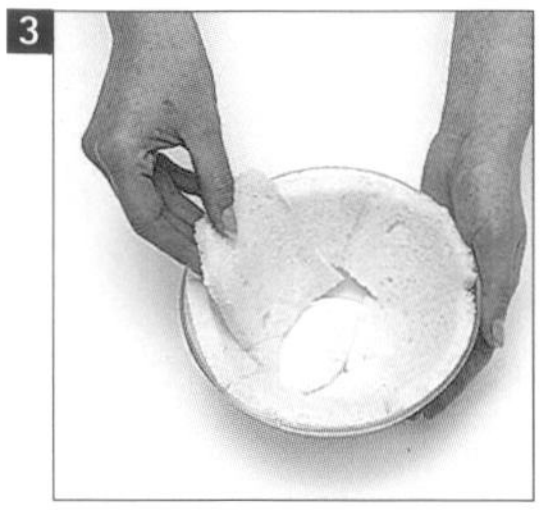

NUTRITIONAL INFORMATION

Calories 174	Sugars 42g
Protein 2g	Fat 0.4g
Carbohydrate . . .43g	Saturates 0g

12 HOURS — 0 MINS

SERVES 4–6

INGREDIENTS

- 1 kg/2 lb 4 oz mixed summer fruit, such as blackberries, redcurrants, blackcurrants, raspberries, loganberries and cherries
- 175 g/6 oz/¾ cup caster (superfine) sugar
- 8 small slices white bread
- low-fat fromage frais, to serve

1 Stir the fruit and caster (superfine) sugar together in a large saucepan, cover and bring to the boil. Simmer for 10 minutes, stirring once.

2 Cut the crusts off the bread slices.

3 Line a 1.1 litre/2 pint/4½ cup pudding basin with the bread, ensuring there are no gaps between the bread slices.

4 Add the fruit and as much of the cooking juices as will fit into the bread-lined bowl.

5 Cover the fruit with the remaining bread slices.

6 Put the pudding basin on to a large plate or a shallow baking tray (cookie sheet). Place a plate on top and weigh it down with cans. Leave to chill overnight in the refrigerator.

7 When ready to serve, turn the summer pudding out on to a serving plate or shallow bowl, cut into slices and serve cold with low-fat fromage frais.

COOK'S TIP

To give the pudding a more lasting set, dissolve 2 sachets (envelopes) or 2 tablespoons of powdered gelatine in water and stir into the fruit mixture. This enables you to turn it out on to the serving plate a couple of hours before serving.

Summer Fruit Clafoutis

Serve this mouth-watering French-style fruit-in-batter pudding hot or cold with low-fat fromage frais or yogurt.

NUTRITIONAL INFORMATION	
Calories 228	Sugars 26g
Protein 9g	Fat 2g
Carbohydrate . . .42g	Saturates 1g

1³/₄ HOURS   50 MINS

SERVES 6

INGREDIENTS

- 500 g/1 lb 2 oz prepared fresh assorted soft fruits such as blackberries, raspberries, strawberries, blueberries, cherries, gooseberries, redcurrants, blackcurrants
- 4 tbsp soft fruit liqueur such as crème de cassis, kirsch or framboise
- 4 tbsp skimmed milk powder
- 125 g/4½ oz/1 cup plain (all-purpose) flour
- pinch of salt
- 60 g/2 oz/¼ cup caster (superfine) sugar
- 2 eggs, size 2, beaten
- 300 ml/½ pint/1¼ cups skimmed milk
- 1 tsp vanilla flavouring (extract)
- 2 tsp caster (superfine) sugar to dust

TO SERVE

- assorted soft fruits
- low-fat yogurt or natural fromage frais

1 Place the assorted fruits in a mixing bowl and spoon over the fruit liqueur. Cover and chill for 1 hour for the fruit to macerate.

2 In a large bowl, mix the skimmed milk powder, flour, salt and sugar. Make a well in the centre and gradually whisk in the eggs, milk and vanilla flavouring (extract), using a balloon whisk, until smooth. Transfer to a jug, and set aside for 30 minutes.

3 Line the base of a 23 cm/9 inch round ovenproof baking dish with baking parchment and spoon in the fruits and juices.

4 Re-whisk the batter and pour over the fruits, stand the dish on a baking sheet and bake in a preheated oven at 200°C/400°F/Gas Mark 6 for 50 minutes until firm, risen and golden brown.

5 Dust with caster (superfine) sugar. Serve immediately with extra fruits, low-fat natural yogurt or fromage frais.

1

2

3

Autumn Fruit Bread Pudding

This is like a summer pudding, but it uses fruits which appear later in the year, such as apples, pears and blackberries, as a succulent filling.

NUTRITIONAL INFORMATION

Calories	178	Sugars	31g
Protein	3g	Fat	1g
Carbohydrate	42g	Saturates	0.1g

12 HOURS — 10 MINS

SERVES 8

INGREDIENTS

900 g/2 lb/4 cups mixed blackberries, chopped apples, chopped pears

150 g/5½ oz/¾ cup soft light brown sugar

1 tsp cinnamon

225 g/8 oz white bread, thinly sliced, crusts removed

1 Place the prepared fruit in a large saucepan with the soft light brown sugar, cinnamon and 100 ml/3½ fl oz of water, stir and bring to the boil.

2 Reduce the heat and simmer for 5–10 minutes so that the fruits soften but still hold their shape.

3 Meanwhile, line the base and sides of a 850 ml/1½ pint pudding basin with the bread slices, ensuring that there are no gaps between the pieces of bread.

4 Spoon the fruit into the centre of the bread-lined bowl and cover the fruit with the remaining bread.

5 Place a saucer on top of the bread and weight it down. Leave the pudding to chill in the refrigerator overnight.

3

4

5

6 Turn the autumn fruit bread pudding out on to a serving plate and serve immediately.

VARIATION

You can use thin slices of plain sponge cake instead of the sliced bread. The sponge will turn a pinkish colour from the fruit juices and the brown edges of the cake will form an attractive pattern of irregular brown lines.

Winter Puddings

An interesting alternative to the familiar Summer Pudding, which uses dried fruits and a tasty malt loaf.

NUTRITIONAL INFORMATION

Calories 447	Sugars 68g
Protein 9g	Fat 11g
Carbohydrate ...80g	Saturates 5g

12 HOURS | 15 MINS

SERVES 4

INGREDIENTS

- 325 g/11½ oz fruit malt loaf
- 150 g/5½ oz/1 cup no-need-to-soak dried apricots, chopped coarsely
- 90 g/3 oz/½ cup dried apple, chopped coarsely
- 425 ml/¾ pint/2 cups orange juice
- 1 tsp grated orange rind
- 2 tbsp orange liqueur
- grated orange rind, to decorate
- low-fat crème fraîche or low-fat natural fromage frais, to serve

1

2

5

1 Cut the malt loaf into 5 mm/¼ inch slices.

2 Place the apricots, apple and orange juice in a saucepan. Bring to the boil, then simmer for 10 minutes. Remove the fruit using a perforated spoon and reserve the liquid. Place the fruit in a dish and leave to cool. Stir in the orange rind and liqueur.

3 Line 4 × 175 ml/6 fl oz/¾ cup pudding basins or ramekin dishes with baking parchment.

4 Cut 4 circles from the malt loaf slices to fit the tops of the moulds (molds) and cut the remaining slices to line them.

5 Soak the malt loaf slices in the reserved fruit syrup, then arrange around the base and sides of the moulds (molds). Trim away any crusts which overhang the edges. Fill the centres with the chopped fruit, pressing down well, and place the malt loaf circles on top.

6 Cover with baking parchment and weigh each basin down with a 225g/8 oz weight or a food can. Chill in the refrigerator overnight.

7 Remove the weight and baking parchment. Carefully turn the puddings out on to 4 serving plates. Remove the lining paper.

8 Decorate with orange rind and serve with crème fraîche or fromage frais.

Crispy-Topped Fruit Bake

The sugar cubes give a lovely crunchy tasted to this easy-to-make pudding.

NUTRITIONAL INFORMATION

Calories	227	Sugars	30g
Protein	5g	Fat	1g
Carbohydrate	53g	Saturates	0.2g

15 MINS   1 HOUR

SERVES 10

INGREDIENTS

- 350 g/12 oz cooking apples
- 3 tbsp lemon juice
- 300 g/10½ oz self-raising wholemeal (whole wheat) flour
- ½ tsp baking powder
- 1 tsp ground cinnamon, plus extra for dusting
- 175 g/6 oz prepared blackberries, thawed if frozen, plus extra to decorate
- 175 g/6 oz light muscovado sugar
- 1 medium egg, beaten
- 200 ml/7 fl oz/¾ cup low-fat natural fromage frais (unsweetened yogurt)
- 60 g/2 oz white or brown sugar cubes, lightly crushed
- sliced eating (dessert) apple, to decorate

1 Preheat the oven to 190°C/375°F/Gas Mark 5. Grease and line a 900 g/2 lb loaf tin (pan). Core, peel and finely dice the apples. Place them in a saucepan with the lemon juice, bring to the boil, cover and simmer for 10 minutes until soft and pulpy. Beat well and set aside to cool.

2 Sift the flour, baking powder and 1 tsp cinnamon into a bowl, adding any husks that remain in the sieve. Stir in 115 g/4 oz blackberries and the sugar.

3 Make a well in the centre of the ingredients and add the egg, fromage frais (unsweetened yogurt) and cooled apple purée. Mix well to incorporate thoroughly. Spoon the mixture into the prepared loaf tin (pan) and smooth over the top.

4 Sprinkle with the remaining blackberries, pressing them down into the cake mixture, and top with the crushed sugar lumps. Bake for 40–45 minutes. Leave to cool in the tin (pan).

5 Remove the cake from the tin (pan) and peel away the lining paper. Serve dusted with cinnamon and decorated with extra blackberries and apple slices.

VARIATION

Try replacing the blackberries with blueberries. Use the canned or frozen variety if fresh blueberries are unavailable.

Fruit & Nut Loaf

This loaf is like a fruit bread which may be served warm or cold, perhaps spread with a little margarine or butter or topped with jam.

NUTRITIONAL INFORMATION

Calories	531	Sugars	53g
Protein	12g	Fat	14g
Carbohydrate	96g	Saturates	2g

1 HOUR

40 MINS

SERVES 4

INGREDIENTS

- 225 g/8 oz/1¾ cups white bread flour, plus extra for dusting
- ½ tsp salt
- 1 tbsp margarine, plus extra for greasing
- 2 tbsp soft light brown sugar
- 100 g/3½ oz/⅔ cup sultanas (golden raisins)
- 50 g/1¾ oz/½ cup no-need to soak dried apricots, chopped
- 50 g/1¾ oz/½ cup chopped hazelnuts
- 2 tsp easy-blend dried yeast
- 6 tbsp orange juice
- 6 tbsp low-fat natural (unsweetened) yogurt
- 2 tbsp sieved apricot jam

1 Sieve the flour and salt into a mixing bowl. Rub in the margarine and stir in the sugar, sultanas (golden raisins), apricots, nuts and yeast.

1

3

4

2 Warm the orange juice in a saucepan but do not allow to boil.

3 Stir the warm orange juice into the flour mixture with the natural (unsweetened) yogurt and bring the mixture together to form a dough.

4 Knead the dough on a lightly floured surface for 5 minutes until smooth and elastic. Shape into a round and place on a lightly greased baking tray (cookie sheet). Cover with a clean tea towel (dish cloth) and leave to rise in a warm place until doubled in size.

5 Cook the loaf in a preheated oven, 220°C/425°F/Gas Mark 7, for 35–40 minutes until cooked through. Transfer to a cooling rack and brush the cake with the apricot jam. Leave the cake to cool before serving.

COOK'S TIP

To test whether yeast bread or cake is done, tap the tin from underneath. If it sounds hollow, the bread or cake is ready.

Fruit Loaf with Apple Spread

This sweet, fruity loaf is ideal served for tea or as a healthy snack. The fruit spread can be made quickly while the cake is in the oven.

NUTRITIONAL INFORMATION

Calories	733	Sugars	110g
Protein	12g	Fat	5g
Carbohydrate	171g	Saturates	1g

1¼ HOURS — 2 HOURS

SERVES 4

INGREDIENTS

- 175 g/6 oz porridge oats (oatmeal)
- 100 g/3½ oz light muscovado sugar
- 1 tsp ground cinnamon
- 125 g/4½ oz sultanas
- 175 g/6 oz seedless raisins
- 2 tbsp malt extract
- 300 ml/½ pint/1¼ cups unsweetened apple juice
- 175 g/6 oz self-raising wholemeal (whole wheat) flour
- 1½ tsp baking powder
- strawberries and apple wedges, to serve

FRUIT SPREAD

- 225 g/8 oz strawberries, washed and hulled
- 2 eating (dessert) apples, cored, chopped and mixed with 1 tbsp lemon juice to prevent browning
- 300 ml/½ pint/1¼ cups unsweetened apple juice

2

6

6

1 Preheat the oven to 180°C/350°F/Gas Mark 4. Grease and line a 900 g/2 lb loaf tin (pan).

2 Place the porridge oats (oatmeal), sugar, cinnamon, sultanas, raisins and malt extract in a mixing bowl. Pour in the apple juice, stir well and leave to soak for 30 minutes.

3 Sift in the flour and baking powder, adding any husks that remain in the sieve, and fold in using a metal spoon.

4 Spoon the mixture into the prepared tin (pan) and bake for 1½ hours until firm or until a skewer inserted into the centre comes out clean.

5 Leave to cool for 10 minutes, then turn on to a rack and leave to cool.

6 Meanwhile, make the fruit spread. Place the strawberries and apples in a saucepan and pour in the apple juice. Bring to the boil, cover and simmer for 30 minutes. Beat the sauce well and spoon into a clean, warmed jar. Leave to cool, then seal and label.

7 Serve the loaf with 1–2 tablespoons of the fruit spread and an assortment of strawberries and apple wedges.

New Age Spotted Dick

This is a deliciously moist low-fat pudding. The sauce is in the centre of the pudding, and will spill out when the pudding is cut.

NUTRITIONAL INFORMATION

Calories	529	Sugars	41g
Protein	9g	Fat	31g
Carbohydrate	58g	Saturates	4g

25 MINS — 1¼ HOURS

SERVES 6–8

INGREDIENTS

- 125 g/4½ oz/¾ cup raisins
- 125 ml/4 fl oz/generous ½ cup corn oil, plus a little for brushing
- 125 g/4½ oz/generous ½ cup caster (superfine) sugar
- 25 g/1 oz/¼ cup ground almonds
- 2 eggs, lightly beaten
- 175 g/6 oz/1½ cups self-raising flour

SAUCE

- 60 g/2 oz/½ cup walnuts, chopped
- 60 g/2 oz/½ cup ground almonds
- 300 ml/½ pint/1¼ cups semi-skimmed milk
- 4 tbsp granulated sugar

1 Put the raisins in a saucepan with 125 ml/4 fl oz/½ cup water. Bring to the boil, then remove from the heat. Leave to steep for 10 minutes, then drain.

2 Whisk together the oil, sugar and ground almonds until thick and syrupy; this will need about 8 minutes of beating (on medium speed if using an electric whisk).

3 Add the eggs, one at a time, beating well after each addition. Combine the flour and raisins. Stir into the mixture. Brush a 1 litre/1¾ pint/4 cup pudding basin with oil, or line with baking parchment.

4 Put all the sauce ingredients into a saucepan. Bring to the boil, stir and simmer for 10 minutes.

5 Transfer the sponge mixture to the greased basin and pour on the hot sauce. Place on a baking tray (cookie sheet).

6 Bake in a preheated oven at 170°C/340°F/Gas Mark 3½ for about 1 hour. Lay a piece of baking parchment across the top if it starts to brown too fast.

7 Leave to cool for 2–3 minutes in the basin before turning out on to a serving plate.

2
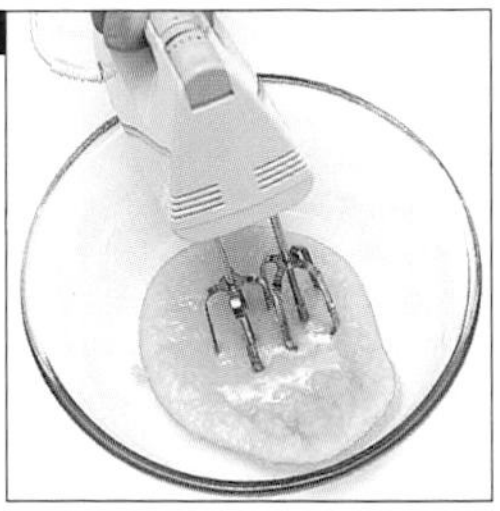

3

3

COOK'S TIP

Always soak raisins before baking them, as they retain their moisture nicely and you taste the flavour of them instead of biting on a dried-out raisin.

Rich Fruit Cake

Serve this moist, fruit-laden cake for a special occasion. It would also make an excellent Christmas cake.

NUTRITIONAL INFORMATION

Calories	772	Sugars	137g
Protein	14g	Fat	5g
Carbohydrate	179g	Saturates	1g

35 MINS

1¾ HOURS

SERVES 4

INGREDIENTS

- 175 g/6 oz unsweetened pitted dates
- 125 g/4½ oz no-need-to-soak dried prunes
- 200 ml/7 fl oz/¾ cup unsweetened orange juice
- 2 tbsp treacle (molasses)
- 1 tsp finely grated lemon rind
- 1 tsp finely grated orange rind
- 225 g/8 oz self-raising wholemeal (whole wheat) flour
- 1 tsp mixed spice
- 125 g/4½ oz seedless raisins
- 125 g/4½ oz golden sultanas
- 125 g/4½ oz currants
- 125 g/4½ oz dried cranberries
- 3 large eggs, separated

TO DECORATE

- 1 tbsp apricot jam, softened
- icing (confectioners') sugar, to dust
- 175 g/6 oz sugarpaste
- strips of orange rind
- strips of lemon rind

1 Preheat the oven to 170°C/325°F/Gas Mark 3. Grease and line a deep 20.5 cm/8 inch round cake tin (pan). Chop the dates and prunes and place in a pan. Pour over the orange juice and simmer for 10 minutes. Remove the pan from the heat and beat the fruit mixture until puréed. Add the treacle (molasses) and rinds. Cool.

2 Sift the flour and spice into a bowl, adding any husks that remain in the sieve. Add the dried fruits. When the date and prune mixture is cool, whisk in the egg yolks. In a clean bowl, whisk the egg whites until stiff. Spoon the fruit mixture into the dry ingredients and mix together.

3 Gently fold in the egg whites using a metal spoon. Transfer to the prepared tin and bake for 1½ hours. Leave to cool.

4 Remove the cake from the tin (pan) and brush the top with jam. Dust the work surface (counter) with icing (confectioners') sugar and roll out the sugarpaste thinly. Lay the sugarpaste over the top of the cake and trim the edges. Decorate with orange and lemon rind.

Chocolate & Pineapple Cake

Decorated with thick yogurt and canned pineapple, this is a low-fat cake, but it is by no means lacking in flavour.

NUTRITIONAL INFORMATION

Calories	199	Sugars	19g
Protein	5g	Fat	9g
Carbohydrate	28g	Saturates	3g

10 MINS 25 MINS

SERVES 9

INGREDIENTS

- 150 g/5½ oz/⅔ cup low-fat spread
- 125 g/4½ oz caster (superfine) sugar
- 100 g/3½ oz/¾ cup self-raising flour, sieved (strained)
- 3 tbsp cocoa powder, sieved (strained)
- 1½ tsp baking powder
- 2 eggs
- 225g/8 oz can pineapple pieces in natural juice
- 125 ml/4 fl oz/½ cup low-fat thick natural yogurt
- about 1 tbsp icing (confectioners') sugar
- grated chocolate, to decorate

2

3

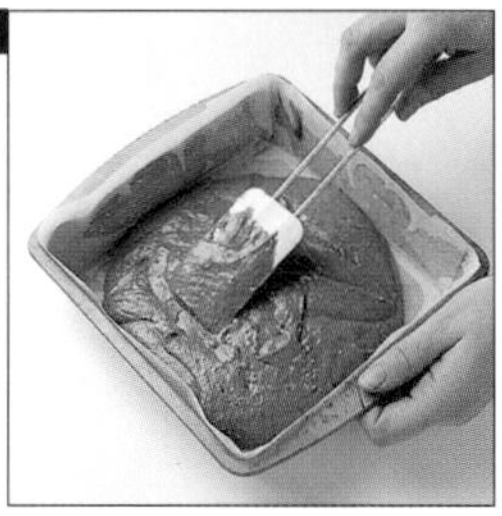

4

1 Lightly grease a 20 cm/8 inch square cake tin (pan).

2 Place the low-fat spread, caster (superfine) sugar, flour, cocoa powder, baking powder and eggs in a large mixing bowl. Beat with a wooden spoon or electric hand whisk until smooth.

3 Pour the cake mixture into the prepared tin (pan) and level the surface. Bake in a preheated oven, 190°C/325°F/Gas Mark 5, for 20-25 minutes or until springy to the touch. Leave to cool slightly in the tin (pan) before transferring to a wire rack to cool completely.

4 Drain the pineapple, chop the pineapple pieces and drain again. Reserve a little pineapple for decoration, stir the rest into the yogurt and sweeten with icing (confectioners') sugar.

5 Spread the pineapple and yogurt mixture over the cake and decorate with the reserved pineapple pieces. Sprinkle with the grated chocolate.

Carrot & Ginger Cake

This melt-in-the-mouth version of a favourite cake has a fraction of the fat of the traditional cake.

NUTRITIONAL INFORMATION

Calories	249	Sugars	28g
Protein	7g	Fat	6g
Carbohydrate	46g	Saturates	1g

15 MINS — $1^1/_4$ HOURS

SERVES 10

INGREDIENTS

- 225 g/8 oz plain (all-purpose) flour
- 1 tsp baking powder
- 1 tsp bicarbonate of soda
- 2 tsp ground ginger
- ½ tsp salt
- 175 g/6 oz light muscovado sugar
- 225 g/8 oz carrots, grated
- 2 pieces stem ginger in syrup, drained and chopped
- 25 g/1 oz root (fresh) ginger, grated
- 60 g/2 oz seedless raisins
- 2 medium eggs, beaten
- 3 tbsp corn oil
- juice of 1 medium orange

FROSTING

- 225 g/8 oz low-fat soft cheese
- 4 tbsp icing (confectioners') sugar
- 1 tsp vanilla essence (extract)

TO DECORATE

- grated carrot
- stem (fresh) ginger
- ground ginger

1 Preheat the oven to 180°C/350°F/Gas Mark 4. Grease and line a 20.5 cm/8 inch round cake tin with baking parchment.

2 Sift the flour, baking powder, bicarbonate of soda, ground ginger and salt into a bowl. Stir in the sugar, carrots, stem ginger, root (fresh) ginger and raisins. Beat together the eggs, oil and orange juice, then pour into the bowl. Mix the ingredients together well.

3 Spoon the mixture into the tin and bake in the oven for 1–$1^1/_4$ hours until firm to the touch, or until a skewer inserted into the centre of the cake comes out clean.

4 To make the frosting, place the soft cheese in a bowl and beat to soften. Sift in the icing (confectioners') sugar and add the vanilla essence (extract). Mix well.

5 Remove the cake from the tin (pan) and smooth the frosting over the top. Decorate the cake and serve.

Banana & Lime Cake

A substantial cake that is ideal served for tea. The mashed bananas help to keep the cake moist, and the lime icing gives it extra zing and zest.

NUTRITIONAL INFORMATION

Calories	235	Sugars	31g
Protein	5g	Fat	1g
Carbohydrate	55g	Saturates	0.3g

35 MINS 45 MINS

SERVES 10

INGREDIENTS

- 300 g/10½ oz plain (all-purpose) flour
- 1 tsp salt
- 1½ tsp baking powder
- 175 g/6 oz light muscovado sugar
- 1 tsp lime rind, grated
- 1 medium egg, beaten
- 1 medium banana, mashed with 1 tbsp lime juice
- 150 ml/5 fl oz/⅔ cup low-fat natural fromage frais (unsweetened yogurt)
- 115 g/4 oz sultanas
- banana chips, to decorate
- lime rind, finely grated, to decorate

TOPPING

- 115 g/4 oz icing (confectioners') sugar
- 1–2 tsp lime juice
- ½ tsp lime rind, finely grated

1 Preheat the oven to 180°C/350°F/Gas Mark 4. Grease and line a deep 18 cm/7 inch round cake tin with baking parchment.

2 Sift the flour, salt and baking powder into a mixing bowl and stir in the sugar and lime rind.

3 Make a well in the centre of the dry ingredients and add the egg, banana, fromage frais (yogurt) and sultanas. Mix well until thoroughly incorporated.

4 Spoon the mixture into the tin and smooth the surface. Bake for 40–45 minutes until firm to the touch or until a skewer inserted in the centre comes out clean. Leave to cool for 10 minutes, then turn out on to a wire rack.

5 To make the topping, sift the icing (confectioners') sugar into a small bowl and mix with the lime juice to form a soft, but not too runny, icing. Stir in the grated lime rind. Drizzle the icing over the cake, letting it run down the sides.

6 Decorate the cake with banana chips and lime rind. Let the cake stand for 15 minutes so that the icing sets.

1

3

4

VARIATION

For a delicious alternative, replace the lime rind and juice with orange and the sultanas with chopped apricots.

Strawberry Roulade

Serve this moist, light sponge rolled up with an almond and strawberry fromage frais (yogurt) filling for a delicious tea-time treat.

NUTRITIONAL INFORMATION

Calories	166	Sugars	19g
Protein	6g	Fat	3g
Carbohydrate	30g	Saturates	1g

30 MINS 10 MINS

SERVES 8

INGREDIENTS

- 3 large eggs
- 125 g/4½ oz caster (superfine) sugar
- 125 g/4½ oz plain (all-purpose) flour
- 1 tbsp hot water

FILLING

- 200 ml/7 fl oz/¾ cup low-fat natural fromage frais (unsweetened yogurt)
- 1 tsp almond essence (extract)
- 225 g/8 oz small strawberries
- 15 g/½ oz toasted almonds, flaked (slivered)
- 1 tsp icing (confectioners') sugar

1 Preheat the oven to 220°C/425°F/Gas Mark 7. Line a 35 x 25 cm/14 x 10 inch Swiss roll tin with baking parchment. Place the eggs in a mixing bowl with the caster (superfine) sugar. Place the bowl over a pan of hot water and whisk until pale and thick.

2 Remove the bowl from the pan. Sift in the flour and fold into the eggs with the hot water. Pour the mixture into the tin and bake for 8–10 minutes, until golden and set.

3 Transfer the mixture to a sheet of baking parchment. Peel off the lining paper and roll up the sponge tightly along with the baking parchment. Wrap in a tea towel (dish towel) and let cool.

4 Mix together the fromage frais (yogurt) and the almond essence (extract). Reserving a few strawberries for decoration, wash, hull and slice the rest. Leave the mixture to chill in the refrigerator until required.

5 Unroll the sponge, spread the fromage frais (yogurt) mixture over the sponge and sprinkle with strawberries. Roll the sponge up again and transfer to a serving plate. Sprinkle with almonds and lightly dust with icing (confectioners') sugar. Decorate with the reserved strawberries.

1

3

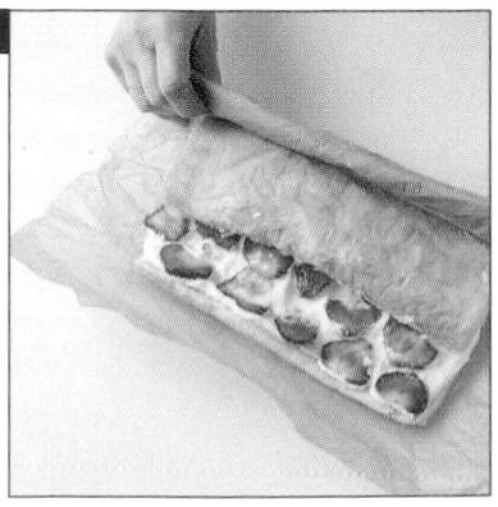

5

Fruity Potato Cake

Sweet potatoes mix beautifully with fruit and brown sugar in this unusual cake. Add a few drops of rum or brandy to the recipe if you like.

NUTRITIONAL INFORMATION

Calories	275	Sugars	44g
Protein	6g	Fat	5g
Carbohydrate	55g	Saturates	2g

15 MINS   1½ HOURS

SERVES 6

INGREDIENTS

- 675 g/1½ lb sweet potatoes, diced
- 1 tbsp butter, melted
- 125 g/4½ oz demerara (brown crystal) sugar
- 3 eggs
- 3 tbsp skimmed milk
- 1 tbsp lemon juice
- grated rind of 1 lemon
- 1 tsp caraway seeds
- 125 g/4½ oz dried fruits, such as apple, pear or mango, chopped
- 2 tsp baking powder

1 Lightly grease an 18 cm/7 inch square cake tin (pan).

2 Cook the sweet potatoes in boiling water for 10 minutes or until soft. Drain and mash until smooth.

3 Transfer the mashed sweet potatoes to a mixing bowl whilst still hot and add the butter and sugar, mixing to dissolve.

4 Beat in the eggs, lemon juice and rind, caraway seeds and chopped dried fruit. Add the baking powder and mix well.

5 Pour the mixture into the prepared cake tin (pan).

6 Cook in a preheated oven, 160°C/325°F/Gas Mark 3, for 1-1¼ hours or until cooked through.

7 Remove the cake from the tin (pan) and transfer to a wire rack to cool. Cut into thick slices to serve.

COOK'S TIP

This cake is ideal as a special occasion dessert. It can be made in advance and frozen until required. Wrap the cake in cling film (plastic wrap) and freeze. Thaw at room temperature for 24 hours and warm through in a moderate oven before serving.

Fruity Muffins

Perfect for those on a low-fat diet, these little cakes contain no butter, just a little corn oil.

NUTRITIONAL INFORMATION

Calories	162	Sugars	11g
Protein	4g	Fat	4g
Carbohydrate	28g	Saturates	1g

10 MINS   30 MINS

MAKES 10

INGREDIENTS

- 225 g/8 oz self-raising wholemeal (whole wheat) flour
- 2 tsp baking powder
- 25 g/1 oz light muscovado sugar
- 100 g/3½ oz no-need-to-soak dried apricots, chopped finely
- 1 medium banana, mashed with 1 tbsp orange juice
- 1 tsp orange rind, grated finely
- 300 ml/½ pint/1¼ cups skimmed milk
- 1 medium egg, beaten
- 3 tbsp corn oil
- 2 tbsp porridge oats (oatmeal)
- fruit spread, honey or maple syrup, to serve

1 Preheat the oven to 200°C/400°F/Gas Mark 6. Place 10 paper muffin cases in a deep patty tin (pan). Sift the flour and baking powder into a mixing bowl, adding any husks that remain in the sieve. Stir in the sugar and chopped apricots.

2 Make a well in the centre of the dry ingredients and add the banana, orange rind, milk, beaten egg and oil. Mix together well to form a thick batter. Divide the batter evenly among the 10 paper cases.

3 Sprinkle with a few porridge oats (oatmeal) and bake for 25–30 minutes until well risen and firm to the touch, or until a skewer inserted into the centre comes out clean. Transfer the muffins to a wire rack to cool slightly. Serve the muffins warm with a little fruit spread, honey or maple syrup.

VARIATION

If you like dried figs, they make a deliciously crunchy alternative to the apricots; they also go very well with the flavour of orange. Other no-need-to-soak dried fruits, chopped up finely, can be used as well.

2

2

3

Paper-Thin Fruit Pies

The extra-crisp pastry cases, filled with slices of fruit and glazed with apricot jam, are best served hot with low-fat custard.

NUTRITIONAL INFORMATION

Calories 158	Sugars 12g
Protein 2g	Fat 10g
Carbohydrate ...14g	Saturates 2g

20 MINS 15 MINS

SERVES 4

INGREDIENTS

- 1 medium eating (dessert) apple
- 1 medium ripe pear
- 2 tbsp lemon juice
- 60 g/2 oz low-fat spread
- 4 rectangular sheets of filo pastry, thawed if frozen
- 2 tbsp low-sugar apricot jam
- 1 tbsp unsweetened orange juice
- 1 tbsp finely chopped natural pistachio nuts, shelled
- 2 tsp icing (confectioners') sugar, for dusting
- low-fat custard, to serve

1 Preheat the oven to 200°C/400°F/Gas Mark 6. Core and thinly slice the apple and pear and toss them in the lemon juice.

2 Over a low heat, gently melt the low-fat spread.

3 Cut the sheets of pastry into 4 and cover with a clean, damp tea towel (dish cloth). Brush 4 non-stick Yorkshire pudding tins (large muffin pans), measuring 10 cm/4 inch across, with a little of the low-fat spread.

4 Working on each pie separately, brush 4 sheets of pastry with low-fat spread. Press a small sheet of pastry into the base of one tin (pan). Arrange the other sheets of pastry on top at slightly different angles. Repeat with the other sheets of pastry to make another 3 pies.

5 Arrange the apple and pear slices alternately in the centre of each pastry case and lightly crimp the edges of the pastry of each pie.

6 Mix the jam and orange juice together until smooth and brush over the fruit. Bake for 12–15 minutes. Sprinkle with the pistachio nuts, dust lightly with icing (confectioners') sugar and serve hot with low-fat custard.

3
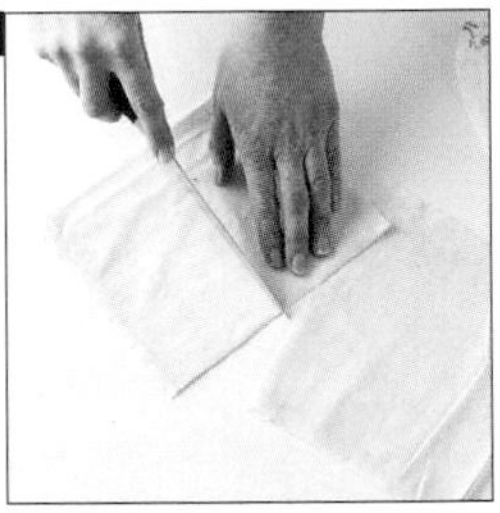

4

5

VARIATION

Other combinations of fruit are equally delicious. Try peach and apricot, raspberry and apple, or pineapple and mango.

Baked Pears with Cinnamon

This simple recipe is easy to prepare and cook but is deliciously warming. For a treat, serve hot on a pool of low-fat custard.

NUTRITIONAL INFORMATION

Calories	207	Sugars	35g
Protein	3g	Fat	6g
Carbohydrate	37g	Saturates	2g

10 MINS 25 MINS

SERVES 4

INGREDIENTS

- 4 ripe pears
- 2 tbsp lemon juice
- 4 tbsp light muscovado sugar
- 1 tsp ground cinnamon
- 60 g/2 oz low-fat spread
- low-fat custard, to serve
- lemon rind, finely grated, to decorate

1 Preheat the oven to 200°C/400°F/Gas Mark 6. Core and peel the pears, then slice them in half lengthwise and brush all over with the lemon juice. Place the pears, cored side down, in a small non-stick roasting tin (pan).

2 Place the sugar, cinnamon and low-fat spread in a small saucepan and heat gently, stirring, until the sugar has melted. Keep the heat low to stop too much water evaporating from the low-fat spread as it gets hot. Spoon the mixture over the pears.

3 Bake for 20–25 minutes or until the pears are tender and golden, occasionally spooning the sugar mixture over the fruit during the cooking time.

1

2

2

4 To serve, heat the custard until it is piping hot and spoon over the bases of 4 warm dessert plates. Arrange 2 pear halves on each plate.

5 Decorate with grated lemon rind and serve.

VARIATION

For alternative flavours, replace the cinnamon with ground ginger and serve the pears sprinkled with chopped stem ginger in syrup. Alternatively, use ground allspice and spoon over some warmed dark rum to serve.

Apricot & Orange Jellies

These bright fruity little desserts are easy to make and taste so much better than shop-bought jellies. Serve them with low-fat ice cream.

NUTRITIONAL INFORMATION

Calories	206	Sugars	36g
Protein	8g	Fat	5g
Carbohydrate	36g	Saturates	3g

4 1/4 HOURS — 25 MINS

SERVES 4

INGREDIENTS

- 225 g/8 oz no-need-to-soak dried apricots
- 300 ml/½ pint/1¼ cups unsweetened orange juice
- 2 tbsp lemon juice
- 2–3 tsp clear honey
- 1 tbsp powdered gelatine
- 4 tbsp boiling water

TO DECORATE

- orange segments
- sprigs of mint

CINNAMON 'CREAM'

- 125 g/4½ oz medium-fat ricotta cheese
- 125 g/4½ oz low-fat natural fromage frais (unsweetened yogurt)
- 1 tsp ground cinnamon
- 1 tbsp clear honey

1

2

4
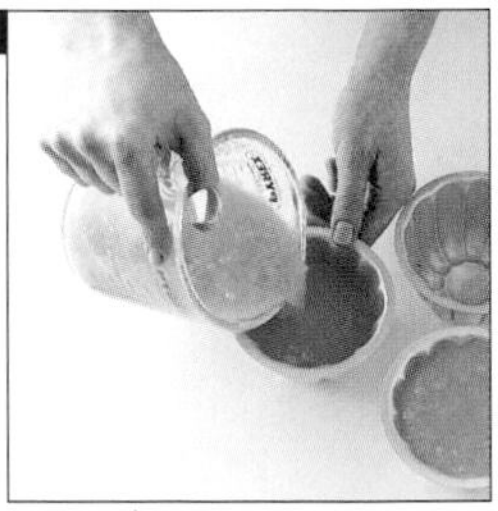

1 Place the apricots in a saucepan and pour in the orange juice. Bring to the boil, cover and simmer for 15–20 minutes until plump and soft. Leave to cool for 10 minutes.

2 Transfer the mixture to a blender or food processor and blend until smooth. Stir in the lemon juice and add the honey. Pour the mixture into a measuring jug and make up to 600 ml/1 pint /2 1/2 cups with cold water.

3 Dissolve the gelatine in the boiling water and stir into the apricot mixture.

4 Pour the mixture into 4 individual moulds (molds), each 150 ml/5 fl oz/2/3 cup, or 1 large mould, 600 ml/1 pint/2 1/2 cups. Leave to chill until set.

5 Meanwhile, make the cinnamon 'cream'. Mix all the ingredients together and place in a small bowl. Cover the mixture and leave to chill until

6 To turn out the jellies, dip the moulds (molds) in hot water for a few seconds and invert on to serving plates.

7 Decorate with the orange segments and sprigs of mint. Serve with the cinnamon 'cream' dusted with extra cinnamon.

Strawberry Meringues

The combination of aromatic strawberries and rose water with crisp caramelized sugar meringues makes this a truly irresistible dessert.

NUTRITIONAL INFORMATION

Calories 145	Sugars 35g
Protein 3g	Fat 0.3g
Carbohydrate ...35g	Saturates 0.1g

1 HOUR | 3½ HOURS

SERVES 6

I N G R E D I E N T S

- 3 egg whites, size 2
- pinch of salt
- 175 g/6 oz/1 cup light muscovado sugar, crushed to be free of lumps
- 225 g/8 oz/1½ cups strawberries, hulled
- 2 tsp rose water
- 150 ml/¼ pint/⅔ cup low-fat natural fromage frais
- extra strawberries to serve (optional)

TO DECORATE

- rose-scented geranium leaves
- rose petals

1

2

4

1 In a large grease-free bowl, whisk the egg whites and salt until very stiff and dry. Gradually whisk in the sugar a spoonful at a time, until the mixture is stiff again.

2 Line a baking sheet with baking parchment and drop 12 spoonfuls of the meringue mixture on to the sheet. Bake in a preheated oven at 120°C/250°F/Gas Mark ½ for 3–3½ hours, until completely dried out and crisp. Allow to cool thoroughly.

3 Reserve 60 g/2 oz/½ cup of the strawberries. Place the remaining strawberries in a blender or food processor and blend for a few seconds until smooth.

4 Alternatively, mash the strawberries with a fork and press through a sieve (strainer) to form a purée paste. Stir in the rose water. Chill until required.

5 To serve, slice the reserved strawberries. Sandwich the meringues together with fromage frais and sliced strawberries.

6 Spoon the strawberry rose purée paste on to 6 serving plates and top with a meringue.

7 Decorate with rose petals and rose-scented geranium leaves, and serve with extra strawberries (if using).

Pears with Maple Cream

These spicy cinnamon pears are accompanied by a delicious melt-in-the-mouth maple and ricotta cream – you won't believe it's low in fat!

NUTRITIONAL INFORMATION

Calories	190	Sugars	28g
Protein	6g	Fat	7g
Carbohydrate	28g	Saturates	4g

10 MINS   25 MINS

SERVES 4

INGREDIENTS

- 1 lemon
- 4 firm pears
- 300 ml/½ pint/1¼ cups dry cider or unsweetened apple juice
- 1 cinnamon stick, broken in half
- mint leaves to decorate

MAPLE RICOTTA CREAM

- 125 g/4½ oz/½ cup low-fat ricotta cheese
- 125 g/4½ oz/½ cup low-fat natural fromage frais
- ½ tsp ground cinnamon
- ½ tsp grated lemon rind
- 1 tbsp maple syrup
- lemon rind, to decorate

1 Using a vegetable peeler, remove the rind from the lemon and place in a non-stick frying pan (skillet). Squeeze the lemon and pour into a shallow bowl.

2 Peel the pears, and halve and core them. Toss them in the lemon juice to prevent discolouration. Place in the frying pan (skillet) and pour over the remaining lemon juice.

3 Add the cider or apple juice and cinnamon stick halves. Gently bring to the boil, lower the heat so the liquid simmers and cook the pears for 10 minutes. Remove the pears using a perforated spoon; reserve the cooking juice. Put the pears in a warm heatproof serving dish, cover with foil and put in a warming drawer or low oven to keep warm.

4 Return the pan to the heat, bring to the boil, then simmer for 8–10 minutes until reduced by half. Spoon over the pears.

5 To make the maple ricotta cream, mix together all the ingredients. Decorate the cream with lemon rind and the pears with mint leaves, and serve together.

1

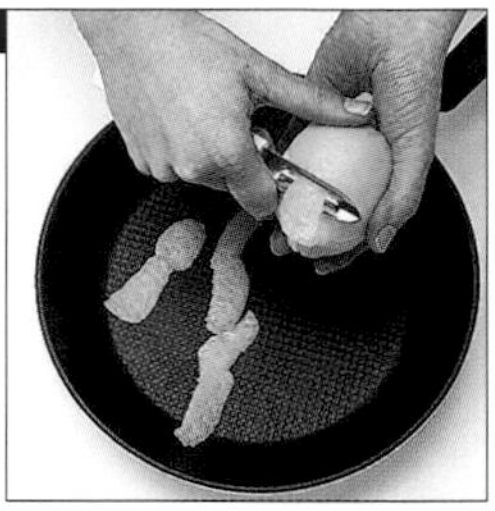

2

3

COOK'S TIP

Comice (Bartlett) or Conference pears are suitable for this recipe. Pears ripen quickly and can bruise easily. It's best to buy them just before you plan to cook them.

Sticky Sesame Bananas

These tasty morsels are a real treat. Pieces of banana are dipped in caramel and then sprinkled with a few sesame seeds.

NUTRITIONAL INFORMATION	
Calories 215	Sugars 38g
Protein 6g	Fat 3g
Carbohydrate . . .41g	Saturates 1g

10 MINS

20 MINS

SERVES 4

INGREDIENTS

- 4 ripe medium bananas
- 3 tbsp lemon juice
- 125 g/4 1/2 oz caster (superfine) sugar
- 4 tbsp cold water
- 2 tbsp sesame seeds
- 150 ml/5 fl oz/2/3 cup low-fat natural fromage frais (unsweetened yogurt)
- 1 tbsp icing (confectioners') sugar
- 1 tsp vanilla essence (extract)
- lemon and lime rind, shredded, to decorate

1 Peel the bananas and cut into 5 cm/2 inch pieces. Place the banana pieces in a bowl, spoon over the lemon juice and stir well to coat – this will help prevent the bananas from discoloring.

2 Place the sugar and water in a small saucepan and heat gently, stirring, until the sugar dissolves. Bring to the boil and cook for 5–6 minutes until the mixture turns golden-brown.

3 Meanwhile, drain the bananas and blot with kitchen paper (paper towels) to dry. Line a baking sheet or board with baking parchment and arrange the bananas, well spaced out, on top.

1

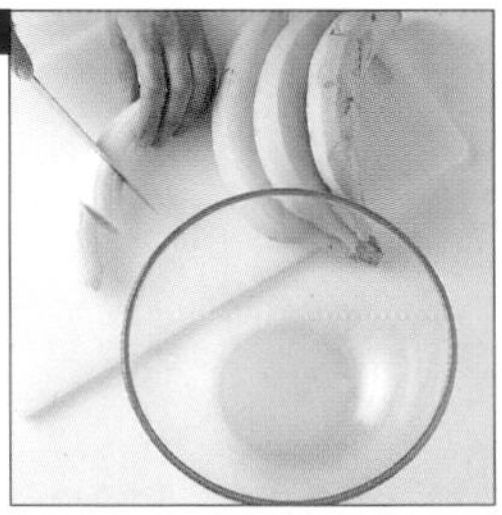

3

4

4 When the caramel is ready, drizzle it over the bananas, working quickly because the caramel sets almost instantly. Sprinkle the sesame seed sover the caramelized bananas and leave to cool for 10 minutes.

5 Mix the fromage frais (unsweetened yogurt) together with the icing (confectioner's) sugar and vanilla essence (extract).

6 Peel the bananas away from the paper and arrange on serving plates.

7 Serve the fromage frais (unsweetened yogurt) as a dip, decorated with the shredded lemon and lime rind.

Summer Fruit Salad

A mixture of soft summer fruits in an orange-flavoured syrup with a dash of port. Serve with low-fat fromage frais (unsweetened yogurt).

NUTRITIONAL INFORMATION

Calories	110	Sugars	26g
Protein	1g	Fat	0.1g
Carbohydrate	26g	Saturates	0g

5 MINS

10 MINS

SERVES 6

INGREDIENTS

- 90 g/3 oz/⅓ cup caster (superfine) sugar
- 75 ml/3 fl oz/⅓ cup water
- grated rind and juice of 1 small orange
- 250 g/9 oz/2 cups redcurrants, stripped from their stalks
- 2 tsp arrowroot
- 2 tbsp port
- 125 g/4½ oz/1 cup blackberries
- 125 g/4½ oz/1 cup blueberries
- 125 g/4½ oz/¾ cup strawberries
- 225 g/8 oz/1½ cups raspberries
- low-fat fromage frais (unsweetened yogurt), to serve

1 Put the sugar, water and grated orange rind into a pan and heat gently, stirring until the sugar has dissolved.

2 Add the redcurrants and orange juice, bring to the boil and simmer gently for 2–3 minutes.

3 Strain the fruit, reserving the syrup, and put into a bowl.

4 Blend the arrowroot with a little water. Return the syrup to the pan, add the arrowroot and bring to the boil, stirring until thickened.

5 Add the port and mix together well. Then pour over the redcurrants in the bowl.

6 Add the blackberries, blueberries, strawberries and raspberries. Mix the fruit together and leave to cool until required. Serve in individual glass dishes with low-fat fromage frais (unsweetened yogurt).

COOK'S TIP

Although this fruit salad is really best made with fresh fruits in season, you can achieve an acceptable result with frozen equivalents, with perhaps the exception of strawberries. You can buy frozen fruits of the forest, which would be ideal, in most supermarkets.

Chocolate Cheese Pots

These super-light desserts are just the thing if you have a craving for chocolate. Serve on their own or with a selection of fruits.

NUTRITIONAL INFORMATION

Calories	117	Sugars	17g
Protein	9g	Fat	1g
Carbohydrate	18g	Saturates	1g

40 MINS   0 MINS

SERVES 4

INGREDIENTS

- 300 ml/½ pint/1¼ cups low-fat natural fromage frais (unsweetened yogurt)
- 150 ml/5 fl oz/⅔ cup low-fat natural (unsweetened) yogurt
- 25 g/1 oz icing (confectioners') sugar
- 4 tsp low-fat drinking chocolate powder
- 4 tsp cocoa powder
- 1 tsp vanilla essence (extract)
- 2 tbsp dark rum (optional)
- 2 medium egg whites
- 4 chocolate cake decorations

TO SERVE

- pieces of kiwi fruit, orange and banana
- strawberries and raspberries

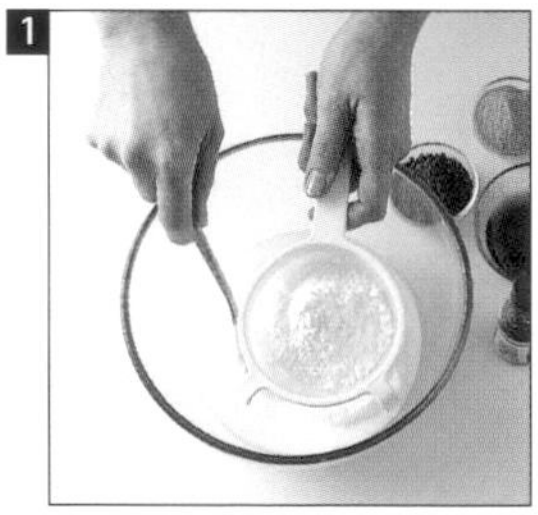

1 Mix the fromage frais (unsweetened yogurt) and low-fat yogurt in a bowl. Sift in the sugar, drinking chocolate and cocoa powder and mix well.

2 Add the vanilla essence (extract) and rum (if using).

3 In another bowl, whisk the egg whites until stiff. Using a metal spoon, fold the egg whites into the chocolate mixture.

4 Spoon the fromage frais (unsweetened yogurt) and chocolate mixture into 4 small china dessert pots and leave to chill for about 30 minutes.

5 Decorate each chocolate cheese pot with a chocolate cake decoration and serve with an assortment of fresh fruit, such as pieces of kiwi fruit, orange and banana, and a few whole strawberries and raspberries.

COOK'S TIP

This chocolate mixture would make an excellent filling for a cheesecake. Make the base out of crushed Amaretti di Saronno biscuits and egg white, and set the filling with 2 tsp powdered gelatine dissolved in 2 tbsp boiling water.

Almond Trifles

Amaretti biscuits made with ground almonds, have a high fat content. Use biscuits made from apricot kernels for a lower fat content.

NUTRITIONAL INFORMATION

Calories	241	Sugars	23g
Protein	9g	Fat	6g
Carbohydrate	35g	Saturates	2g

1¼ HOURS 0 MINS

SERVES 4

INGREDIENTS

- 8 Amaretti di Saronno biscuits
- 4 tbsp brandy or Amaretti liqueur
- 225 g/8 oz raspberries
- 300 ml/½ pint/1¼ cups low-fat custard
- 300 ml/½ pint/1¼ cups low-fat natural fromage frais (unsweetened yogurt)
- 1 tsp almond essence (extract)
- 15 g/½ oz flaked (slivered) almonds, toasted
- 1 tsp cocoa powder

1

3

4

1 Place the biscuits in a mixing bowl and using the end of a rolling pin, carefully crush the biscuits into small pieces.

2 Divide the crushed biscuits among 4 serving glasses. Sprinkle over the brandy or liqueur and leave to stand for about 30 minutes to allow the biscuits to soften.

3 Top the layer of biscuits with a layer of raspberries, reserving a few raspberries for decoration, and spoon over enough custard to just cover.

4 Mix the fromage frais (unsweetened yogurt) with the almond essence (extract) and spoon over the custard. Leave to chill in the refrigerator for about 30 minutes.

5 Before serving, sprinkle with toasted almonds and dust with cocoa powder.

6 Decorate the trifles with the reserved raspberries and serve at once.

VARIATION

Try this trifle with assorted summer fruits. If they are a frozen mix, use them frozen and allow them to thaw so that the juices soak into the biscuit base – it will taste delicious.

Spun Sugar Pears

Whole pears are poached in a Madeira syrup in the microwave, then served with a delicate spun sugar surround.

NUTRITIONAL INFORMATION	
Calories 166	Sugars 41g
Protein 0.3g	Fat 0g
Carbohydrate ...41g	Saturates 0g

20 MINS 35 MINS

SERVES 4

INGREDIENTS

- 150 ml/¼ pint/⅔ cup water
- 150 ml/¼ pint/⅔ cup sweet Madeira wine
- 125 g/4½ oz/½ cup caster (superfine) sugar
- 2 tbsp lime juice
- 4 ripe pears, peeled, stalks left on
- sprigs of fresh mint to decorate

SPUN SUGAR

- 125 g/4½ oz/½ cup caster (superfine) sugar
- 3 tbsp water

1 Mix the water, Madeira, sugar and lime juice in a large bowl. Cover and cook on HIGH power for 3 minutes. Stir well until the sugar dissolves.

2 Peel the pears and cut a slice from the base of each one so they stand upright.

3 Add the pears to the bowl, spooning the wine syrup over them. Cover and cook on HIGH power for about 10 minutes, turning the pears over every few minutes, until they are tender. The cooking time may vary slightly depending on the ripeness of the pears. Leave to cool, covered, in the syrup.

4 Remove the cooled pears from the syrup and set aside on serving plates. Cook the syrup, uncovered, on HIGH power for about 15 minutes until reduced by half and thickened slightly. Leave to stand for 5 minutes. Spoon over the pears.

5 To make the spun sugar, mix together the sugar and water in a bowl. Cook, uncovered, on HIGH power for 1½ minutes. Stir until the sugar has dissolved completely. Continue to cook on HIGH power for about 5–6 minutes more until the sugar has caramelized.

6 Wait for the caramel bubbles to subside and leave to stand for 2 minutes. Dip a teaspoon in the caramel and spin sugar around each pear in a circular motion. Serve immediately, decorated with sprigs of mint.

1

2

3

COOK'S TIP

Keep checking the caramel during the last few minutes of the cooking time, as it will change colour quite quickly and continue to cook for several minutes after removing from the microwave oven.

Tropical Fruit Fool

Fruit fools are always popular, and this light, tangy version will be no exception. Use your favourite fruits in this recipe if you prefer.

NUTRITIONAL INFORMATION

Calories	149	Sugars	25g
Protein	6g	Fat	0.4g
Carbohydrate	32g	Saturates	0.2g

35 MINS 0 MINS

SERVES 4

INGREDIENTS

- 1 medium ripe mango
- 2 kiwi fruit
- 1 medium banana
- 2 tbsp lime juice
- ½ tsp finely grated lime rind, plus extra to decorate
- 2 medium egg whites
- 425 g/15 oz can low-fat custard
- ½ tsp vanilla essence (extract)
- 2 passion fruit

1 To peel the mango, slice either side of the smooth, flat central stone. Roughly chop the flesh and blend the fruit in a food processor or blender until smooth. Alternatively, mash with a fork.

1

2

4

2 Peel the kiwi fruit, chop the flesh into small pieces and place in a bowl. Peel and chop the banana and add to the bowl. Toss all of the fruit in the lime juice and rind and mix well.

3 In a grease-free bowl, whisk the egg whites until stiff and then gently fold in the custard and vanilla essence (extract) until thoroughly mixed.

4 In 4 tall glasses, alternately layer the chopped fruit, mango purée and custard mixture, finishing with the custard on top. Leave to chill in the refrigerator for 20 minutes.

5 Halve the passion fruits, scoop out the seeds and spoon the passion fruit over the fruit fools. Decorate each serving with the extra lime rind and serve.

VARIATION

Other tropical fruits to try include paw-paw (papaya) purée, with chopped pineapple and dates or pomegranate seeds to decorate. Or make a summer fruit fool by using strawberry purée, topped with raspberries and blackberries and cherries.

Cottage Cheese Hearts

These look very attractive when they are made in the French coeur à la crème china moulds, but small ramekins could be used instead.

NUTRITIONAL INFORMATION

Calories	114	Sugars	19g
Protein	9g	Fat	1g
Carbohydrate	19g	Saturates	0.4g

1¼ HOURS — 0 MINS

SERVES 4

INGREDIENTS

- 150 g/5½ oz low-fat cottage cheese
- 150 ml/5 fl oz/⅔ cup low-fat natural fromage frais (unsweetened yogurt)
- 1 medium egg white
- 2 tbsp caster (superfine) sugar
- 1–2 tsp vanilla essence (extract)
- rose-scented geranium leaves, to decorate (optional)

SAUCE

- 225 g/8 oz strawberries
- 4 tbsp unsweetened orange juice
- 2–3 tsp icing (confectioners') sugar

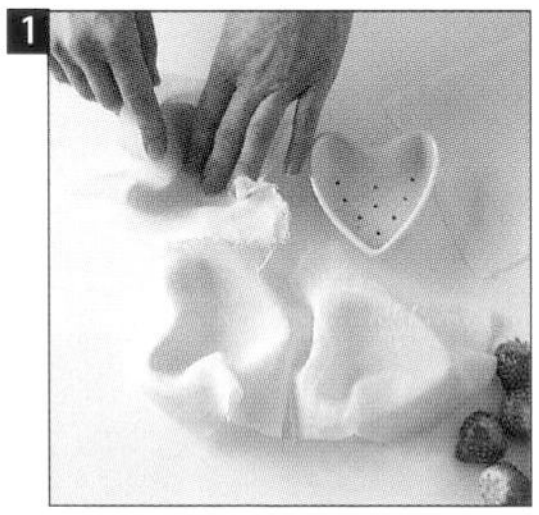

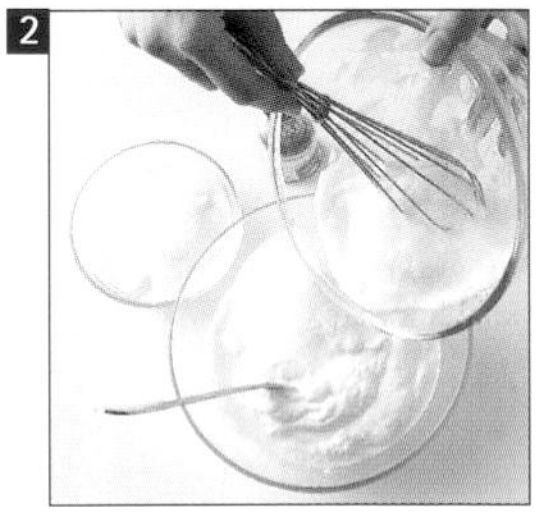

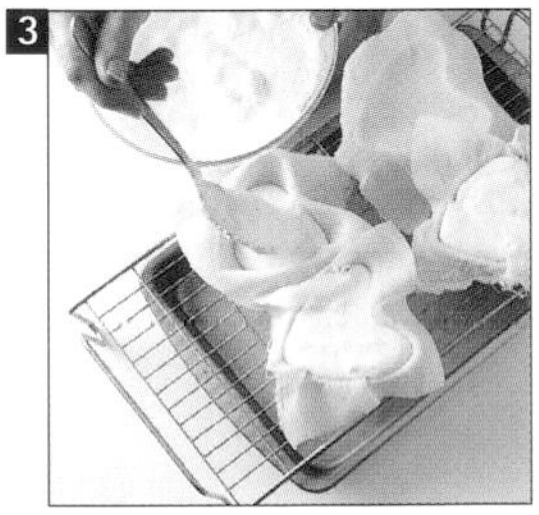

1 Line 4 heart-shaped moulds (molds) with clean muslin (cheesecloth). Place a sieve (strainer) over a mixing bowl and using the back of a metal spoon, press through the cottage cheese. Mix in the fromage frais (yogurt).

2 Whisk the egg white until stiff. Fold into the cheeses, with the caster (superfine) sugar and vanilla essence (extract).

3 Spoon the cheese mixture into the moulds and smooth over the tops. Place on a wire rack over a tray and leave to chill for 1 hour until firm and drained.

4 Meanwhile, make the sauce. Wash the strawberries under cold running water. Reserving a few strawberries for decoration, hull and chop the remainder.

5 Place the strawberries in a blender or food processor with the orange juice and process until smooth. Alternatively, push through a sieve (strainer) to purée. Mix with the icing (confectioners') sugar to taste. Cover and leave to chill in the refrigerator until required.

6 Remove the cheese hearts from the moulds and transfer to serving plates.

7 Remove the muslin (cheesecloth), decorate with strawberries and geranium leaves (if using) and serve with the sauce.

Orange Syllabub

A zesty, creamy whip made from yogurt and milk with a hint of orange, served with light and luscious sweet sponge cakes.

NUTRITIONAL INFORMATION

Calories	464	Sugars	74g
Protein	22g	Fat	5g
Carbohydrate	89g	Saturates	2g

1½ HOURS — 10 MINS

SERVES 4

INGREDIENTS

- 4 oranges
- 600 ml/1 pint/2½ cups low-fat natural yogurt
- 6 tbsp low-fat skimmed milk powder
- 4 tbsp caster (superfine) sugar
- 1 tbsp grated orange rind
- 4 tbsp orange juice
- 2 egg whites
- fresh orange zest to decorate

SPONGE HEARTS

- 2 eggs, size 2
- 90 g/3 oz/6 tbsp caster (superfine) sugar
- 40 g/1½ oz/6 tbsp plain (all-purpose) flour
- 40 g/1½ oz/6 tbsp wholemeal (whole wheat) flour
- 1 tbsp hot water
- 1 tsp icing (confectioners') sugar

2

2

3

1 Slice off the tops and bottoms of the oranges and the skin. Then cut out the segments, removing the zest and membranes between each one. Divide the orange segments between 4 dessert glasses, then chill.

2 In a mixing bowl, combine the yogurt, milk powder, sugar, orange rind and juice. Cover and chill for 1 hour. Whisk the egg whites until stiff, then fold into the yogurt mixture. Pile on to the orange slices and chill for an hour. Decorate with fresh orange rind and sponge hearts.

3 To make the sponge hearts, line a 15 × 25 cm/6 × 10 inch baking tin (pan) with baking parchment. Whisk the eggs and caster (superfine) sugar until thick and pale. Sieve, then fold in the flours using a large metal spoon, adding the hot water at the same time.

4 Pour into the tin (pan) and bake in a preheated oven at 220°C/425°F/Gas Mark 7 for 9–10 minutes until golden and firm to the touch.

5 Turn on to a sheet of baking parchment. Using a 5 cm/2 inch heart-shaped cutter, stamp out hearts. Transfer to a wire rack to cool. Lightly dust with icing (confectioners') sugar before serving with the syllabub.

Mixed Fruit Brûlées

Traditionally a rich mixture made with cream, this fruit-based version is just as tempting using natural (unsweetened) yogurt as a topping.

NUTRITIONAL INFORMATION

Calories	165	Sugars	21g
Protein	5g	Fat	7g
Carbohydrate	21g	Saturates	5g

5 MINS 5 MINS

SERVES 4

INGREDIENTS

- 450 g/1 lb prepared assorted summer fruits (such as strawberries, raspberries, blackcurrants, redcurrants and cherries), thawed if frozen
- 150 ml/5 fl oz/¾ cup half-fat double (heavy) cream alternative
- 150 ml/5 fl oz/¾ cup low-fat natural fromage frais (unsweetened yogurt)
- 1 tsp vanilla essence (extract)
- 4 tbsp demerara (brown crystal) sugar

1 Divide the prepared strawberries, raspberries, blackcurrants, redcurrants and cherries evenly among 4 small heatproof ramekin dishes.

2 Mix together the half-fat cream alternative, fromage frais (unsweetened yogurt) and vanilla essence (extract) until well combined.

3 Generously spoon the mixture over the fruit in the ramekin dishes, to cover the fruit completely.

4 Preheat the grill (broiler) to hot.

5 Top each serving with 1 tbsp demerara (brown crystal) sugar and grill (broil) the desserts for 2–3 minutes, until the sugar melts and begins to caramelize. Leave to stand for a couple of minutes before serving.

COOK'S TIP

Look out for half-fat creams, in single and double (light and heavy) varieties. They are good substitutes for occasional use. Alternatively, in this recipe, omit the cream and double the quantity of fromage frais (yogurt) for a lower fat version.

Pavlova

This fruit meringue dish was created for Anna Pavlova, and it looks very impressive. Use fruits of your choice to make a colourful display.

NUTRITIONAL INFORMATION			
Calories	321	Sugars	37g
Protein	3g	Fat	18g
Carbohydrate	37g	Saturates	11g

1½ HOURS   1½ HOURS

SERVES 8

INGREDIENTS

- 6 egg whites
- ½ tsp cream of tartar
- 225 g/8 oz/1 cup caster (superfine) sugar
- 1 tsp vanilla flavouring (extract)
- 300 ml/½ pint/1¼ cups whipping cream
- 400 g/14 oz/2½ cups strawberries, hulled and halved
- 3 tbsp orange-flavoured liqueur
- fruit of your choice, to decorate

1 Line a baking (cookie) sheet with baking parchment and mark out a circle to fit your serving plate. The recipe makes enough meringue for a 30 cm/12 inch circle.

2 Whisk the egg whites and cream of tartar together until stiff. Gradually beat in the caster (superfine) sugar and vanilla flavouring (extract). Whisk well until glossy and stiff.

3 Either spoon or pipe the meringue mixture into the marked circle, in an even layer, slightly raised at the edges, to form a dip in the centre.

4 Baking the meringue depends on your preference. If you like a soft chewy meringue, bake at 140°C/275°F/Gas Mark 1 for about 1½ hours until dry but slightly soft in the centre. If you prefer a drier meringue, bake in the oven at 110°C/225°F/Gas Mark ¼ for 3 hours until dry.

5 Before serving, whip the cream to a piping consistency, and either spoon or pipe on to the meringue base, leaving a border of meringue all around the edge.

6 Stir the strawberries and liqueur together and spoon on to the cream. Decorate with fruit of your choice.

2

3

5
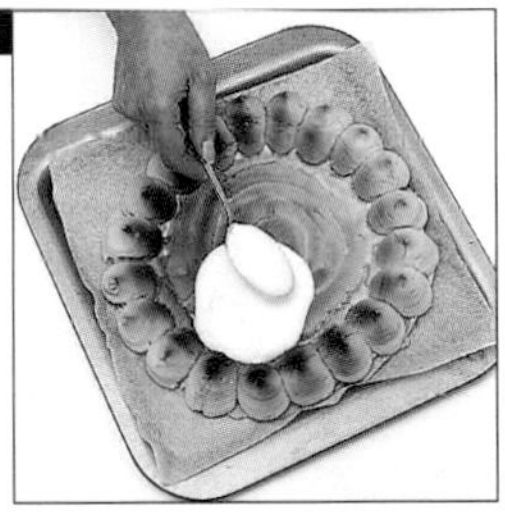

COOK'S TIP

If you like a dry meringue, you can leave it in the oven on the lowest setting overnight. However, do not use this technique with a gas oven – but in an electric oven or solid fuel cooker it would be fine.

Almond Cheesecakes

These creamy cheese desserts are so delicious that it's hard to believe that they are low in fat.

NUTRITIONAL INFORMATION

Calories 361	Sugars 29g
Protein 16g	Fat 15g
Carbohydrate ...43g	Saturates 4g

1¼ HOURS — 10 MINS

SERVES 4

INGREDIENTS

- 12 Amaretti di Saronno biscuits
- 1 medium egg white, lightly beaten
- 225 g/8 oz skimmed-milk soft cheese
- ½ tsp almond essence (extract)
- ½ tsp finely grated lime rind
- 25 g/1 oz ground almonds
- 25 g/1 oz caster (superfine) sugar
- 60 g/2 oz sultanas (golden raisins)
- 2 tsp powdered gelatine
- 2 tbsp boiling water
- 2 tbsp lime juice

TO DECORATE

- 25 g/1 oz flaked (slivered) toasted almonds
- strips of lime rind

1 Preheat the oven to 180°C/350°F/Gas Mark 4. Place the biscuits in a clean plastic bag, seal the bag and using a rolling pin, crush them into small pieces.

2 Place the crumbs in a bowl and bind together with the egg white.

3 Arrange 4 non-stick pastry rings or poached egg rings, 9 cm/3½ inches across, on a baking tray (cookie sheet) lined with baking parchment. Divide the biscuit mixture into 4 equal portions and spoon it into the rings, pressing down well. Bake for 10 minutes until crisp and leave to cool in the rings.

4 Beat together the soft cheese, almond essence (extract), lime rind, ground almonds, sugar and sultanas until well mixed.

5 Dissolve the gelatine in the boiling water and stir in the lime juice. Fold into the cheese mixture and spoon over the biscuit bases. Smooth over the tops and chill for 1 hour or until set.

6 Loosen the cheesecakes from the tins using a small palette knife or spatula and transfer to serving plates. Decorate with flaked (slivered) toasted almonds and strips of lime rind, and serve.

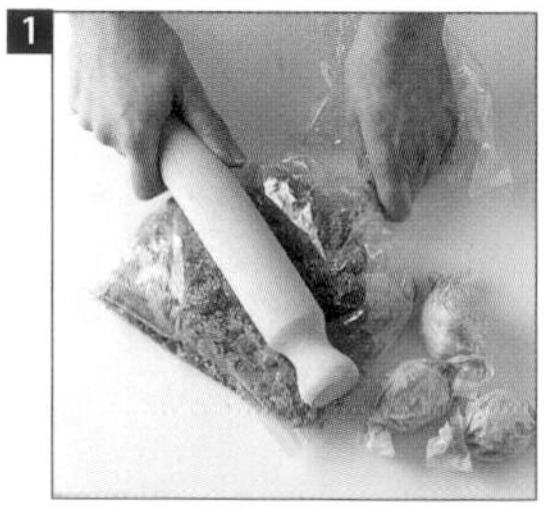

Mocha Swirl Mousse

A combination of feather-light yet rich chocolate and coffee mousses, whipped and attractively served in serving glasses.

NUTRITIONAL INFORMATION

Calories 130	Sugars 10g
Protein 5g	Fat 8g
Carbohydrate 11g	Saturates 5g

1¼ HOURS

0 MINS

SERVES 4

INGREDIENTS

- 1 tbsp coffee and chicory essence (extract)
- 2 tsp cocoa powder, plus extra for dusting
- 1 tsp low-fat drinking chocolate powder
- 150 ml/5 fl oz/⅔ cup low-fat crème fraîche, plus 4 tsp to serve
- 2 tsp powdered gelatine
- 2 tbsp boiling water
- 2 large egg whites
- 2 tbsp caster (superfine) sugar
- 4 chocolate coffee beans, to serve

1 Place the coffee and chicory essence (extract) in one bowl, and 2 tsp cocoa powder and the drinking chocolate in another bowl. Divide the crème fraîche between the 2 bowls and mix both well.

2 Dissolve the gelatine in the boiling water and set aside. In a grease-free bowl, whisk the egg whites and sugar until stiff and divide this evenly between the two mixtures.

3 Divide the dissolved gelatine between the 2 mixtures and, using a large metal spoon, gently fold until well mixed.

4 Spoon small amounts of the 2 mousses alternately into 4 serving glasses and swirl together gently. Chill for 1 hour or until set.

5 To serve, top each mousse with a teaspoonful of crème fraîche, a chocolate coffee bean and a light dusting of cocoa powder. Serve immediately.

COOK'S TIP

Vegetarians should not be denied this delicious chocolate dessert. Instead of gelatine use the vegetarian equivalent, gelozone, available from health-food shops. However, be sure to read the instructions on the packet first as it is prepared differently from gelatine.

1

2

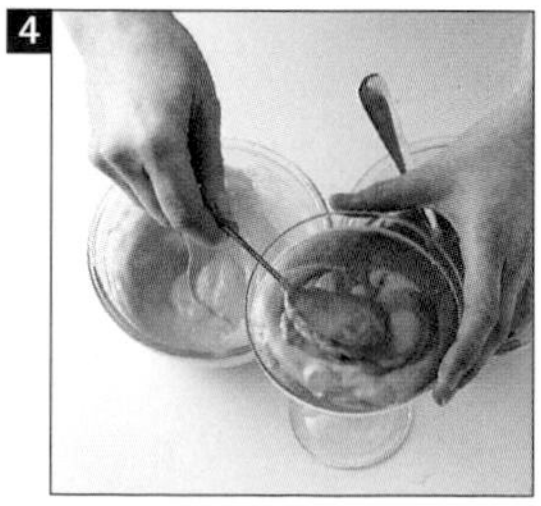
4

Index